Mass Media and Historical Change

Mass Media and Historical Change

Germany in International Perspective, 1400 to the Present

Frank Bösch

Translated by Freya Buechter

berghahn
NEW YORK • OXFORD
www.berghahnbooks.com

Published by
Berghahn Books
www.berghahnbooks.com

English-language edition
©2015 Berghahn Books

German-language edition
©2011 Campus Verlag GmbH
Mediengeschichte. Vom asiatischen Buchdruck zum Fernsehen

All rights reserved. Except for the quotation of short passages
for the purposes of criticism and review, no part of this book
may be reproduced in any form or by any means, electronic or
mechanical, including photocopying, recording, or any information
storage and retrieval system now known or to be invented,
without written permission of the publisher.

Library of Congress Cataloging-in-Publication Data
Bösch, Frank, 1969-
 [Mediengeschichte. English]
 Mass media and historical change: Germany in international perspective, 1400 to the present / Frank Bosch; translated by Freya Buechter. -- First Edition.
  pages cm
 Includes bibliographical references and index.
 ISBN 978-1-78238-625-4 (hardback) -- ISBN 978-1-78238-626-1 (ebook)
 1. Mass media--History. 2. Journalism. I. Title.
 P90.B6387 2015
 302.2309--dc23

2014039945

British Library Cataloguing in Publication Data
A catalogue record for this book is available from the British Library

ISBN 978-1-78238-625-4 (hardback)
E-ISBN 978-1-78238-626-1 (institutional ebook)

Contents

Introduction: Approaches to Media History	1
1. The Breakthrough of Typographic Printing	13
Asia as the Cradle of Printing	13
A Media Revolution? The Dissemination of Gutenberg's Invention	19
Social and Cultural Consequences of Printing	30
2. The Establishment of Periodicals	39
Newspapers as a New Medium	39
The Newspaper and Periodical Market in the Eighteenth Century	48
Interpretations, Effects and Usage of Periodicals	55
3. The Media and the Road to Modernity	62
The Media, Revolutions and Nationalism, 1760–1848	62
Politics and Society in the Age of Magazines and the Popular Press	77
Globalisation, Colonialism and Media Transformation	91
4. Modernity, World Wars and Dictatorships	103
Film and Media Culture before and during the First World War	103
Golden Years? Media and 'Mass Culture' of the 1920s	113
Fascist Dictatorships and the Second World War	123
5. The Media during the Cold War	137
Media and Socialism in the GDR	137
Media and the Establishment of Democracy in West Germany	145
A Global Television Age?	155
Epilogue: The Internet Age from the Perspective of Media History	167
Bibliography	175
Index	197

Introduction

Approaches to Media History

The significance of the media can hardly be overestimated. They transmit, create and store information and in so doing influence perception, knowledge and memory. They put their seal on politics, economy and culture and are an important part of free-time activity and daily discourse. Exceptional events such as wars and revolutions are bound up with the media, as are long-term developments and interpretive patterns like nationalism, religious and ideological groupings and gender roles. Seen in this light, the media are not merely a virtual 'mirror' of something 'real', but are themselves part and parcel of social realities. The family sitting in front of the television and the politician reading a newspaper are as real as the media themselves, their contents and their creators. They often seem invisible. Yet the simple act of believing in the media's power can cause people to change the way they act and speak. Nowadays, the media themselves regularly emphasise their own importance, and the role of the media in elections, armed conflicts and in society in general has become newsworthy.

The historical significance of the media did not begin with the Internet age. If the media are interpreted in the broadest sense as a means of communication, then they have been an essential component of human history since the beginning, because gestures, speech and writing have always structured human communication. Even if one considers 'only' the technical 'mass media', as this book does, it is clear that these have played a defining role at least since the advent of printing, which gave numerous people regular access to collective communication sources. Furthermore, each new medium in its turn altered perceptions, actions and meanings because one and the same concept is formulated, understood and interpreted differently depending on whether it appears on parchment, in a pamphlet or on television.

Thus this book shows how new media have emerged and have been used since the invention of printing and how they have influenced societal developments. The social and cultural history of the media rather than the history of technology and ideas will be given priority. It is the intention of this book to provide an overview of the evolution of media and their impact on societies, and to point out various approaches and suggestions to encourage future research.

Almost every international study has and maybe needs a certain point of view. Unlike other studies, this book does not focus mainly on the American or British perspective. On the one hand, it looks at international and transnational developments in the Western world and in other countries in which a new media market emerged. Besides Western Europe and the United States, China and Japan in particular will be addressed. On the other hand, the German perspective stands in the centre of this transnational study, as it might offer a different view to the familiar debates and research in the United States and Britain.

There are good reasons to choose such a perspective. Many new media emerged in early modern Germany, like the printing revolution in the fifteenth century and the first newspaper in 1605. Germany was the biggest media market in the world in terms of the number of journals, newspapers and pamphlets published up until the nineteenth century. Even in the twentieth century, when the United States became the leading country in the development and distribution of media, German film studios, printing houses and broadcasting stations were still amongst the strongest internationally. Furthermore, German mass media were to a great extent part of transnational networks and developments. German book printers spread their knowledge throughout Europe and founded newspapers in other countries. In the twentieth century, German media stood in the centre of international conflicts – due to the world wars, Allied occupation and the Cold War, but also due to globalised media markets. Especially those chapters about media and fascism and about the Cold War will analyse East and West Germany in the context of Western and socialist developments. Finally, there is a long and rich German tradition of research in national and international media history, which is not that well known in the English-speaking world so far. Consequently, this book offers an alternative view to those very few books on international media history, which take an anglophone perspective and seldom pick up German literature (cf. Briggs and Burke 2002; Chapman 2005; Simonson et al. 2012).

At the same time, this introduction into media history wants to break up the traditional national master narratives and perspectives of single countries. For instance, the history of book printing did not start in Europe, but in East Asia. Consequently, this book starts with the history of printing in China and Korea and compares these developments to those in Europe, and especially Germany. And due to the fact that popular journalism first arose in the United States and Britain, these countries and their influence play a significant role in the chapters concerning nation building and modernity. Media have always connected across borders, even when they stimulated national movements or prejudices against other countries. Consequently, the research of media should have an international perspective, especially when we look at the circulation of news or media techniques.

Research Traditions

Analyses of media development have a long tradition. Studies about newspapers abounded in Germany as early as the last third of the seventeenth century, including the first Ph.D. thesis on newspaper developments (sources in: Kurth 1944; Pompe 2004: 35f.). In the middle of the nineteenth century in particular, comprehensive accounts intended to underline the historical power of the press appeared in many West European countries in the wake of liberal movements: in France they were authored by Léonard Gallois (1845) and Eugène Hatin (8 vols, 1859–61), in England by Frederick Knight Hunt under the programmatic title *The Fourth Estate* (1850), and in Germany by Robert Prutz, who described journalism as one of the 'excellent tools' for the 'democratic principle of history' (Prutz 1845: 84). An early international newspaper history, including a descriptive summary, even appeared at this time (cf. Coggeshall 1856). Since the end of the nineteenth century, numerous studies on a variety of media have followed, carried out in the disciplines of economics, history, sociology and philology.

At the same time, examining the historical role of the media is a certain novelty. This is especially true concerning historical scholarship, which did not begin an intensive debate of their significance until the 1990s. Also, media studies have expanded their historical research in recent decades. This increased historical interest is due to the media's omnipresence in the Internet age. In this process, computer and Internet have historicised the now 'old' media, rendering them objects of research. Furthermore, this 'cultural turn' has strengthened awareness of communication, focusing the attention of researchers on popular culture as well as media-based perceptions and discourses. In fact, even our present-day term 'media' is new. The American expression 'mass media' had already surfaced in the 1920s, but it was not until the 1950s that this term ('Medien') was adopted in a country like Germany to describe communication tools capable of reaching a vast audience (for the history of the term, see Hoffmann 2002). Researchers initially spoke of 'journalism' or 'communication'.

The question of defining the term 'media', but also the methods and focal points of media history are highly controversial, especially among German researchers. Anglo-Saxon media accounts are much more pragmatic: usually they eschew debates about terminology, and proceed from the vernacular meaning of 'media' in the sense of 'mass media' and use this in their media history (Briggs and Burke 2002; Chapman 2005; Williams 2010). Also, studies titled as 'communication history' prefer a general definition of communication and concentrate on mass media like print, film, radio, television and 'new media' (Simonson et al. 2012: 1). In Germany the concepts of 'media' and 'media history' operate very differently, depending on which research field is at work. The approaches taken by media historians of the social and communication sciences (*Kommunikationswissenschaft*) are very clearly differentiated from those of cultural media studies (*Medienwissenschaft*, often translated as 'Media Culture Studies').

Communication studies is the discipline that has been analysing media history for the longest. It was established in the United States during the 1920s as a way to examine the function of public opinion with the tools of social science. In the 1920s, many American scholars published studies on the historical content and impact of the press and publishers. During the following decade, the propaganda of European dictatorships was the primary factor triggering empirical research of media influence, with Harold Lasswell and Paul F. Lazarsfeld conducting groundbreaking studies about radio and opinion polls. In general, the 1970s are seen as the period when communication history emerged as an important field (see a brilliant survey in Simonson et. al. 2013: 13–57).

In Germany, and in Western Europe generally, studies of journalism and newspapers (*Zeitungswissenschaft*), which use the approaches of historians and the humanities, have also gained a foothold at several universities since the 1920s. Since the 1960s the field of communication studies in (West) Germany has increasingly adopted American approaches, which are more sociological in character. To the present day a narrow concept of 'the media' (i.e. press, radio, cinema and television) is typical here, interpreting them primarily as technical tools 'suitable for disseminating messages to a potentially unlimited public' (Wilke 2008: 1; Stöber 2003, Vol. 1: 10).

In marked dissociation from traditional studies on press history so far, media studies oriented towards cultural studies have been established in many Western countries since the 1970s. One starting point was the new openness of literary studies towards pop culture; another was the wide reception of Marshall McLuhan's interpretation of the media. McLuhan propagated a wide definition of media: he saw them as bodily extensions, among which he included things like eyeglasses, money and the wheel (McLuhan [1964] 2001). According to McLuhan, the actual message of a medium lies in its social effects, the alteration of the yardstick, speed or pattern it brings to the human condition. Consequently, many Western countries have witnessed the appearance of studies that inquire into the relationship between media and cultural practices, and postulate the defining power of media practices for the general developments of societies in certain periods (e.g. Poe 2010). Within the sphere of media studies there are heterogeneous schools with ethical, philosophical or technical focal points, united predominantly by their culture-studies approach and their broad interpretation of the media concept. Thus their media accounts quite openly define the object of their research as 'interaction coordinators' (Hörisch 2004: 66) or as 'complex, entrenched transmission facilities that organise and regulate communication' (Faulstich 2006a: 8). Because of this broad interpretation, their media histories often begin in pre- or early history or in antiquity. Thus 'Woman and the Sacrificial Rite' were considered the first media, since they represented 'sacred communication principle' (ibid.: 18), or fire, tools and the human voice (Hörisch 2004: 30–39). Depending on the school of thought, priority is given to the aesthetic analysis of various media products (especially films) as well as the changes that have taken place in knowledge, order, practices and perceptions during the course of media formation. The wide reception of the cultural study approaches of the 'Birmingham School' (like Stuart Hall and John Fiske) has led to a different perception of the audience as active individuals decoding messages.

Historical scholarship dealing with research in media history lies somewhere between these disciplines. Media analysis was long frowned upon by historians, since journalists and journalistic sources were held to be dubious and historical scholars used archival sources as a means of establishing distance. The German historian Martin Spahn made an early attempt in 1908 to re-evaluate media sources at the International Congress of Historical Sciences, where he voiced the prognosis that the press 'would become the most valuable of all sources for every chronicler of modern history' (Spahn 1908). Consequently, as a professor in Cologne, he called for the establishment of a national newspaper museum and sponsored many papers on press history. Moreover, since the end of the nineteenth century a number of historical studies on individual media have appeared. These have addressed aspects of journalistic policy and control, specific media such as pamphlets and newspapers, and leading figures in publishing. At least some newspaper histories were published in the first half of the twentieth century. However, most historians continued to regard the media merely as sources to be accessed occasionally for the purpose of enlivening an illustration or unobtrusively investigating causes and effects.

A first increase in historical media studies can be found in the 1970s, when the emergence of social and cultural history supported the interest in popular culture and media history. Seminal writings about the underground press and the rumours circulating prior to the French Revolution were especially influential in this context (Darnton 1982). International research on printing in the context of the Reformation received additional impetus as well (like Elizabeth L. Eisenstein 1979). Nevertheless, only since the late 1990s has there been an overwhelming increase in the number of publications on media history that differ in their methodology.

The concept of media as now understood in the context of historical scholarship has become quite diverse. Yet historians tend to prefer a narrow interpretation of the term, and they concentrate their studies on technically produced mass media for broad audiences. The majority of historians define media as artefacts whose purpose it is to enable communication and fulfil tasks such as recording, storage, transmission, multiplication and reproduction, playback and processing of information (Crivellari and Sandl 2003: 633). In general, the media history branch of historical scholarship concerns itself less with the media themselves than with their respective social, cultural and political significance.

If one makes up a balance sheet of these examples of research trends, there has been a change from studying media history towards studying the mediality of history (Crivellari et al. 2004: 30). From this perspective, the historical view of the media not only represents a new specialisation within historical scholarship (like political, social or economic history), but is grounded in modernity, and in particular in modern historical processes, contemporary experience and personal memory (Lindenberger 2004). This does not mean that one must proceed from a kind of media-technological determinism, as some media scientists postulate (Poe 2010). The nature of the roles played by the media depends on prevailing social parameters and media users. Furthermore, one must be wary of concentrating too strongly on the effects of media, which can hardly be determined in detail in any case.

Media respond to societal needs and thus are a part of history as a whole. The million-fold increase in demand that determines their function and modus operandi was not created simply through technical innovations but rather by a social framework and users, who in turn generate needs. In any case, the new media have always concurrently changed the old and occasionally pushed them aside. Now and again the new media have taken on the structures of the old, establishing their own logics that in turn redound on society. Why new media come into existence at all, and then manage to assert themselves, has been attributed to various needs, such as higher speed as a power resource (Virilio 1989), new technology for waging war (Kittler 1995), greater focus on the senses (Hörisch 2004: 14) and improving the function of previous media (Stöber 2003 Vol. 2: 216).

The assumption that there would be continual media innovation was contrasted with the concept of compacted 'media upheavals' that would manifest themselves in discourse, society and technology (Käuser 2005). Such upheavals in media history tend to go hand in hand with history in general. Seen in this light, the introduction of printing in Europe marked the end of the Middle Ages and the beginning of the Modern Era; the Enlightenment in the eighteenth century corresponded to the establishment of periodicals, and the late nineteenth century, which witnessed the birth of the mass press, telegraphy, photography, phonograph and film, is considered the beginning of Classical Modernity. The expansion of digital media during the 1990s also corresponded to a new epochal turning point.

Accounts that discuss the international media history are rare. Next to a few international handbooks about the history of specific media such as newspapers (Smith 1979) or films (Nowell-Smith 1996), two studies have recently appeared that proceed from British and American perspectives in making international comparisons. The British scholar Jane Chapman published a well-written, concise introduction to the history of journalism and the media since 1789, but focusing primarily on the twentieth century (Chapman 2005). The most comprehensive study so far is the *Social History of the Media* by the historians Asa Briggs and Peter Burke (2002), which is even more concerned with the respective historical roles played by the media, especially the mass media, since the introduction of printing.

Current Research on German Media History

Research on German media history has a long tradition, but it is in many respects not as advanced as the one in Britain or the United States. Anyone interested in getting information about the broad development of German media history already has a few very different overviews at his/her disposal. An example of the German cultural media studies communication science (*Medienwissenschaften*) is Jochen Hörisch's (2004) essayistic account in which he takes an original look at media in the broadest sense, presenting attributes ascribed to the media, beginning with fire. However, he gives less information about concrete media producers, users or contents. Several publications from the perspective of the German cultural media studies were published by Werner Faulstich (abridged version: Faulstich 2006a/b; multi-volume 1996ff.). His 'cultural history of the media' asks which control and orientation functions were taken over by the respective media, from the 'human media' (woman, priest, etc.) and 'formative media' (wall, sheet, etc.) to print, electronic and digital media. However, mass media are rarely mentioned here and reviewers criticised many fundamental mistakes in Faulstich's books. The German *Handbuch der Mediengeschichte* [Handbook of Media History] (Schanze 2001) and the partly historical *Handbuch der Medienwissenschaften* [Compendium of Media Studies] (Leonhard et al. 1999–2002) focus more on high culture (like theatre, music, books and film) and also briefly introduce various approaches to the subject, such as media law, media sociology and media pedagogy, but neither book gives specific consideration to historical scholarship. A new introductory work for undergraduates (Böhn and Seidler 2008) gives a brief presentation of typological characteristics of each individual media innovation. Previous media histories from the field of communication science clearly had a different emphasis; they concentrated mainly on the specific history of press, radio and television as well as their producers, and on the dissemination, control and reception of these media (Stöber 2003; Wilke 2008). These studies are similar to introductory works about other Western countries like Great Britain (Williams 2010) and the United States (Fellow 2005). However, they were less interested in the historical context and more in the media itself.

Looking at current studies on German media history, one can highlight different main areas of research. Since historians have long accorded politics a privileged position, one aspect receiving much attention is the relationship between the media and politics. Older studies stressed the methods of censorship and repression that targeted both media and public, whether these were found in absolutistic regimes, constitutional monarchies, dictatorships or democracies. Newer studies have more closely examined the deliberate participation of rulers in public communication, ranging from the 'propaganda' of monarchs to the types of communication used in wars or political campaigns (Gestrich 1994; Burkhardt 2002). Most recently, the question has been posed in reverse: How has change in the media caused political change? The latter is analysed as a communication space whose symbolic make-up is strongly defined and constituted by the media (cf. e.g. Bösch 2009). In this perspective it even becomes possible to study the prevailing media foundation of such classic 'arcane areas' as foreign policy (Geppert 2007; Bösch and Hoeres 2013).

Another focal point of German media history, which is much more related to social history, is the examination of public spheres. This analysis first came up with Jürgen Habermas's book *Untersuchungen zu einer Kategorie der bürgerlichen Gesellschaft* (1962/1989), and continued on an international scale after it was translated into English nearly thirty years later as *The Structural Transformation of the Public Sphere* (1989) (cf. e.g. Calhoun 1992; Barker and Burrows 2002). In the forefront were the questions of who could participate in public communication, what consequences this would have for the formation of social groupings, and how media and personal communication would interact. By now, public spheres were quite openly being defined as generally accessible communication spaces. The plural here underlines the assumption that there are also sub-spaces that may differ in ideological, functional and regional ways (Requate 1999; Führer, Hickethier and Schildt 2001). Many studies exist for the Early Modern Era, but this concept was hardly used for contemporary history. Recent research has analysed how the public spheres interacted in the media and in assemblies – for example at protests, in social movements and in parliaments (Stamm 1988; Vogel 2010).

Only a few studies researched the concrete usage of media and their significance for daily life. Here too one finds important impulses originating in the

Early Modern Era, such as studies on reading practices (Würgler 2009: 97). Studies dealing with the twentieth century have researched public and private usage of the 'mass media' based on social class differences (Schildt 1995; Führer 1996; Ross 2008). Up to and into the 1950s, it was difficult to discover exactly which media people chose to access, what significance these had for their daily lives and how they spoke about them, since no surveys on media usage are available for this period. For this reason researchers have used, for instance, informers' reports about audience behaviour in cinemas during dictatorships (Paech and Paech 2000; Stahr 2001), or about conversations about newspapers at the time of the German Empire (Bösch 2004). Media usage in the GDR was determined by questioning contemporaries (Meyen 2003).

More and more studies on German media history became interested in the question how newly evolving media transformed society, social practices and perceptions (methodology based on communication science: Behmer et al. 2003). At the same time, new media are themselves understood as components, expressions and consequences of societal change. There were early studies on the societal effects of new media technology in relation to book printing (Eisenstein [1979] 2005), as well as to fields like the history of crime (Curtis 2001; Müller 2005), consumption, brand name products in everyday life (Gries 2003), and the role of the media in the urban culture of Berlin around 1900 (Fritzsche 1996). In the course of this, the concept of 'medialisation' (or 'mediatisation') was established as a means of understanding the media's increasing penetration of societal systems, their socialising effects and the mutual impact of media and social change (Meyen 2009; Daniel and Schildt 2010: 23).

In contrast to British and American media history, studies on Germany have seldom used biographical approaches. While several biographies of major Anglo-Saxon publishers like Lord Northcliffe and William Randolph Hearst are available, nothing comparable as yet exists for German media moguls like Ullstein, Scherl and Mosse, and there is only a very recent biography of such a key figure as Axel Springer, who was the biggest news publisher in Europe post-1945 (Schwarz 2008). The most groundbreaking studies are those dealing with group biographies among nineteenth-century journalists from the standpoint of social history (Requate 1995), and the transition to critical journalism around 1960 from a generational vantage point (Hodenberg 2006). It would have been especially desirable to have more studies on the daily work routine of 'ordinary' journalists in the twentieth century, and of foreign correspondents (Esser 1998; Bösch and Geppert 2008).

Instead, manifold studies concentrated on the contents of print media. Before the 1980s, many of these viewed historical events as they were reflected in specific newspapers and journals and occasionally in films, but hardly ever in radio or television content. Although they revealed the ideological profile of individual media, there is good reason why this approach has lost importance. There has been a recent flurry of approaches that analyse discourse, examine the contents of various media to discover changes in interpretive patterns and relate these to more general changes (for instance about media and religion: Hannig 2010). A cultural history of this type can make use of events and processes to explain the interpretations called up by the media and the consequences that ensue (cf. Lenger and Nünning 2008).

Recent studies are less interested in printed articles than in Visual History. They analyse repetitive forms of pictures and their symbolic content. Since the 1990s this has been freed from the high-culture aesthetics of art history and has tapped into pictorial sources like simple prints, postcards, photographs, films, caricatures and advertisements (Jäger 2009). The plea for an Iconic Turn or Pictorial Turn at the same time stressed the claim that pictures do not merely illustrate something but rather generate an independent symbolism beyond their textual sources. Now the concept of Visual History has established itself in historical scholarship, in order to 'examine pictorial sources as media that condition ways of seeing, define patterns of perception, convey means of interpreting history and organize the aesthetic relationship of historical subjects to their social and political reality' (Paul 2006: 25). Iconic pictures from the twentieth century that demonstrate this can be found in the two famous volumes of *Das Jahrhundert der Bilder* (The Century of Pictures), edited by Gerhard Paul (Paul 2008/9), which has no equivalent in international research as yet. However, historical scholarship on German media history has hardly concerned itself with the moving pictures of television. Some initial studies on how television deals with the Nazi past (Horn 2009) and on the cultural and political upheavals of 1968 (Vogel 2010) have opened up new avenues.

Historical media research remained nation-oriented for a long time. In recent years the interest in transnational and comparative approaches on German media history has been growing, too. Some transnational studies have inquired into mutual relationships and transfers spanning several countries, for example wartime journalism in the Early Modern Age (Schultheiß-Heinz 2004), media communication and diplomacy (Hoeres 2013), or in the Cold War (Imre 2013). Other transnational studies looked at telegraphy in the nineteenth century (Wenzlhuemer 2010) and broadcasting (Badenoch, Fickers and Henrich-Franke 2013). Future studies on the general transnational or global history would be well advised to consider the impact of media structures, which often make transfer processes possible.

The state of the sources might be another reason why media-historical research has so far developed slowly in Germany. What exists is a wilful conglomerate of abundance and scarcity: on the one hand mass media sources such as pamphlets, newspapers, films and television programme guides have been preserved in almost daunting numbers, and this demands a methodically well-considered choice. On the other hand there is an extremely poor state of transmission history for sources providing historical contextualisation: editorial files for newspapers, publishing houses and radio stations are often not available in German archives. The same applies to unpublished journalistic works, and sources and data about media users and reception prior to 1945. There is also only scant information about radio programmes of the 1920s and 1930s, and television broadcasts of the 1950s and 1960s. The source situation is also worse in Germany than in neighbouring countries. While American and British journalists began to write their memoirs and donate their correspondence to archives at a fairly early date, in Germany even the collected material of large publishing houses is very limited for the period before 1933. Accessing radio sources is especially difficult in Germany. Countries like Italy, France and the United States have provided online access for some important film and television sources, but in Germany examining radio and television archives is extremely expensive and access is often arbitrarily regulated. The digitalisation of pre-1945 German newspapers is also comparatively underdeveloped, whereas in the United States, Britain and Austria a great deal of historical press material is digitally accessible. Nevertheless, there are sufficient sources available for future research on media history. For example, there are numerous detailed editions of printed graphics (e.g. Harms 1985ff.; Paas 1984). Newspapers from the seventeenth and eighteenth centuries are on file in the *Institut für deutsche Presseforschung* in Bremen and in the newspaper section of the State Library in Berlin. The 'ZDB-Opac' displays the editions and locations of all newspapers and periodicals. Also, at least a few German newspapers are digitally accessible – some free of charge, like the *Augspurgische Ordinari Postzeitung* (1770–95) – while others like the *Vossische Zeitung* (1918–34) and the *FAZ* (from 1949) can only be viewed by licence in major libraries. The film department of the Berlin branch of the Federal Archives collects sources for films of all genres dating back to the beginnings of cinema. Accessing radio and television programmes is more difficult, but the German Radio Archives in Frankfurt and Babelsberg (for GDR material) has enabled an initial entrée. Sources for individual (West) German programmes can be found in the archives of the different broadcasting stations. If one looks for German (TV) films, a good alternative is provided by the media libraries of universities, which can be used for purposes of research.

The present volume has been written from the German perspective and from the perspective of a historian. Nevertheless it often makes use of approaches and findings from other disciplines. Its intention is to highlight the development of new media and their respective societal significance on the basis of research. Hence it addresses the momentous role played by the respective media during various epochs and their significance for such pivotal events in human history as the Reformation, revolutions, wars and dictatorships. Beyond that, the comparative and transnational orientation of this book will attempt to set some new accents of its own. Because its size necessitates some limitations, this volume will concentrate on 'mass media' – technological media that enable indirect communication with an anonymous, widely scattered public. For this reason some important technological means of communication like the phonograph record, photography and the telephone will only be dealt with in passing. As far as the time frame goes, 'only' the six hundred years since the end of the Middle Ages will be addressed. Also, the computer and the Internet will only be considered within the context of a summing up in the Epilogue, since digitalisation has only relatively recently begun to exert broad social and cultural influence.

This study tries to focus on Germany on a transnational basis. However, it must be said that, especially in regard to the twentieth century with its great media-historical complexity, comparisons can only be made by means of examples. The state of research also sets boundaries because the media-historical studies that exist are mainly concerned with the industrialised countries of the West and only in a limited way with Eastern Europe, South America, China and Japan.

Chapter 1

The Breakthrough of Typographic Printing

Asia as the Cradle of Printing

The invention of modern book printing is inextricably linked to the name of Gutenberg. Gutenberg was considered by American journalists to be the most important 'Man of the Millennium', and his work was seen as the central turning point between the Middle Ages and the modern era. This, of course, is rather a Western point of view. For in actual fact, letterpress printing had already been invented centuries before in China; and even in Korea, a printing method using movable metal type was practised from the 1230s onwards. The famous Gutenberg Bible is therefore not the oldest surviving book that was printed using this technique. In fact, a copy of the Korean Jikji is kept in the Parisian Bibliothèque National, which was produced in 1377 using movable type. A history of modern mass media intended not to reflect an overly Eurocentric perspective should thus commence in Asia – in China and Korea in particular, but also in Japan. A new and comprehensive interpretive bibliography offers an excellent introduction to this topic (Walravens 2007).

The approach adumbrated above is ideal for re-discussing existing theses on the social and cultural causes and consequences of book printing. To date, the field of media studies, as well as historical works investigating the social effects of modern printing, have tended to largely ignore or even negate the relevance of the Asian development. Marshall McLuhan's media study, for instance, mentions Asia only incidentally. The fact that no industrialisation took place in China despite the early invention of book printing is briefly established in two sentences: 'The purpose of printing among the Chinese was not the creation of uniform repeatable products for a market and a price system. Print was an alternative to their prayer-wheels and was a visual means of multiplying incantatory spells, much like advertising in our age' (McLuhan [1962] 2011: 40). In his famous work on book printing in the early modern period, the German media historian Michael Giesecke emphasised that in China and Korea, printing had only had a limited effect until it was re-imported from Europe. The author claims that in Korea, book printing had only served as a means for institutional communication, but had no relevance in everyday life. The reason for this, according to Giesecke, lies not in the complexity of the language. Rather, he determines that any desire to change the dominating social and political circumstances, if indeed such desires existed, would not have been associated with communication media (Giesecke 1991: 128–30). Other historians and scholars of communication and bibliography studies wholly ignored printing progress in Asia or simply cited the technical superiority of the German innovation.

A glance at existing literature on the Asian development provides a different outlook. From a research perspective, a technical comparison between Asia and Europe is less productive than the consideration of the different social and cultural dimensions of media changes. It is striking that, unlike in the Western world, the invention of book printing in Asia happened quite inconspicuously and was not tied to an association with one man's sudden stroke of genius. What was considered a revolutionary act in the West occurred rather as a long-term evolution in the East. Neither exact dates nor names of inventors have been passed on; and in general, Chinese sources scarcely broach the issue of printing before the sixteenth century (McDermott 2006: 9–13). The development period, in fact, spanned over a thousand years, and pivotal innovations were of transnational occurrence. The Chinese, for instance, produced high-quality paper as early as the first century AD, and its use then spread across the whole of Central Asia during the following centuries. Similarly, in the first half of the eighth century, woodblock printing emerged in China and Korea and was subsequently adopted by the Japanese in the same century. The book market flourished in the eleventh century, leading to some experimentation with movable ceramic type in China around 1040. Although this invention never asserted itself, the notion was taken up in Korea and reformed in the shape of metal type. Individual Korean scholars have dated the first letterpress prints as far back as the eleventh century; however, most experts suspect the formation period to be around 1230, although no corresponding prints have survived from that period (Moon-Year 2004: 32; Seong-Rae 2004: 26). All of these inventions were regarded by the renowned art historian and expert on East Asia, Lothar Ledderose, as part of a Chinese 'modular system', in which various distinct forms of mass production continued to emerge over several centuries (Ledderose 2000).

The great demand for books which encouraged such inventions and triggered high-circulation publications in China and Korea was the product of various developments. Firstly, it resulted from the well-organised Chinese education and assessment system for administrations, which the Koreans adopted in the tenth century (Sohn 1972: 218). From the Chinese Song period onwards (960–1279), books provided a means to gain social and political advancement, and thus attain more prestigious positions (McDermott 2006: 85). Although the state demanded the standardisation of study material, a dynamic book market with competing works of preparatory literature evolved. Aspirants to the civil service even tried to impress with their own writings (Chow 2004: 242).

Secondly, the governments played a prominent role with regard to media expansion. In China, the ministerial printing office did not merely produce administrative instructions, official dynasty histories, and exam preparation literature. Rulers also distributed books which they regarded as commercially or politically important (Brokaw 2005: 17). This was even more widespread in Korea. Here, in 1403, the king had a metal foundry set up, which initiated prints, developed print techniques, and even organised the paper and ink production and nationwide distribution. Besides the royal printing house and governmental bodies, the Korean sovereigns also authorised monasteries, private study institutions, local government agencies in the provinces, and private individuals to engage in the business of printing. However, this central organisational system tended to restrict the expansion of the new media in Korea (Sohn 1972: 230; Lie 2003: 19, 36–43).

At the same time, the rulers of East Asia promoted the preservation of accumulated knowledge in large libraries. Around 1420, the inventory of the imperial library in China already comprised approximately twenty thousand titles containing one hundred thousand printed works (*juan*), with students being granted access to libraries belonging to the Chinese imperial college (McDermott 2006: 50, 116). Surprisingly, the Chinese book market suffered less from constraints than the European one. According to the studies of Kai-Wing Chow, neither the contents nor the number of printers were regulated by sovereigns until sometime in the eighteenth century – in contrast to Europe (Chow 2004: 251). Naturally, this too facilitated the emergence and expansion of the medium.

Thirdly, the newly emerging print and book market is not to be understood merely as a means to secure authority. It is also to be viewed in the context of everyday social and cultural practices. Books played a central role in the form of gifts because they were valued as aesthetic objects in private collections, and also served to secure loyalty within the state (McDermott 2006: 85; Seong-Rae 2004: 31). Whereas profit-orientation was the main trigger behind the dynamics of the Western book market, it had only marginal bearing in Korea before the mid-seventeenth century (Burke 2000: 175), doubtless impeding the production dynamics initially aimed at by the sovereigns. By contrast, an increasingly commercial book market flourished in China, particularly in the middle of the sixteenth century. Chinese books covered quite a broad range of topics, from religious matters to guidebooks and light fiction (Chow 2004: 245). The books' contents, however, also demonstrated that printing did not automatically cultivate the practice of individual authorship. In many cases, various texts were combined; others were re-issued under different titles (Brokaw 2005: 20).

Fourthly, religion contributed greatly to the upsurge of print media in Asia. Large collections of Buddhist texts and numerous Buddhist book illustrations substantiate the fact that the Buddhist faith fuelled the heyday of printing in Korea until the end of the Goryeo Dynasty (918–1392) and constituted printing as a religious act. Neo-Confucian writings, which later became the focus of the printing business, aspired to a certain degree a text standardisation such as existed in Western Europe. Accordingly, the oldest surviving book worldwide is a collection of Buddhist lore written by a Zen master, most commonly referred to as Jikji and printed in 1377 using metal type. Similarly, in the Joseon Dynasty (1392–1910), printing served the promotion and enforcement of Neo-Confucianism as the new state doctrine. Illustrated prints in particular were intended to propagate the Confucian canon of values nationwide from the fifteenth century onwards. However, printing was not solely utilised for the propagation of religions and modes of behaviour. The fact that the mere act of duplicating religious writings was considered a step on the way to salvation served to further increase the immense circulation figures. This was particularly evident in Japan in the 760s, when the empress had approximately one million holy scriptures printed for pagodas (*Dhâranî*) (Giesecke 2007: 428; Yukawa 2010: 246).

The Asian development also proved that it was by no means inevitable that, even after its invention, movable type printing should become the dominant system in the field of media technology. Despite its early breakthrough, it played only a marginal role in China until the nineteenth century, whilst at the same time in Korea movable type printing coexisted with the method of xylography ('woodcut'). High-circulation books continued to be manufactured using woodcut, whereas movable types were intended for standardised texts, special editions, or anything produced on a smaller scale. In the 1590s, two events were responsible for bringing this technique to Japan also. At the same time that the Japanese were at war with Korea, where they looted printing equipment and abducted printers, a Portuguese missionary introduced them to the Western printing practice. The latter was subsequently prevalent in Japan for a brief period, but its popularity soon diminished (Yukawa 2010: 282). It was only in the 1860s that movable type printing asserted itself after the encounter with the Western world.

One explanation as to why typographic printing failed to establish itself to the same extent as it did in Europe is rooted in the complexity of the writing system. In particular, the task of typesetting the countless number of Chinese characters was economically unprofitable, since labour costs for carving were significantly lower. This, in turn, enabled the provision of low-priced books. No less important was the power of typographic traditions. Although in the 1440s a simplified Korean alphabet evolved, it was not until the nineteenth century that it was able to prevail over the well-established use of Chinese characters, as scholars were reluctant lest it precipitate an alienation from Neo-Confucianism. It has therefore been assumed that – had a successful simplification of script taken place – letterpress printing would have developed a similar dynamic to that in Europe (Sohn 1972: 227). This, however, may be refuted by drawing a comparison with Japan, where a simplified Chinese script did indeed exist, but no comparable printing tradition developed.

Aesthetic traditions also influenced the dissimilar developments. As calligraphy was highly valued in China, Korea and Japan, woodblock printing was more suitable for their needs. To a large extent, luxurious books even continued to be handwritten for a considerable time. In Japan and Korea, the value system created a rather distanced attitude, giving privilege to the art of fancy lettering and the combination of image and writing (Giesecke 2007: 437). Furthermore, the continued use of xylography entailed lower initial investment costs and also had a cost-cutting effect in regard to technical know-how, thus providing wider access to printed texts. Consequently, minimum circulation was not a primary concern, and printers had higher mobility (Brokaw 2005: 8, 15). Especially in China, the xylographic method enabled a virtually unlimited number of reprints because of the large clientele, despite the woodblocks demanding much storage space. While in the West the capital-intensive printing machines were only available to a few rich and central cities, such as Lyon, Paris, Venice and Amsterdam, over in China an important advantage of xylography was that it enabled the regional spread of the printing trade. Scholars of Asian studies thus quite rightly condemn the deprecation of Asian woodblock printing practices, which from a European perspective have often appeared as nothing more than an underdeveloped intermediate stage on the way to Western book printing (cf. Chow in Baron et al. 2007: 175).

In Asia, the zenith of the printing period did not immediately succeed the groundbreaking inventions, but rather occurred with some delay. Since political rulers exerted strong influence over the book production, changes of dynasty were not without consequence. This was demonstrated by the large expansion of the book market in Korea, in particular during the reign of Sejong (1418–1450). Today, there remain 114 printed titles which can be assigned to the method of movable type printing, with circulation ranging between one hundred and three hundred copies, and 194 titles identified as xylographic prints covering a circulation of at least three hundred and maybe up to ten thousand copies (Sohn 1998: 28). Book production thus not only served to stabilise the new regime, but also to promote Neo-Confucian state doctrine, with the intention of thrusting aside Buddhism by means of new rituals and scriptures. A study of the flourishing Chinese book market between 1550 and 1650 moreover reveals cultural and socio-historical causes. During this time, a rapid increase in population stimulated the demand for books, and production costs could be kept low due to the large number of workers (Chow 2004; Brokaw 2005: 10). Also, book distribution was improved during this period. Since a collective written language existed in China despite hundreds of different dialects (but seldom used in books), the entire country was targeted for distribution. This had not only economic significance, but the media market also contributed to imagining China as an entity and, at least potentially, promoting a collective public sphere. This strengthened China's cultural coherence, which, however, remained visual. After all, printing did not contribute to the establishment of a collective spoken vernacular language (Chow 2004: 245) – in contrast to Europe, where Latin had established itself as the written language and increasingly gave way to vernacular print-work from the sixteenth century onwards.

These findings on the development of printing caution us not to deduce causalities from media innovations too hastily. Printing was evidently responsible for a whole range of consequences. At the same time, the above examples illustrate that the element of technical distinction should never lead one to assume the socio-cultural meaninglessness of Asian print media. It is thus imperative to view xylographic printing in Asia not so much as an artistic pre-stage of movable type printing, but rather as a self-contained medium in Asia (Chow 2004: 246).

With a view to the Asian continent, it is reasonable to ask how far Gutenberg himself knew of and was inspired by its development. Based on a rather limited number of literary references, there is some speculation that reports on Asian printing practices found their way to Europe through Mongolian conquerors or tradesmen along the Silk Road, but there is no conclusive evidence to support this (cf. Sohn 1972: 217, 228; Kapr 1988: 113–20). However, even the technical differences alone illustrate the independence of Gutenberg's letterpress printing from the Korean invention. Gutenberg's manual casting procedure for letter reproduction, which enabled him to produce an unlimited number of facsimiles of the same letters, in itself constitutes a distinctive technique of type making. The typesetting methods also differed, as the Koreans used standardised printing plates with fixed framing (Lie 2003: 74; Yukawa 2010: 356). Also, whilst it is well known that Gutenberg's invention operated with a mechanical printing press, the Koreans practised hand printing until the nineteenth century. Due to this technical discrepancy, it has been argued that Asian book manufacturing should not be described by the same terms that are applied to Gutenberg's procedure (Giesecke 2007: 400–404). At the very least, however, one must recognise that there are two separate paths of mediatisation which only merged slowly over time by means of cultural encounters, initiated mainly – in the book business – by missionaries. The fact that the Gutenberg Bible and the Korean Jikji have been exhibited alongside each other during the past few years suggests that these differing paths to a media society are increasingly attracting public attention (Engels 2003).

A Media Revolution? The Dissemination of Gutenberg's Invention

In comparison to the evolutionary development in Asia, which spanned over one thousand years, Gutenberg's invention emerged rather suddenly. The introduction of movable type printing has accordingly been conceived of as a media revolution (Eisenstein [1979] 2005), and on the basis of Marshall McLuhan's work, the belief in the power of new media technology to change society has been emphasised (McLuhan [1962] 2011; Giesecke 1991). Since 1540, Gutenberg's invention has been celebrated every one hundred years; at first with poems of praise, and then in the nineteenth century with elaborate performances (Estermann 1999). Whether it is to be regarded as a revolution in the sense of a sudden upheaval, however, has been a matter of controversy among academics. Today there is a tendency, particularly in historical studies, to classify Gutenberg's printing practice as a long-term change, because its potential for innovation during its first few centuries did not unfold to the extent that the term 'revolution' suggests. Uwe Neddermeyer thus concludes in his extensive study on the development from handwriting to book printing that, in regard to Gutenberg's invention, no strong transformation or break in the history of the book can be detected in respect of either contents and design or recipients and reception. He refers to it rather as the trigger for a considerable acceleration phase within a longer period (Neddermeyer 1998: 552; also Eisermann 2003: 307; Schanze 1999). Even the American historian Elizabeth L. Eisenstein, in the new edition of her classic work on 'print revolution', refers to it as a 'long revolution' taking place between 1450 and 1470 (Eisenstein 2005: 335; on the debate on Eisenstein, cf. Baron et al. 2007).

Several observations reinforce the classification of Gutenberg's invention as a long-term process. A crucial sign is the quantitative rise in book production in the Middle Ages, which can be observed in Germany, Italy, France and England in roughly the same period. After this first peak in the thirteenth century, another considerable increase in book production followed around 1370, shortly after the Black Death had subsided; for parchment had now been superseded by paper, which was available at a considerably lower cost (Neddermeyer 1998: 291–307). The flourishing of universities, the expansion of urban administration, and the increasing effort to create a legal norm were all connected to this development. In Germany, text production was carried out to a large extent by monks, nuns, and secular clergy. Given that their share of the population was on the increase, this, too, marked an important precondition.

Also supporting the argument for a long-term process is the circumstance that handwritten and printed books continued to be co-produced for some centuries after Gutenberg's invention, underlining the 'coexistence and cooperation' of old and new media (Schanze 2001: 300; Dicke and Grubmüller 2003). In contemporary perception, this transitional phase also manifested itself as a 'process-like occurrence' (Ott 1999: 176). Printing clearly dominated the book-manufacturing business in Germany, France and Italy around 1500, but news, at least, continued to be distributed in handwritten form. This smooth transition was also reflected in text forms and modes of communication up to the beginning of the sixteenth century: content, style, paper, font, reception and price levels only changed gradually in the time prior to Gutenberg and after (Eisermann 2003: 307–9; Neddermeyer 1998: 24). Even the sales market reveals this continuity: movable type printing was able to meet the demands of the established market. However, a certain overproduction was recorded, leading to a price slump in the second half of the fifteenth century, which in turn made the medium affordable to the broader masses.

Assigning the printing press to a long-term period of change also appears plausible if one relates it to other inventions of the time. Media scholar Werner Faulstich thus argues that, from a media perspective, the dawn of the Modern Era should be dated to the early fifteenth century when various innovations coincided. For even in the decades around 1400, paper making and paper mills as well as print making and block books began to spread. Subsequently, scriptoria, where texts were produced on demand, and the expansion of the postal service, initiated in particular by Franz von Taxis in 1490, followed. From this, Faulstich perceives a change in dominance, shifting from that of *Mensch-Medien* (human media) to that of new print media: from storyteller to pamphlet, and from herald to diplomat (Faulstich 2006a: 121, 139). The process-like nature of these phenomena can further be highlighted by taking a more European view. After its development in China, the art of paper making reached Spain as early as the twelfth century via the Arabs. In the following century, the practice also spread to Italy, whose use of paper-making factories in this period has been substantiated.

Moreover, the age of printing in Europe as well was marked not by the printed word but rather by the printed image. Woodcut can be traced back to the early fifteenth century in Germany. Thus this was not only the beginning of the typographic era and of 'printed memory', but indeed also a period of increasing visualisation, ranging from the depiction of saints to artistic images, and from emblems to cityscapes and maps. The latter were compiled and released in print in the sixteenth century, demonstrating a thitherto largely unknown spacial knowledge (Würgler 2009: 7, 118). Up to ten thousand copies could be created from a single woodblock. The demand for this – primarily religious – commercial art can be ascribed to late medieval lay piety, a way of life which stands for individual religiousness.

Concurrently, the process-like nature of the 'media revolution' also accentuates Gutenberg's invention in itself. His printing technique is considered to be a groundbreaking compilation of the previously named innovations; hence the term 'printing' defines Gutenberg's stroke of genius rather imprecisely. Consensus prevails that the core element of his invention is not so much his pressing technique – a concept which he adapted from the working methods of the winemakers in the Rhineland – but rather his casting method, which facilitated identical, precise and unlimited reproduction (Neddermeyer 1998: 8; Giesecke 1991: 71, 106).

Gutenberg's motives for his invention are disputable. In recent research, the supposition that Gutenberg sought to discover quick and easy ways of mass production, as may seem to be the case in retrospect, has been put into perspective. Michael Giesecke above all has argued that Gutenberg was much more intent on pursuing a plan to improve writing aesthetically and create an even and harmonious script (Giesecke 1991: 138–43). The sumptuous design of his Bible in particular supports this thesis. According to Giesecke, it was precisely because Gutenberg did not strive for simple and quick reproduction technologies that his invention triumphed, on account of the aesthetic superiority of his mechanical production devices. Nonetheless, Gutenberg was also a man of business who endeavoured to make a good economic profit and not merely defray high investment costs, and he indeed achieved his financial goal. This is corroborated by the fact that Gutenberg printed functional literature that was in high demand and promised a high profit, at a rapid pace, including for instance essential grammar books, letters of indulgence, and broadsides. Even his magnificent Bible had a high profit margin (Kapr 1988: 180, 193; Stöber 2000: 25–27). Uwe Neddermeyer actually opined that the invention arose in the German-speaking world precisely because the demand for inornate functional literature was higher than for example in Italy, where a somewhat larger market for sumptuous books had developed (Neddermeyer 1998: 379). Ultimately, it is Gutenberg himself who links these research positions by having proved that it is possible for aesthetic and economic aims to complement one another.

From Mainz, the printing technique spread across Europe over the following centuries. Printing was already practised in 90 cities in 1480, with the number rising to 252 within the following twenty years. In the early stages, a third of all printing locations were situated in the Heiliges Römische Reich (the Holy Roman Empire), as the reign of the emperor is officially called; later, the same encompassed a fifth of all printing locations. The first conspicuous details are the strong regional differences respecting the transfer of new media technology. The wealthy northern Italian cities now constituted the most important core areas. As private book ownership had already established itself, the demand for print-work was particularly high (Fremmer 2001: 288). Generally speaking, northern Italian cities made for very appealing printing locations – thanks to their political structure, their economic wealth, and, as a result of their well-established universities, their high level of education (Richardson 1994). Even though Paris and Lyon attracted printers for similar reasons, printing technology expanded considerably more slowly into other areas of France, not least due to the effects of the Hundred Years' War (Chartier and Martin 1989). In England, though, there were no printing houses until 1476, the year in which the cloth merchant William Caxton established the very first one on his return from Cologne, where he had been on business and had learned the art of book printing (Kuskin 2006). The number of books printed in England remained smaller than in Italy, France and the Reich up until 1560, and the book market remained 'provincial' until sometime in the seventeenth century, the reasons for which may be found in the economic and political situation during and after the Wars of the Roses (Burke 2000: 193). In addition, the number of manuscripts produced in England had been comparably low even before this, so the printing trade could not build on a previously established book market in the late fifteenth century. This, of course, also confirms that printing was strongly dependent on previously established cultural constellations.

When turning to Eastern Europe and the Orient, this culturally conditioned regional discrepancy becomes distinctly visible. In the orthodox East, printing was hardly able to gain ground, whether due to the limited extent of alphabetisation or concerns about worldly and ecclesiastical direction. The reforms of Peter the Great in the early eighteenth century marked the first turning point in facilitating the dissemination of printing in Russia. The first printing house in St Petersburg was constructed in about 1711, after the one in Moscow was unable to handle the workload. In spite of this, the trade with handwritten texts continued to dominate the Russian streets. When the patriarchal printing house began to issue prayer books and primers galore in the seventeenth century, it was once again the Church that gave impetus to the printing trade (Plambeck 1982: 53). A noteworthy expansion of the printing business, however, took place only towards the end of the eighteenth century, in the reign of Catherine the Great.

New media technology was suppressed even more rigidly in the Ottoman regions. Even though the import of worldly print-work was permitted from the end of the sixteenth century onwards, printing houses did not evolve until sometime in the eighteenth century. The Napoleonic campaigns, in particular, were responsible for introducing some of the first printing presses to the Arab world – a fact which is recognised as a historical turning point in Arabian historiography as well (cf. Roper, in Baron et al. 2007: 250). In South East Europe, printing also failed to develop to any significant extent under Ottoman occupation. Consequently, the first printing house in long-term use emerged only in 1577 in Upper Hungary; in Bratislava, it was even as late as 1610 (Komorová 2007: 186). The 'media revolution' of Gutenberg's invention was in this respect not even a European, but for some time rather a West European, manifestation whose powerful development, even in these parts, occurred only in certain core regions.

The European transfer of new media production often took place as a result of the emigration of German printers. Italy, Flanders, France and Spain were destinations of particular interest because higher profits could be expected. Occasionally, the print-work produced by Germans in Italy was then sold back to Germany, for as a result of the West European dissemination of printing, export centres were rapidly evolving. Their purpose was to provide other European countries with literature, even targeting their clientele with print-work in their respective vernacular language. In the fifteenth and sixteenth centuries it was the city of Venice that constituted the largest printing location worldwide (Burke 2000: 190). North of the Alps, Cologne soon played a large part, with Basel and Antwerp, in particular, following shortly after, and the distribution area of the book trade extending all the way to Portugal and England (Neddermeyer 1998: 395–99). The Central European region which stretched from Flanders to South Germany and Lombardy thus formed the centre of the new medium. Of slightly less importance than the export and emigration of printers was the transmission of the new printing technique through printed instructions. The art of printing was initially regarded as knowledge which was not divulged through printing manuals, until the first ones appeared in the seventeenth century (Giesecke 1991: 71). This, too, underpins the dominant role of economic interests, although in this case it rather impeded the expansion of the new medium.

The fact that this invention had sprung from the mind of a German, and was therefore also promoted by the Germans, generated a certain sense of superiority in contemporary self-perception. In the Holy Roman Empire of the German Nation, the notion was thus articulated that the German invention had much improved the cultural reputation of the Reich, which would no longer appear as a 'land of barbarians' to Italy (Füssel 1999: 48; Scholz 2004: 21). Such statements are on occasions interpreted as evidence (a bit far-reaching) that Gutenberg's invention promoted a premature formation of proto-national identity.

When viewing contemporary perceptions of this invention in general, one sees that in Western Europe positive assessments predominated to an extent not attained by later changes in the media landscape. Even critics largely welcomed the printing press and merely denounced its misuse. The clergy, in general, also approved. A statement in praise of the good readability of the Gutenberg Bible made by Pope Pius II in 1455 is actually on record. Printing was repeatedly described as a gift from God, and in the fifteenth century, clerics had already begun to appreciate the flawless transfer, the exactness of the copy, and the advantage to be gained by believers who could more independently engage in the study of religious texts. The disadvantage, in the mind of contemporaries, was the increasing circulation of vernacular texts, as well as the alleged mass production of redundant books and the printers' greed for profit. The abundance of books in particular had already been criticised in the time before the invention (Giesecke 1991: 161, 169; Neddermeyer 1998: 384; Scholz 2004: 12–18).

In contemporary perception, credit was soon given to the new medium for not restricting itself to a particular target group (Scholz 2004: 18). Not least out of commercial interest, printers saw to it that books became available to a wide audience. As shown by an evaluation of prefaces written by printers from Lyon in the sixteenth century, they addressed the growing group of educated, wealthy citizens, who had been discovered as an additional target group next to that of scholars, with a somewhat educational claim (Vogel 1999: 272). Having said that, the actual number of literates around 1500 is exceedingly difficult to determine. It is estimated that 2 per cent of the population in the German territories were readers (around three hundred thousand). One century later, the estimate number of readers had doubled (Würgler 2009: 94).

Regional, confessional, and gender-related differences as well as the urban–rural gradient make estimation difficult. Men in urban areas and reformed Protestants had a higher rate of alphabetisation. The highest rates in Europe can probably be found in northern Italian cities, where about a third of all boys attended school, and 10 to 20 per cent of all residents were thus able to read in a city such as Venice (Fremmer 2001: 67; Grendler 1989: 77). Generally, it is thought that at least in the Central European cities up to 10 per cent of people were able to read, and that from 1450 onwards readers from the urban middle classes increasingly gained on the literate clergy (10–30 per cent according to Würgler 2009: 95). However, print-work reached significantly more people, which becomes clear when considering broadsides. For in the sixteenth century, texts were still intended primarily to be read out in churches, public spaces and inns, and not for the individual, silent reader (Körber 1998:

302). Broadsides and pamphlets, in particular, therefore reached a countless number of illiterate people.

The usage of the new print media was also dependent on its language, its form, its content and its price. If one reflects on the contents of the printed book, a certain continuity in relation to the Middle Ages is detectable during the first few centuries. In the early phases, the medieval standard works were printed in greater number. A change in content did not occur in the Reich until about 1520. During this time, the market for vernacular writings by reformers as well as occult works increased (Zika 2007). Most books, particularly in the sixteenth century, were religious in content. Liturgical books and school books (Latin grammar books) reached high sales numbers, but ancient literature also constituted 10 to 15 per cent of the market (Neddermeyer 1998: 426–40).

Likewise, printers did not widen the language spectrum for the market's heterogeneous readership until the sixteenth century. Before 1500, of the thirty thousand existing print-works, 70 to 80 per cent were written in the language of the Church, in Latin (Füssel 1999: 76). At around 1480 the circulation of print-works in the national language decreased at first because Latin, with an eye to Europe-wide export, was an effective means to increase sales (Neddermeyer 1998: 544). However, economic considerations finally led printers to publish a greater amount of vernacular print-work towards the end of the century (Barbier 2007: 40). From 1520 onwards, its proportion of printed titles in Italy and the Reich climbed to 50 per cent; in France the same happened in 1560. In particular, light fiction, prose novels of the late Middle Ages, popular history, self-help books and fables were published in the respective vernaculars, although Latin continued to dominate the book sector until the end of the seventeenth century. Remarkably high circulation was achieved by German books on the liberal arts, which were geared towards educated people in urban areas (Füssel 1999: 76–78, 90). This again underscores that the new media technology took some time to recognise its opportunities and target audiences that were not open to previous medieval handwriting methods, and how it eventually brought about change.

Leaflets and Pamphlets

The book market was certainly only one result of the new media technology, and at least with regard to circulation, not even the most significant. Pamphlets, leaflets, so-called *Neue Zeitungen* (new newspapers) and calendars had a strong appeal, as people particularly in rural areas valued the advice they contained on everyday life. Even though these media are not clearly distinguishable, different typologies can be made out relative to form and content, with whose help it is possible to illustrate their social significance. Leaflets (*Flugblatt*) played a key role in the early modern period. The term 'leaflet', which alludes to its rapid distribution, was coined in 1787. The term 'broadside' seems more appropriate. In most cases these prints combined text and image on a single page, ranging from official notes to political, religious, scientific and literary contents (Schilling 1990; Wilke 2000: 20). Compared to multiple-page chapbooks, they did not usually include evaluations which may have had an instigative effect, but tended to be of an informative, albeit moralising character.

The leaflet is significant on a number of different levels. Its economic dimension, to begin with, furthered both expansion and versatile circulation. Owing to the low production costs and high distribution figure, it was a profitable medium for printers, whose potential Gutenberg had also recognised. The price of a leaflet was at least equal to the hourly wage of a workman, with the average circulation figure being around a thousand to fifteen hundred copies. The often lurid character of the titles further illustrates printers' keen sales orientation.

Secondly, leaflets can be understood as part of the political communication in the fifteenth century, as a means to exercise power. Broadsides were thus often posted clearly visible in public spaces, especially in times of conflict such as feuds, wars, and legal issues (Eisermann 2003: 290). This again demonstrates the continuity of previous communication techniques, since typography and layout were mostly congruent with medieval modes of writing (ibid.: 294). In contrast to today, freely sold leaflets were not connected with political protest. In cases in which they did contain political criticism, this was, according to Michael Schilling, usually in conformity with the authorities. If this was not so, any existing criticism was at least outbalanced by uplifting comments (Schilling 1990: 199). However, early broadsides did occasionally encourage political action. The contemporary scholar Sebastian Brant, for instance, reported on the meteorite which struck in 1492 near Ensisheim, interpreting it as a bad omen in regard to the French and Burgundians, and prompting King Maximilian to proceed against them (Füssel 1999: 98). Hence, the leaflet stood for direct communication with the sovereigns. Although leaflets refrained from a denunciation of politics, it is believed that they encouraged political criticism and damaged the sovereign's reputation (Schilling 1990: 200).

Thirdly, leaflets were a form of information media, actually turning ongoing processes into events through their regular and comprehensive reporting. Thus in 1502, the term 'new newspapers' was already in use, referring to the not yet periodical but certainly up-to-date news which they delivered (Lang 1987: 57–60). Sensationalism is a distinct, often-mentioned characteristic. While spectacular images depicting violent scenes or 'miracles' were intended as an incentive to buy, texts were often emotionally charged (Schilling 1990:

76–90). Recent research, though, stresses that their news reporting was chiefly of a political-military nature and that sensations were less common than has been assumed (Pfarr 1994: 124). News travelled all the way to the Ottoman Empire and America, and was furnished with various verification strategies. According to Schilling, such news was seldom subject to scrutiny in the sixteenth century. In the ensuing century, however, people gradually began to question news contents (Schilling 1990: 140).

Closely associated with this is, fourthly, the significance of broadsides as a means of social disciplinary action. In the depiction of crimes, the punishment of the offender always took centre stage. It often concluded with religiously based moral passages which provided a guideline for exclusion, crisis management, and the (re-)establishment of order. On the basis of such reports, printing contributed to the standardising of perception – for instance, how deformities or comets were to be interpreted (Mauelshagen and Mauer 2000: 104). In other words, leaflets were also a medium intended to influence.

Despite their similarity, leaflets did differ from pamphlets in several ways. Pamphlets (in German: *Flugschriften*) were usually of a smaller format, were made up of several pages, including more text passages, were aimed to a greater extent at influencing the reader, and often had a somewhat polemic undertone. Authors published their work anonymously for the most part, and their various text forms were primarily concerned with questions of religion, politics, or legal issues. Some historians waive such functional ascriptions and merely define pamphlets as multi-page, non-periodical, self-contained writings (Harms 1989: 622; Repgen 1997: 50). After all, elaborate statistical examinations of 3,100 pamphlets from the reformation period have demonstrated that they were chiefly informative and seldom 'pugnacious-polemic' (Köhler 1986: 261–64). In international research, in fact, they are considered as printwork, 'which was intended sometimes to inform, but usually to persuade the reader about current events', regardless of their scope (Harline 1987: 3). The term 'pamphlet' thus describes a specific literary genre (Raymond 2003: 25). When observing the emergence of pamphlets in respective countries but in an international context, it is striking that their greatest expansion is found in times of social conflict. In Germany, they began to thrive as early as 1517 during the course of the Reformation, moving from Latin polemic papers to German pamphlets. Neighbouring Western countries also showed this crescive trend, albeit slightly later in the second half of the sixteenth century. Its incipience in the Netherlands can be pinpointed to 1565, and a second detectable upsurge in the years after 1607, when an increasing number of polemic papers surfaced in connection with the beginning of the revolt of the Seventeen Provinces against Spain, the founding of the Dutch Republic, and the start of the Eighty Years' War. However, these papers remained an important part of the Netherlands' public culture of political discussion, the more so as there was particularly little monitoring of leaflets (Harline 1987: 227). The fact that in the seventeenth and eighteenth centuries the culture of pamphlets spread in England and the Netherlands, in particular, is evidence that this medium was not merely an expression of crises, but rather signified the formation of a public space. In doing so, this media innovation constituted a stabilisation of the principle of competing interests (Mörke 2005: 18, 31).

In the context of the religious conflicts in France in the 1560s, chapbooks also gained significance (Latimer 1976). In particular the campaign against minister Concini (1614–1618) is considered as the high point of this medium (Sawyer 1990). Besides criticising the crown, they were also utilised by Richelieu for the systematic defence of Louis XIV (Klaits 1976: 7). Although, from 1550, pamphlets were also used during religious conflict in England, these print-works bore no significant meaning for political life (Raymond 2003: 15). Indeed, dissemination increased from 1580 onwards, but it would take until sometime in the seventeenth century before this medium would be of central importance, which was particularly the case in relation to the 1640s Civil War. Pamphlets established critical, public debates on political issues and thus became a model for public speeches (Raymond 2003: 26; Zaret 2000). Two factors in particular speak in favour of their use in situations of conflict: for one, it was safer to express one's opinion in print than to state it in person; and secondly, pamphlets put more pressure on the rulers, as they produced the impression of addressing the common people, possibly offering an incentive for rebellion. As shown by Craig E. Harline in the case of the Netherlands, sovereigns were thereupon more inclined to respond with the public legitimation of their actions (Harline 1987: 229). The claim that rulers now justified their behaviour publicly with the aid of chapbooks can also be seen in the case of the Duchy of Prussia. Duke Albert, for instance, defended his conversion to Lutheranism in 1526 in a pamphlet; and similarly, in 1577, the city of Danzig explained that it would not surrender to Poland (Körber 1998: 159). Rulers thus left the realm of arcane politics, at least to some extent.

Simultaneously, the authorities also availed themselves of the new media. According to Falk Eisermann, the first people to launch printing in the Reich were in the medium to upper echelons of politics (legates, councilmen and chancellery workers), and, from about 1480 onwards, the political leader (Eisermann 2003: 307), as Emperor Maximilian I is seen as the first sovereign to make systematic use of Gutenberg's invention. He had print-work prepared and distributed in order to influence people's disposition on important events, such as his election in 1486, his captivity in Flanders, and the Imperial Reform (Reichsreform) of Worms in 1495 (Eisermann 2002). Additionally, he distributed printed Reichstag invitations containing war reports as well as calls for war against the Turks. During conflicts in Venice, he even used leaflets in Italian for propaganda purposes by dropping them behind the front line suspended from balloons. Last but not least, his circulation of print-work was an attempt to secure his posthumous fame (Füssel 1999: 102–4).

This political utilisation of media entailed censorship in all European nations. Subsequent to previous ecclesiastical surveillance, secular and clerical censorship developed at the end of the fifteenth century. Starting in the 1520s, with the amount of critical discourse in printed media gradually increasing, restrictive laws came into being, such as pre-censorship (1529) and the requirement to display imprint (1530) in the Reich (Eisenhardt 1970: 29; Hemels 1982: 32; Wilke 2000: 36). In addition, restrictions were made with regard to printing locations, giving precedence to university towns, royal seats and imperial cities in the Reich, and London as well as the two university towns Oxford and Cambridge in England (Briggs and Burke 2002: 50). Religious and confessional aspects initially took precedence over political ones in censorship laws. This circumstance did not change until the second half of the eighteenth century (Eisenhardt 1970: 153). Moral and ethical misdemeanours were punished chiefly in connection with other offences (Schilling 1990: 201). Besides territorial censorship under the superintendence of the emperor, there was ecclesiastical surveillance which in regard to Protestants was also carried out at the territorial state level.

Censorship edicts and their justification are pre-eminent for identifying the powerful effect attributed to print media by contemporaries. When viewing the practical implementation of censorship laws, however, one may find that researchers have on various occasions projected the police state regime of the *Vormärz* in the early nineteenth century onto the early Modern Era. More recently, on the other hand, scholars have emphasised the limits of censorship in the sixteenth and seventeenth centuries, spurred on by investigations of the underground journalism of French hacks prior to 1789. These include the omission of imprints, the stating of false names and places of publishing, the smuggling of books from abroad, and the local censorship practice. Not only did censorship rules differ regionally, there was also a considerable leeway in applying them. Various sovereigns, for instance, did not implement the emperor's decisions. Moreover, many of them commissioned people who were already entrusted with other tasks, such as preachers or professors, with media supervision, instead of appointing special control committees. Not least, punishments were discriminative and arbitrary. In order to demonstrate respect for the much-maligned nation of Scotland, the Duchy of Prussia even imposed the death penalty on someone for launching a vituperative attack. Some cases of long prison sentences are also recorded. In other comparable instances, though, punishments were usually lenient or restricted to 'mere' exile (Körber 1998: 271). France, on the other hand, dealt with her perpetrators more stringently (Minois 1995). Generally speaking, however, it was certainly possible for media dynamics to avoid political control.

To conclude, the findings so far have revealed that Gutenberg's invention was no 'media revolution' in the sense that it triggered sudden changes. Rather, his innovation of media technology was embedded in a wide range of cultural changes in the Middle Ages, and it required several decades to unfold its individual forms, contents and impact.

Social and Cultural Consequences of Printing

The foregoing examples have already outlined many of the varied effects directly linked with the new media. However, media scholars in particular, as well as some historians, have stressed even more strongly the wide-ranging social consequences resulting from the expansion of Gutenberg's printing technique. In doing so, they associated media change with processes of modernisation, which paved the way to the Modern Era culturally, socially, economically and politically (Giesecke 1991; Eisenstein 2005; Hörisch 2004; Faulstich 2006a; McLuhan 2011). Most straightforward are doubtless those effects which were directly linked to the printing technology. The expansion and acceleration of text and image production led to a transnational consolidation of communication, as print-works provided a common basis of reference. This advanced the academic network, whose foundation had its roots in the Renaissance period, and facilitated the accumulation of knowledge for other social strata. Simultaneously, this development improved the economic relations between scholars and those businessmen who made printing and distribution possible (Eisenstein 2005: 28; Burke 2000: 20).

Also, printing resulted in a tangible rise of alphabetisation. Although more recent studies reveal an increase in the number of literates around 1370 (i.e. before the invention of printing), figures show that a considerably higher proportion of laypersons learned to read in the sixteenth century (Neddermeyer 1998: 536). In East European countries, on the other hand, where the printing trade initially had difficulties gaining ground, literacy rates rose only marginally. It is debatable, however, to what extent reading practices changed – from public readings to private, silent reading habits – but there is some evidence that a shift began to take place as early as the Middle Ages (Stein 2006: 159; Griep 2005: 197).

Other, more extensive theses on the social consequences of printing appear convincing at first, but can be challenged by drawing a comparison to the previously outlined development in Asia. Against the background of economic aspects, McLuhan has argued that printing was able to develop modern markets because it represented a central consumer good in itself (McLuhan 2011: 236). A glance towards Korea, however, proves that it was indeed possible for this new medium to expand primarily within a state-run distribution system, without going hand in hand with a capitalistic structure (Lie 2003). McLuhan's socio-economic theses are also derived from the attribute of printing he considers most distinct – the principle of uniform reproduction. This led to the widely held deduction that the printing press had been the first assembly line and the first mass production industry, and had thus effected uniform mass production and industrialisation (McLuhan 2011: 142f.). But once again the comparison with Asia is a warning against too readily conjecturing causalities, as neither printing techniques nor mass circulation entailed the concept of Fordism.

The standardisations which had resulted from printing – including, for instance, increasingly homogenised text forms, images, maps and diagrams as well as the harmonisation of calendars and dictionaries – promoted the formation of a collective body of knowledge (Eisenstein 2005: 23, 56), leading to the assumption that printing implied linguistic standardisations. Its development ostensibly led to a harmonisation of writing styles and dialects and thus to the establishment of national languages. This seems to correlate with the linguistic appeal of Bible translations in different countries, from a long-term perspective as well, especially since an increase in vernacular prints from the sixteenth century onwards has been substantiated. Yet printed Protestant Bible translations should not be overrated, as vernacular languages asserted themselves concurrently in countries with major confessional differences, for example the Reich, England, France, Italy and Bohemia (cf. Gilmont 1998).

This should nevertheless be put into perspective. For in religious and academic communication at least, Latin continued to prevail for quite some time, while the significance of dialects, on the other hand, did not diminish because of printed language. What is more, the comparison with China underscores that a uniform written language must by no means result in an automatic eradication of dialects. On the contrary, it tended to remain on a somewhat rarefied level relative to the spoken language. Considering that dialects did not pale in significance until sometime in the twentieth century, it appears that language standardisation occurred not only in connection with the education system, but particularly in conjunction with the dissemination of electronic media such as radio and television. Even in the case of national languages, uniform modes of writing did not develop in Germany until later, arising primarily in the wake of the general standardisation efforts emanating from nineteenth-century nationalism. One must equally relativise the claim that nationalism evolved on the grounds of printing in the sixteenth century, as Benedict Anderson, amongst others, argues in his much cited work (Anderson [1983] 2006: 31–48). Anderson argues in a brief footnote that printing had no revolutionary impact in China, because of the absence of capitalism there (ibid.: 46). He roots his most pivotal argument not only in the establishment of national languages, but also in the awareness of contemporaneous media use. Researchers on the topic of nationalism, however, hold the view that this phenomenon developed as late as the second half of the eighteenth century, while any previous cognition should be reduced to a sense of affiliation at the most (Jansen and Borggräfe 2007: 26).

McLuhan's notion that printing induced a novel conception of scribes as authors, as well as the concept of intellectual property, have been much referred to. Printing is thus thought to have been the agent for the evolving of individuals as inventors with a claim to originality, whereby 'change itself [became] the archetypal norm of social life' (McLuhan 2011: 177). Indeed, disputes on plagiarism and disputes about authorship increased in quantity during the Renaissance and portended the birth of the author (Burke 2000: 176). Many creators of past innovations – such as the mirror, spectacles and the mechanical clock – had remained unknown, whilst the image of the inventor now appeared to rise to that of a prototypic character of the Modern Era (Hörisch 2004: 130). To begin with, the emphasis on individual names on the covers of books, catalogues and images was conducive to this trend, even though the original intention was to stimulate sales. Book covers have thus been perceived as the birth of advertisement (Saenger 2005: 197; Eisenstein 2005: 33). One may also add that censorship laws such as the obligatory imprint, as well as prosecution in case of non-compliance, forced people to regard texts as individual creations. The emergence of paramount figures like Luther, Da Vinci and Galilei also seems to confirm this evolution of creative individuals as being a result of printing.

The associated assumption that printing had generally encouraged individualisation bears even more truth. As Neil Postman argued, printed texts prompted individual reflection; they also evolved on the basis of personal avowals (Postman [1982] 2011: 27–32). When contrasting these discoveries with the Asian development, however, it once again becomes clear that the birth of individualism was not necessarily impacted by printing. After all, authorship initially had hardly any significance in Asia, and no mention was made of the inventors of new media technologies. Furthermore, self-manifestation cannot have been so effortlessly and rapidly achieved in Western Europe either; for why else do we have so little biographical knowledge of perhaps the greatest poet and playwright of all time, William Shakespeare. It was not an anomaly for printed texts to be published anonymously or under false names – the proportion of anonymous print-work in seventeenth-century England rose to a full 30 per cent (Raymond 2003: 169). Another conflictive aspect is whether this alleged individualisation is compatible with the simultaneously postulated standardisation of society through the technology of printing. Elisabeth Eisenstein has attempted to elucidate this discrepancy by claiming that standardised writing was precisely what encouraged efforts to develop a personal touch (Eisenstein 2005: 72, 104).

It is without doubt that printing changed the way knowledge was imparted, leading to modifications in visual and textual contents. Broadsides gradually assumed the task of news distribution, which had previously been assigned exclusively to the Church (Eisenstein 2005: 104). And since economic aspects increasingly steered textual selection, printing also facilitated the rejection of canonical texts. This novel way of accumulating knowledge also altered the art of preserving memories, which is why printing has been designated the 'engine of immortality' (McLuhan 2011: 230). The preservation in print, the storing of knowledge in libraries, and cataloguing and indexing with the aid of bibliographies thus modified the selection mechanisms of memory culture. At the same time, printing transformed the places associated with written communication. According to Frieder Schanze, scriptoria were turned into offices in the Modern Era; libraries became places of study for individually working scholars, and for competitive reasons, the theatre concentrated increasingly on physicality (Schanze 2001: 233–39). The dissemination of school books changed the course of lessons as early as the sixteenth century, and the Church also transformed its communication by means of the immediate utilisation of printing, which Michael Giesecke has interpreted as 'a rationalisation of office communication' (Giesecke 1991: 223–30, quote 230). Ecclesiastical rituals are also said to have been harmonised.

The most convincing as well as the most difficult statement to prove is McLuhan's arguably most significant thesis, which describes typography as a natural resource that 'shapes not only private sense ratios but also patterns of communal interdependence' (McLuhan 2011: 186). In his work, he detects a hierarchical shift from the aural to the visual sense, making homogeneous visual perception the characteristic of 'typographic man'. One objection to this has been that medieval contemporaries had already perceived similar changes (Neddermeyer 1998: 21, 550). Eric Alfred Havelock stressed very early on that such an alteration of perception was detectable even in the ancient world, namely in the transition between oral and written culture – a view which met with much criticism. Contrariwise, public reading did not die out in 1500, but, on the contrary, remained the norm for at least another two centuries after the emergence of typography. The argument of 'visual culture' at first appears convincing with regard to the educational sector, with textbooks now more frequently serving as the chief source of knowledge, and learning examples being increasingly accompanied by images (Eisenstein 2005: 40–45). However, this area of life also reveals the limits of the visual age. For despite the expansion of the book market, it is common knowledge that schools and even universities continued to adhere rigidly to teaching methods like spoken dialogues and lectures. Other domains also demonstrate the simultaneous expansion of speech and writing, such as in the form of sermons or songs (Briggs and Burke 2002: 46).

Judging from intuition, one may plausibly argue that the establishment of print media cultivated logical rationalism: an assumption hardly to be proved. According to some research, it was not just the printed contents of texts, but to a much greater extent their new medial formation which changed people's mindsets, its power lying in the argumentative and rule-governed new structure (McLuhan 2011). Claims have also been made that higher literacy rates contributed to enhancing the capacity for abstract thinking. The fact that printing enabled an increase in the use of display formats such as diagrams, charts and maps (i.e. illustrations not suited for public reading) has also been seen as an aid to improving abstraction skills and rationalism. Neil Postman developed this assumption even further by claiming that reading and abstraction skills had been necessary to create a gap between adults and children, and thus constitute childhood (Postman 2011: 20).

Evidently, the establishment of printing also had political implications for power relationships, social communities and political order. Media scholars have postulated that printing activated critique on authorities and the demise of hierarchies, because printed text assumed a new authority (Postman 2011: 23–33). Early political protests, particularly the Reformation and the German Peasants' War, 1524 to 1526, serve as examples (Beyer 1994: 85–88). Essentially it can hardly be contested that chapbooks and pamphlets established a form of discourse in the broadest sense by challenging political authorities and thus forcing them to justify themselves and their actions – in some cases at least (Harline 1987: 227; Körber 1998: 381). On the other hand, at the same time, according to Michael Schilling, printing led to stricter regimentation and disciplinary action on the part of the sovereigns by means, for example, of printed legal documents such as police orders, or texts on moral standards (Schilling 1990: 215).

How far the invention of printing was able to alter existing social orders can be highlighted particularly well using the example of the Reformation. The connection between the Reformation and media change has been stressed by representatives of various academic disciplines. It is thought that printing was directly responsible for the outcome of the Reformation (Eisenstein 2005: 208; Burkhardt 2002: 35–48), which is thereby conceived as a media event (Hamm 1996). It has been referred to as a revolution of religion and communication which brought about a structural change in sacral communication (Lottes 1996: 252, 260). Undisputed is the fact that new media not only influenced the Reformation, but that the Reformation in turn shaped the media landscape by causing it to expand, become vernacular and develop new formats. In spite of all this, a comprehensive media history on the Reformation period has not been attempted, even though Anglo-Saxon literature, in particular, addresses the issue of Reformation 'propaganda' more than once (Scribner 1981; Edwards 1994; Gilmont 1998).

Doubtless, the change in religious communication cannot be ascribed merely to Luther or any other great reformer. The Church quickly embraced new media technology in the first centuries after the invention of printing, whether for religious interaction, such as the printing of indulgence letters, or reform efforts, such as the Council of Basel (Eisermann 2002: 305; Giesecke 1991: 229, 273–76). Prior to Luther, eighteen printed copies of the Bible in the German language were already in existence, making use of the new media potential despite the poor translation (Füssel 1999: 110). At the end of the fifteenth century, moreover, and before Luther's achievement, a wave of piety surfaced and proved to be quite media compatible. This included, for instance, the increase in devotions, foundations and pilgrimages; the trade with devotional articles; and the indulgence system. Because of this, devotional books and images reached high circulation figures even before the Reformation (Lottes 1996: 249; Beyer 1994: 78).

Nevertheless, the media expansion accompanying the Reformation in the German Reich had thitherto been unparalleled. Book production rose in 1517 and peaked in 1523, when chapbooks, too, had an immense circulation. Hans-Joachim Köhler has calculated that eleven thousand prints were produced between 1520 and 1526 alone, with circulation revolving around eleven million copies, keeping in mind that the population of the Reich amounted to approximately twelve million people (Köhler 1986: 250, 266; overview in Mörke 2005: 130–35). Luther himself contributed significantly. For besides his Bible translation, he was by far the most successful author of his time. As many as 219 chapbooks are attributed to him, and around a hundred thousand copies of his small Catechism were printed up to 1563. The Reformation also encouraged laymen to take a stand in print, and not least, the media triggered a Europe-wide discussion: for one, Reformation writings found their way to foreign countries, and this, in turn, generated the production of refutations (Gilmont 1998). Even the public libricide of Luther's writings, reaching from London to Poland, was part of this media event (see Raymond 2003: 13; Kawecka-Gryczowa and Tazbur 1998: 424). Thus, Wittenberg – and not Mainz – has pointedly been declared as the actual origin of the 'Gutenberg-Galaxy' (Weyrauch 1995: 2).

To what extent did Luther intend a medial 'mass mobilisation' against the Roman Catholic Church? Firstly, it is striking that Luther did not compose leaflets, even though they would have reached a notably larger audience. Instead, his chapbooks chiefly addressed the educated people. However, these texts were in turn simplified and tailored to popular culture by other authors, particularly from Nuremberg, and partially distributed free of cost for propaganda purposes (Heintzel 1998: 215). Another objection that has been articulated is the opinion that Luther's chapbooks were not always as polemically persuasive as his famous Peasants' War writing, 'Against the Murderous,

Thieving Hordes of Peasants' from 1525, and that some of his writings had a rather matter-of-fact tone to them, such as 'On the Freedom of a Christian' from 1520 (Hamm 1996: 142). In taking up everyday experiences and culminating in criticism, particularly of the Pope, it was primarily the pictorial illustrations accompanying his texts that were characterised by polemic and personalised antitheses (Scribner 1981: 243–46).

Moreover, Luther attached great value to a productive connection between printed text and verbal communication. His translated and newly composed lyrics and the way he directly addressed his readers underscore this. This 'oral writing' (Lottes 1996: 256) can also be found in sermons that drew on Luther's writings. Luther's 'principle of Scripture', which implied that faith could be derived only from the Holy Bible ('sola scriptura'), is in perfect agreement with the new print media. Reformers' attempts at persuasion were not restricted to texts. They used visual material, such as images of Luther himself, of pious peasants or caricatured opponents, as in the much quoted 'Passional Christi and Antichristi' from 1521 (Scribner 1981: 148–89; Stöber 2000). In general, the wide dissemination of the Lutherans must also be defined through visualisation, even though polemic visualisations were mostly annotated (Beyer 1994: 184). Luther's fondness for images underscores why Reformation media were embellished with illustrations in Germany, while Calvinism in France availed itself of music (Würgler 2009: 20). In this way, a diverse 'reformatory public' emerged (Wohlfeil 1984) and communicated on an inter-medial level transcending class. One should not underestimate the rise of Europe-wide consequences of this literary preservation of Protestantism, which resulted in the spread of printing into regions of Eastern Europe, where it had scarcely taken root before (Kawecka-Gryczowa and Tazbur 1998: 413; cf. Gilmont 1998).

Media scholars such as Werner Faulstich, in particular, assigned the successful outcome of the Reformation to the fact that different media techniques were used compared to the Roman Catholic Church. While reformers took advantage of the new print media, the Roman Catholic Church mainly used the 'old Mensch-media' in the Counter Reformation, i.e. priests or preachers (Faulstich 2006a: 145). In fact, the Roman Church hardly responded medially until the Diet of Augsburg of 1530, even though early popular prints also mocked Luther visually as a confederate of the devil (Scribner 1981: 229–32). According to Alexander Heintzel's findings, representatives of the Roman Church started their counter-propaganda, mainly initiated by the Jesuits, only after the Council of Trent in 1563 (Heintzel 1998: 214). But not even the famous Jesuit drama was able to achieve a comparably broad effect, as it, too, concentrated on the use of 'Mensch-media'. Of course, one may counter that the spread of the Reformation was also precipitated by 'Mensch-media' such as priests, and that its continued use by the Roman Church means that their forms of communication were indeed successful. The Counter-Reformation also developed a novel form of visual politics; however, as shown by Jens Baumgarten, it had no great effect on supporters of the Protestant faith, but rather served to consolidate its own followers (Baumgarten 2004).

It is important not to view the dissemination of printing with merely hierarchical-ecclesiastical intentions in mind, but to take into consideration the printers' economic outlook. They offered their services to Catholic rulers as well, for instance in Spain, Portugal, France, and the Habsburg Empire, without, however, being able to expand their markets accordingly. Although more recent research emphasises the fact that the position of the Catholic Church regarding the vernacular translation of the Holy Scriptures was by no means consistent (Gilmont 1998: 473), the prohibition of vernacular popular editions for Catholic laymen in non-reformed regions slowed down the printing business (Eisenstein 2005: 192–99). Because of the Reformation, the Roman Church suffered the loss of many printing locations in the Reich – with a few exceptions, such as Cologne – which made the exertion of influence and censorship difficult. Many printers emigrated north from Oberdeutschland, causing the book market to expand and to relocate its centre.

While the expansion of print media did not automatically provoke criticism of hierarchies, its central role in times of controversy was evident when religious conflicts arose in the second half of the sixteenth century in Western Europe. Even in France, where Reformation efforts failed, estimates reveal about thirteen hundred printed religious texts between 1511 and 1551, with a total circulation of around one million copies. In 1525, the Parisian theological faculty prohibited the translation of reformatory writings, but prints from Antwerp and Geneva supplied the country with texts. Reformatory writings emerged at the same time as counter-reformatory ones, both reaching maximum distribution in the 1540s (Higman 1996: 14–22). The religious conflicts in France, the Eighty Years' War of the Dutch against Spain, and the pamphlet culture in the religiously charged English Civil War (1642–1649) further exemplify how religious issues gave a certain dynamic to the printing culture and vice versa (Raymond 2003: 164, 202–75).

These considerations on the role of printing during the Reformation again highlight the fact that the media development generated clearly visible social changes. Nonetheless, it must be emphasised that many academic theses introduced in this work on the effect of media changes are somewhat far reaching in parts, and should perhaps be understood as intellectual stimuli for future research on related sources rather than as provable findings. It has been shown that the verification of causal relations is difficult, in the first place because postulated changes did not occur directly after the invention of the new medium. For as can be seen, Gutenberg's innovation was a milestone in a general upheaval rather than a media revolution, its development spanning some two hundred years even within the Reich. Michael Giesecke, who certainly postulated extensive effects to a greater extent than other authors of recent studies, casually points out in his book that the consequences of the media change were dependent on the wishes and concerns of the environment (Giesecke 1991: 124). If this statement is taken seriously, printing can be seen as a type of catalyst which activated a series of unforeseen processes. When considering Asia as well as the various discrepancies within Europe, one must conclude that the cultural diversity of the different regions was of great importance, for this was what the expansion and effects of media depended on.

CHAPTER 2

The Establishment of Periodicals

Newspapers as a New Medium

Newspapers and magazines are still counted among those mass media which exert the most influence in the realms of politics, culture and society. Nevertheless, the invention of the periodical press in 1605 is not classified as a turning point in remembrance culture or in historical studies. Until today, even major encyclopedic works have mostly failed to consider the inventor of the newspaper, Johann Carolus, worthy of an entry. Nor did contemporaries often bring up the issue of the new medium. It was not until newspapers were established Europe-wide in the last third of the seventeenth century that an intensive debate emerged on the subject (Pompe 2004). While communication studies have long stressed the social significance of early newspapers, historians are now also beginning to emphasise their importance. In the German context, Wolfgang Behringer in particular refers to the emergence of newspapers as a media revolution in whose course the interplay of the postal network and newspapers 'contributed considerably to changing the view of the world within a generation' (Behringer 1999: 81).

One reason why the rise of the newspaper was generally not considered as a 'media revolution' was the fact that no technical innovation was linked with it. In fact, printing techniques hardly changed between the age of Gutenberg and the French Revolution. This underlines the argument that technical changes were not a prerequisite for media developments, but that the form and acquisition of media were shaped rather by cultural, political and social preconditions. Linguistically, the invention of the newspaper also fails to constitute a distinct break: on the one hand, the German term *Zeitung* (originally meaning 'news') had been used from around 1500 to denote non-periodical leaflets containing the latest news (so-called *Neue Zeitungen*, 'New Newspapers'). On the other hand, *Zeitung* only succeeded in asserting itself as a term for this specific medium in the nineteenth century. At the same time, other terms circulated in Europe, such as *Aviso* (advertisements), *Relationen* ('accounts'), *Gazette, Nouvelle, Courante, Mercurius,* and *Post* or *Newsbooks,* the latter being referred to in England under the collective term of 'pamphlets' (Raymond 2003: 101). Another reason why the seventeenth century newspaper attracted little interest might have been that it was only one medium of many in the press sector. Pamphlets continued to predominate and interacted with newspapers intertextually as well as with regard to production and reception until the eighteenth century (Bellingradt 2011). The interplay of oral, literal and typographic information provided an economically grounded media system, which shaped the formation of opinions in the seventeenth century (Scholz Williams and Layfer 2008; Arndt and Körber 2010).

The specific character and novelty of the newspaper were achieved through the fusion of four criteria attributed to older types of media: its periodicity, its quality of being up-to-date, universality of content, and publicity, i.e. accessibility for everyone (such is the definition of the newspaper since Otto Groth (1948: 339f.). Similar to Gutenberg's invention, it tied in with existing communication techniques. Thus some media scientists regard 'human media' (e.g. singers or preachers) as important precursors of the newspaper, as they disseminated news periodically and promptly (Faulstich 1998: 212–14, 224). More important for the establishment of periodical papers, however, was the postal system, whose primary form of communication, namely the letter, and distribution logistics served as central requirements (Behringer 2003: 412–17). The printed press would thus, from the fourteenth century, draw upon handwritten 'newspapers' – letters written by correspondents and used for spreading (chiefly economic) news within a well-established network in Western Europe and the Middle East (Gravesteijn, in North 1995: 63–66). By this means, merchants, sovereigns and city councillors were able to gather relevant economic and political information on a regular basis. Particularly well known are the *Fugger-Zeitungen* from the sixteenth century, since they have been exceptionally well preserved. Another forerunner were the single-page leaflets, which were also referred to as *Neue Zeitungen* due to the fact that they tended to include the latest news. The so-called *Messrelationen*, which comprised pieces of news on around one hundred pages, usually semi-annually, and were sold at fairs, also advanced the development of periodicity since the 1580s (Rousseaux 2004). As with book printing, it was a case of smooth transition. Handwritten newspapers survived until well into the eighteenth century, particularly in rigid, absolutist systems such as France and the Habsburg Monarchy (Popkin 2005: 24).

This transition can be clearly demonstrated by the example of the Strasbourg printer Johann Carolus (1575–1634), who issued the first newspaper known to us today. Initially, Carolus duplicated handwritten notices. After acquiring a printing press and founding one of the major printing houses on the Upper Rhine, he created a printed newspaper called *Relation aller Fürnemmen und gedenckwürdigen Historien...* (newspaper of all important and memorable histories...), a by-product combining his work as a printer and distributor of news (Welke in Welke and Wilke 2008). In 1605, he filed a request for a concession on his invention before the municipal council. His location in Strasbourg had the advantage of being the hub of the postal system; moreover, messages were exchanged there between the German and French territories. Thus for a second time, a key invention of media history emerged in the Rhineland, abetted by the region's population density, compression of information and open trading culture.

In Western Europe, the invention of the newspaper was in the air at the beginning of the seventeenth century. From the 1580s, printed news from France and the Netherlands had increasingly appeared in England. By 1592 it could be purchased in London at fairly regular intervals (*News of France on the First of the Month of March*), and in the following year on set dates (Raymond 2003: 105–7). Dutch media historians occasionally assert that the first newspaper published worldwide originated in Amsterdam in 1609 (Wijfjes, in Broersma 2007: 61). What is certain is that in 1605 the Archdukes granted a printer from Antwerp the privilege of regularly publishing 'great events', particularly for the military (Morineau 1995: 34). Accordingly, newspapers spread quickly in the region.

As is the case with the history of print, huge discrepancies are evident in the spread of the newspaper in seventeenth-century Europe. The German-speaking regions at the time boasted about two hundred newspaper titles, which was more than the rest of Europe combined. Moreover, they were regionally diversified, so that in the year 1669, seventeen of the thirty-two European cities with newspapers were situated in the German Holy Roman Empire, whereas centralised states such as Sweden, Denmark, England and France only had newspapers printed in their capitals (Ries 1977: 179). Yet there were also vast differences within the empire. At first newspapers were mainly produced in the south and around Thuringia and Saxony, but with the exception of Cologne and Hamburg, hardly at all in the northern and western parts of Germany. The explanation lies in the particular cultural, economic and political framework of these regions as well as their population density. Thus despite its central location, hardly any long-running newspapers emerged in the Electorate of Hanover before the eighteenth century for reasons of low demand and authoritarian restrictions (Küster 2004: 138–57).

Newspapers experienced an early and widespread expansion in the Netherlands, starting in 1618. As was the case in the Holy Roman Empire, the country's polycentric and religiously heterogeneous structure fostered this development, as did the local printing tradition and urban prosperity. The influence of politics on the spread of the new medium was also evident in northern Italy: despite affluence and high literacy rates, newspapers did not appear there until 1636, as they had formerly been prohibited by the authorities. As with printing, expansion proceeded only tentatively in the north and especially the east of Europe. The first newspaper published in the Swedish language did not appear until 1645, the first Danish one in 1672, and the first Polish one in 1661 (Welke and Wilke 2008: 234). In Russia, newspapers only began to establish themselves in the course of Peter the Great's reforms, from 1702, as a means to mobilise the populace for the war against Sweden and to inform about domestic and foreign policy (Plambeck 1982: 39–43; McReynolds 1991: 16). However, since profits remained low because of limited readership, most newspapers and periodicals were short-lived (Marker 1985: 167). In Hungary, too, the periodical press only began to develop in the eighteenth century during Maria Theresia's era of enlightened absolutism. Above all, the country's almost complete lack of urban middle-class culture inhibited press expansion (Bachleitner and Seidler 2007; Balogh and Tarnói 2007). In those parts of Europe belonging to the Ottoman Empire, newspapers were not introduced until sometime in the nineteenth century. In Bulgaria, for instance, the first long-running weekly paper appeared in print in 1848 (Gesemann 1987: 230). Therefore, if the invention of the newspaper is to be understood as a media revolution, it is clear that it only occurred in parts of Western Europe in the seventeenth century.

Nonetheless, the newspaper was an internationally connective medium that triggered various transfers. As with book printing, it was German printers who first spread the new invention, with the Dutch following suit. Thus it came about that the first English and French newspapers in 1620 were actually translations of the Dutch *Courante uyt Italien, Duytslandt* …, which from 1622 were published rather sporadically by English printers under titles such as *Weekly News from Italy* … (Raymond 2003: 130; Schultheiß-Heinz 2004: 33). In Poland, the first papers to be circulated were in German, and starting in 1634, two printers from Germany published newspapers in their native tongue in Denmark for three decades before the first Danish periodicals were issued (Nielsen, in Welke and Wilke 2008: 198). In Sweden, German printers even undertook the task of creating an official Swedish newspaper whose contents and design were modelled on and thus closely resembled a Hamburg paper (Ries, in Dooley and Baron 2001: 238). Most of the newspapers which emerged in the second half of the eighteenth century in Hungary were also written in German, since they were aimed primarily at educated, German-speaking Upper Hungarians (Czibula, in Blome 2000: 115; Balogh and Tarnói 2007).

Enforcing restrictions on newspaper distribution was also common practice in many North and West European countries, where the authorities only permitted a limited number of loyal newspapers. The *Gazette*, for instance, which had originally been produced in support of the King and significantly involved Cardinal Richelieu, remained the only official newspaper in France until the mid-eighteenth century (Klaits 1976; Saada, in Welke and Wilke 2008: 181). The governmental censorship commission Maître de la Librairie gained importance in the seventeenth century vis-à-vis previous censorship authorities such as the Church, university and parliament. Similarly, only one official newspaper existed in Sweden until 1731, which was entitled *Ordinari Post Tijdender* and issued by a government delegate (Ries 2001: 240). The Viennese *Wiennerische Diarium* of 1703 established itself in like manner as the sole German newspaper for the next sixty years, during which it was also classified as the semi-official mouthpiece of the Habsburg Emperor (Duchkowitsch 1978; Gestrich, in Daniel 2006: 25). At the same time, the international press market was also able to evade such news surveillance, if there was sufficient demand. Thus numerous French newspapers from the Republic of the Netherlands and the Holy Roman Empire of the German Nation were in circulation as early as the seventeenth century. Various newspapers emerged, particularly in border regions, in order to take advantage of the dissimilar censorship practices in places like Altona, which was next to Hamburg then, but under Danish administration (Böning 2002: 53).

A large variety of newspapers were available in parts of the Holy Roman Empire and the Netherlands thanks to their greater freedom of press. In the Netherlands many censorship decrees did in fact exist, but they were scarcely implemented, except perhaps in cases where foreign authorities felt slighted by news reports (Haks, in Koopmans 2005: 173). In the Holy Roman Empire, the pre-censorship rules for printing practices, namely the *Wormser Edikt* of 1521, also applied to newspaper publishing. But a number of territories again facilitated unrestricted news exchange, for sovereigns assigned censorship to local authorities who displayed varying levels of severity. Control of news distribution chiefly took the form of printing patents in the Empire and less in the shape of text editing, let alone the threat of imprisonment. In seventeenth-century England there were phases when either method was applied. On the one hand the *London Gazette* came into being as a semi-official royalist newspaper based on a French model, and its monopoly lasted three decades. Yet apart from this period, freedom of the press evolved much earlier in England than in any other European country. During the 1640s English Civil War, a huge number of critical newspapers competed against each other, which explains why the British press was considered the most powerful in all of Europe (Mendle, in Dooley and Baron 2001: 61). After a period of severe censorship in the second half of the seventeenth century, which had led to a deterioration of the press, the abolition of the 'Licensing Act' of 1695 brought about the first freedom from censorship worldwide. This immediately fostered a boom in the press market and a considerable increase in political news reports (Sommerville 1996: 120).

Despite these strong differences in media policy, the West European newspapers were surprisingly similar in content and form. In contrast to today, news items were mostly arranged in the order in which they were received rather than according to relevance, thus splitting events up into a list of isolated incidences (see Schröder 1995: 214, 229). In order to inspire trust and highlight its up-to-dateness, each message was preceded by the time and place at which it was received, even though, depending on distance, events might date back several weeks, and so printers scarcely intervened by editing news reports from their foreign correspondents. Consequently, articles had linguistic deficiencies and were difficult to understand. The number of foreign words and technical terms was fairly high, and the many intermittently mentioned people, locations and details required firm background knowledge. The personalisation of news reports, on the other hand, made them more accessible (Schröder 1995: 146, 269; Schultheiß-Heinz 2004: 105–11).

European newspapers were also of a striking similarity in respect of content. Foreign affairs predominated, with regional reports constituting less than a tenth of the news (Morineau, in North 1995: 37; Schultheiß-Heinz 2004: 271; Haks, in Koopmans 2005: 169). Whilst news coverage of America and the Orient was not uncommon, on the whole it was centred on neighbouring European countries. The Holy Roman Empire especially was often the focus of the foreign press (Wilke 1986: 80). International journalism was strongly interwoven as far as content was concerned; however, as reports were passed from paper to paper the news was also altered (Dooley 2010).

Regional events were covered mostly by pamphlets. Since they were often produced in the same print shops as periodicals, one can say that the division of responsibilities was intermeshed (Bellingradt 2011). The fact that newspapers scarcely published local or regional news could be accounted for by fear of censorship. In periods of greater freedom of press, the amount of local and domestic news coverage did in fact increase, for example during the English Civil War in the 1640s, and the revolutions of 1789 and 1848. Yet even in comparatively liberal regions such as the Netherlands, reporting chiefly consisted of news from abroad. In order to explain the newspapers' choice of topics one must also see them in relation to their readers' interests: it was doubtless more convenient to communicate regional incidents verbally or via pamphlet journalism, with sensationalist news such as miraculous births being primarily disseminated by broadsides and rarely published in newspapers.

In nearly all European newspapers, military references took up by far the most space. In Germany they accounted for as much as 70 to 80 per cent of all articles during the battle-ridden summer months, and as much as 40 per cent in the winter (Adrians 1999: 185f.; Neumann, in Blühm and Gebhardt 1987: 315). The spread of newspapers was closely connected with war as well: their expansion throughout Western Europe and all the way to England did not transpire until the beginning of the Thirty Years' War. War reporting did not merely serve to satisfy curiosity but could be essential for survival because it enabled citizens to plan possible means of escape. By the same token, the English periodical press did not establish itself until the events of the Irish Rebellion and the Civil War in 1641/42 (Raymond 1999: 13–26).

Economic news, on the other hand, only played a marginal role. In West European newspapers it only accounted for a small percentage of the total number of articles, and revolved mainly around incoming ships' cargoes and the economic consequences of natural disasters (Schultheiß-Heinz 2004: 151f.; Wilke 1984: 125, 130). However, seventeenth-century newspapers already contained advertisements, albeit only a few. The first advertising agency in Paris can be traced back to the 1630s and supplied the semi-official *Gazette* (Saada, in Welke and Wilke 2008: 187). While on the Continent advertisements had begun by primarily promoting books, a flourishing market for advertising developed in England. In addition to book and job adverts, from the 1670s onwards the semi-official *London Gazette* also reported on the establishment of businesses and lost articles (Winkler, in ibid.: 143). Moreover, advertisers such as the *City Mercury* and the *Weekly Advertiser* were launched at an early stage in England, thus also establishing the medium of the newspaper as an instance of local communication.

Newspaper reports were overwhelmingly non-partisan and at most adopted the judgements of their correspondents (Weber 1999: 29, 36; Schröder 1995: 334; very pointedly: Schönhagen 1998: 291). More recent research on reports about the Thirty Years' War, however, has revealed that comments, assessments and biased reporting were more frequent than had previously been assumed (Adrians 1999: 185f.; Behringer 2003: 369f.). A study on war reporting in four Western countries has also shown that not only semi-official papers such as the French *Gazette*, but newspapers in general often gave patriotic praise to the positions taken by their own territories (Schultheiß-Heinz 2004: 217, 236–56, 273). Even Dutch newspapers, which were hardly subject to political monitoring, had a patriotic tone to them (Morineau 1995: 39), and in 1703 in Austria the *Post-tägliche Mercurius* emerged as a newspaper which took a clear stand on topics such as the War of the Spanish Succession (Duchkowitsch 2009: 312).

The most intensive partisanship of newspapers was to be found in England. In the context of the 1640s Civil War, newspapers emerged which either aggressively supported the monarch (e.g. *Mercurius Aulicus, Mercurius Pragmaticus*) or militantly supported Parliament and the republican idea (e.g. *Mercurius Politicus, The Moderate*) (Raymond 2003: 26–79; Mendle 2001: 61). So although the dawn of editorialised newspapers must be dated back further than is generally accepted, fiery political and religious discussions were left to the pamphleteers. This once again illustrates that early newspapers must be understood as part of a media network comprising leaflets and broadsides as well as handwritten newspapers, and that they alternately both influenced and distinguished themselves from one another.

Generally newspapers were surprisingly well informed and their reporting proved to be fairly detailed for the time. Using the example of the 1648 Peace of Westphalia, Konrad Repgen has demonstrated that even dossiers, which historians classify as secret sources, appeared in contemporaneous newspapers with reasonable accuracy (Repgen 1997: 48f., 83). Furthermore, from the very beginning of the Thirty Years' War, newspapers printed handwritten correspondences considered by researchers to have been secret (Weber 1999: 28). The example of the War of the Spanish Succession (1702–1713) highlights that in the case of the Netherlands, newspapers were just as well informed as the most knowledgeable politician of the time would have been (Haks, in Koopmans 2005: 181). These findings enhance the value of early newspapers as research sources and stakeholders in history.

Specificities about newspaper authors and correspondents are hard to pinpoint, since they also wrote anonymously for fear of censorship. Early 'journalists' are thought to have been fairly young and 'at a transitional stage in their professional lives between their academic training and a hoped-for full-time job, in accordance with the career ideal of the Early Modern Era' (Arndt 2006: 109). Publishing a newspaper could mean great opportunities for profit as well as high risks, since many newspapers failed after only a short while in the business. Depending on the scope of their news reporting, correspondents who worked in cities that served as information hubs, such as Vienna (South East Europe), Hamburg (Northern Europe) or Cologne (North West Europe) could earn a respectable amount of money, depending on the length of the articles, and this constituted about a fifth of all newspaper costs. They were often 'experts in the orbit of power', such as military or state officials (Weber, in Kutsch and Weber 2002: 18; Blühm and Engelsing 1967: 29f.). Be that as it may, they seldom travelled to the scenes of events, despite the fact that as many as 1,666 war correspondents that actually travelled to theatres of war have been recorded for the Netherlands (Morineau 1995: 38).

Existing information about publishers of early newspapers is somewhat more substantial. Previous assumptions that postmasters were chiefly the ones to publish newspapers, since they could immediately make use of the transmitted information, have been refuted for the German territories. Rather, it was the printers themselves who collected reports and hired editors. Occasionally, even scholars would employ a hired printer (Arndt 2006: 102). In the seventeenth century, thirty-five women who had taken over their late husbands' trades in accordance with guild precepts managed such print shops in German regions (Welke 1971: 6f.). Of course, if one views Europe as a whole, differences are obvious. Postmasters played a significant role in Sweden, for instance, where they had a monopoly position as newspaper publishers. In France, where the semi-official *Gazette* largely enjoyed a monopoly position, the dependent state of editors is striking: they were either related to the family of the privileged newspaper publisher Renaudot, came from aristocratic or ecclesiastical circles, or were intellectuals such as poets or historians who received state pensions.

Newspapers already had a fairly wide-ranging readership in the seventeenth century. Academics, government officials and the upper classes were their primary target groups, but tradesmen, craftsmen, soldiers and women were also part of their audience. The annual subscription for a Hamburg newspaper would cost a craftsman from Cologne about 2 per cent of his annual income, which was a handsome sum but still affordable (Würgler 2009: 39). Since newspapers were read out in inns, shops and other public places, in the cities at least, even illiterate people could get information as listeners (Winkler 1998: 811). The wives of wealthy men were not the only women with access to newspapers. Printed news was equally available to women who kept inns or pubs, coffee house staff, housemaids and female newspaper sellers, to name a few. Even if these women were unable to read, it was easier for them to discover something about the content of the paper with the help of literates with whom they came into contact. Yet the disparity between East and West is undeniable: while readerships were drawn from a wide range of society in the United States, England, and the Netherlands, the Russian audience consisted mainly of aristocrats and a few wealthy merchants (Plambeck 1982: 51). Even in absolutist France, it is estimated that half of all readers belonged to the aristocracy while the remainder came chiefly from wealthy backgrounds (Censer, in Barker and Burrows 2002: 161).

Numbers and circulation were quite low at first. It is estimated that in the late seventeenth century the average circulation figure in the German territories ranged between three and four hundred copies, which meant that the total of all newspapers amounted to around twenty or twenty-five thousand copies. Newspapers such as the French *Gazette* or the English *London Gazette* of the 1680s, which were issued in restrictive absolutist countries, quickly attained a high circulation of more than one thousand copies. Nevertheless, the available number of newspaper copies remained low, even if one takes into account those which were imported from abroad. According to recent estimates there were at least thirty readers per newspaper per country, adding up to a very respectable weekly readership in Western Europe (Bellingradt 2011; as many as forty readers are suggested by Winkler 1998: 810). Papers were not only passed on within households, to neighbours or inns; institutions such as universities, schools, public offices and monasteries also had subscriptions. Courts and city councils usually received complimentary copies. Collective subscription quickly became common as well. The earliest newspaper-reading community proven to have existed was in Kitzingen in 1614, and their paper was shared by between twelve and twenty-one dignitaries following a set order of rotation (Welke, in Dann 1981: 36). In this respect the newspaper can be considered a mass medium even in the seventeenth century, notwithstanding the fact that it was not until the eighteenth century that the periodical press experienced a much stronger expansion.

The Newspaper and Periodical Market in the Eighteenth Century

At first glance, newspapers did not change significantly in the eighteenth century. Foreign news reports and articles on military topics continued to dominate the newspaper landscape, while local and rational-critical commentary remained scarce. Therefore the line between the Baroque Era and the Era of Enlightenment should not be drawn too sharply in media history (Fischer et al. 1999: 13; Wilke 2008: 82). Some changes nevertheless occurred in the newspaper market that are particularly noteworthy from an international perspective.

Newspaper circulation shot up on an international level in the eighteenth century, even though hardly any innovations had occurred in printing technology. In the second half of the eighteenth century, the total number of publications doubled in the German territories, reaching an average of approximately 600, while the number of newspapers climbed to between 200 and 250, resulting in over 300,000 copies per week (see Welke 1977: 78f.). Circulation figures were similarly high in England, where the numbers of newspapers and print runs had spiralled rapidly since the introduction of widespread press freedom in 1695. Thanks to the use of revenue stamps, reliable figures are on record. In 1750, 9.4 million stamps were disbursed (approximately 180,000 per week), and in 1800 the number reached 16.4 million (around 315,000 per week). In addition, unauthorised copies as well as the illegal *Unstamped Press* were available (Barker 2000: 30). In France, weekly circulation rose to at least 44,000 in the 1770s, with the *Gazette de France* reaching its peak in the 1750s with approximately 15,000 copies and the few remaining papers accounting for a circulation figure of at least several thousand (Censer 1994: 215). Again, wars and conflicts were chiefly responsible for the sudden international rise in newspaper copies, for example the Seven Years' War (1756–1763), the American War of Independence and the French Revolution. Newspapers thus contributed markedly to the development of national and international spheres of communication in the eighteenth century.

The framework conditions of the international press also changed in the eighteenth century. Generally, censorship shifted from religious to political matters and became more centralised and bureaucratic. The Era of Enlightenment by no means signified an uninterrupted advance towards press freedom. In fact, international developments proved to be rather different. Whereas a change of sovereign entailed stricter censorship in 1780s Prussia, Austria moved in the opposite direction; for although censorship regulations were stringent, they were badly organised (Küster 2004: 70; Haefs and Mix 2006). Towards the end of the 1750s, France began to tolerate an increasing number of foreign papers; at the same time, however, foreign newspapers were newly produced with government support for the domestic market, such as the *Journal de Genève* in 1772 and two years later the *Journal de Bruxelles* (Censer, in Barker and Burrows 2002: 173). Freedom of the press was established in stages in Sweden and Denmark in the 1770s, where only a very few loyal newspapers had been permitted in the seventeenth century.

Even in liberal England development did not proceed smoothly. Between 1712 and 1819, newspaper taxes were increased eight times, leading to a price rise and a consequently reduced circulation. Additionally, members of the government were bribing newspapers and suing publishers for libel. But although one should not idealise freedom of the press in England, such measures started to wane in the mid-eighteenth century. The illegal *Unstamped Press*, which entirely dispensed with tax stamps, was already on the increase in the 1740s. Higher profits resulting from a rise in advertisements and circulation made the press less vulnerable to corruption. The Republican politician and journalist John Wilkes succeeded in achieving a reduction in libel cases from the 1760s onwards by means of his campaigns and court cases (Barker 2000: 31, 72, 92). Particularly in the 1770s and 1780s, the media in Europe were generally granted more freedom of reporting before fears of upheaval triggered a backlash towards the end of the century.

Innovations pertaining to content are evident in eighteenth century North America. Initially newspapers established themselves rather tentatively: after a failed attempt in 1690, the first long-standing newspaper emerged in 1704 under the name *Boston Newsletter*. A gradual development of the newspaper market commenced in the 1720s, resulting in the publication of a dozen papers in 1740. The stringent licensing policies and the bribery of the colonial administration impeded the development of the press at first; however the scope of these limitations varied within the American colonies (Copeland, in Barker and Burrows 2002: 145–48). The centre of the press was located on the coast and mainly represented by Boston, which counted twenty thousand inhabitants and formed the hub of the postal system. The slow pace of urbanisation, a decayed infrastructure, and the disconnection from European lines of communication all seemed to militate against the development of an innovative and expanding press.

This constellation, however, was ultimately responsible for the creation of a newspaper profile which still has resonance today. Due to a lack of foreign news, regional and local reports played a much larger role for North American newspapers than they did in Europe. Reports on crime and entertainment news were also more frequent (Burns 2006: 87; cf. Wilke, in Blühm and Gebhardt 1987: 292). As in England, advertisements quickly acquired a significant status. The papers' tendency towards opinion-laden and belligerent news reporting was also reminiscent of their English counterparts. The American tradition of 'Crusading Journalism' began to some extent in 1721 with the *New England Courant* by James Franklin, who demanded freedom of press and accused the British government of corruption. A spectacular case against the *New York Weekly Journal* reduced repressions against newspapers through libel suits (Burns 2006: 55–62, 104f.).

Moral and value-oriented contents intermingled with political positioning. It was Benjamin Franklin – journalist, inventor and later one of the Founding Fathers of the United States – who established this connection between moral, political and social commitment in the American press. He turned his newspaper into a political forum that encouraged its readership to participate by sending in commentaries, and by means of financial help, advice, new mail routes and paper mills he established links to over thirty printers from North to South in order to propagate his approach. By 1755, eight out of the total number of fifteen North American newspapers were partners of Franklin or worked in close connection with him (Frasca 2006: 196–204). In this manner the press became an engine in America's fight for independence.

A few individual changes in contents can also be made out in Western Europe. England bore the most striking similarity to the developments in North America. The proportion of regional reports, partisan commentaries, and 'sensationalist' news increased, as well as the number of advertisements. Some German newspapers also made innovative changes to their content. The *Hamburgische unparteyische Correspondent* for instance was the first to introduce a kind of culture section, which played a part in evolving the *gelehrten Artikel* (scholarly article). Other newspapers added light-hearted instructive text segments. Political criticism was at least attempted by a few papers, such as Friedrich Daniel Schubart's *Deutsche Chronik* or Wilhelm Ludwig Wekhrlin's *Das Felleisen*, earning the journalists prison sentences in these specific cases (Wilke 2008: 89). Overall, however, newspapers were still virtually free of commentary.

Another media innovation of the eighteenth century was the German *Intelligenzblätter* (Intelligence sheet), which presented official information and advertisements. They cropped up in Britain and France, for instance, in the form of provincial advertisers. They established their own genre alongside newspapers and periodicals. In the German-speaking area, roughly two hundred of such *Intelligenzblätter* came into existence, starting in 1722 (Böning, in Fischer et al. 1999: 89f., 103; Doering-Manteuffel et al. 2001). Appearing first on a weekly and later on a semi-weekly basis, they printed job advertisements, birth notices, and obituaries, as well as advertisements for works of literature. Some were issued by private individuals, but especially in Prussia the state acted as publisher, securing a monopoly on advertisements in 1727 and consequently on the *Intelligenzblätter*. The innovation here was that the papers were regionally based: also, they were issued in small towns where the advertisements became part of the local living environment (Böning, in Fischer et al.: 91–96). Their print run was fairly large, counting five hundred to a thousand copies on average, not least due to low prices. Since the *Intelligenzblätter* were available in public buildings and sometimes purchased by administrations, officials, monasteries, hospitals and inns via forced subscriptions, their reach was considerable and they represented an important connection between urban and rural areas. Furthermore, over and above pro-government statements, the advertisers developed editorial sections which also contributed to public enlightenment. These include educational articles, practical advice, and economic and agricultural reports (ibid.: 89f.; Blome, in Dooley 2010). Humorous and literary texts also appeared. Another innovation was the interplay with the readers, who were encouraged to send in written contributions, which helped the papers to shape interactive public spheres despite their affiliation with the state.

That said, an exceedingly strong impact in terms of media innovations in eighteenth-century Europe must be ascribed to the periodical, which was not merely a child of the Enlightenment and the public sphere, but rather their prime agent. Periodicals were not published as frequently as newspapers, their content was specialised and they were not so much focused on currentness. They engaged more in rational-critical debate and imparted general knowledge beyond the politics of the day, which was dealt with in detailed articles.

Periodicals rapidly developed a range of different formats, which were adapted and copied transnationally, with groundbreaking impulses being provided by France and England. The Parisian *Journal des savants*, for instance, which was first published in early 1665, is considered the first scientific periodical, followed three months later by *Philosophical Transactions* in England. In the field of entertainment and literary periodicals, the French *Mercure Galant* (from 1672) provided important impetus. In the establishment of moral weekly periodicals, the English *Tatler* (1709) and *Spectator* (1711) represented key influences which were fast imitated in Germany with only few alterations. Recent studies have actually stressed that some types of periodicals had their roots in Germany. The Hamburg journal *Erbauliche Ruh-Stunden* (1676), for instance, is considered an early version of moral weekly periodicals, and the Nuremberg *Der Verkleidete Götter-Bothe*

Mercurius (1674–75) is seen as an early historical-political journal (Böning, in Welke and Wilke 2008: 298f.). The *Relationes Curiosae* (1683–91), another Hamburg periodical, is an example of a magazine that spread knowledge of the world along more popular lines (Egenhoff 2008). One might conclude that, contrary to Jürgen Habermas's later theses, scientific and historical-political rather than literary periodicals represented the starting points of the public sphere.

Even though the periodical did not emerge exclusively in the German regions, the greatest variety of this new medium was to be found there. Approximately seven thousand different titles of periodicals were assigned to the period before 1830, even though a large proportion was only published for a short duration. In terms of numbers, the market was dominated by scholarly papers that were initially oriented towards universal academic discourse and later divided into specific academic disciplines. Historical periodicals were particularly numerous, followed by theological journals (Wilke 2008: 96). On the other hand, political magazines were quantitatively of much less significance. They initially documented governmental actions, and in the last third of the eighteenth century became reform-oriented companions to contemporary German politics (for example the *Politische Journal* and the *Staats-Anzeiger*). On top of this, a large market developed for entertainment periodicals aimed at educating the reader morally as well as culturally. The morally edifying weeklies had particularly high circulation figures. They made use of different genres such as fables, dialogues and poetry in order to impart general knowledge and Christian middle-class values to a diverse readership. In so doing, they also appealed to women. Finally, literary periodicals were especially characteristic of the eighteenth century. Besides reviews they printed short literary works and offered readers the opportunity to send in their own contributions. Periodicals appealed to various target groups and at the same time were conducive to the shaping of respective social groups. Especially during the boom in the last third of the eighteenth century, diverse magazines based on people's interests, profession, generation and gender began to appear. Thus, forty-three youth journals emerged between 1770 and 1789 in Germany, particularly in northern regions (Uphaus-Wehmeier 1984: 42). Titles such as *Der Zögling*; *Wochenschrift zum besten der Erziehung der Jugend*, *Pädagogische Unterhandlungen*; *Moralische Erzählungen* and *Jugendzeitung* revealed their pedagogic orientation. Much like that of the moral periodicals, their goal was to entertain as well as to instruct. In this context, younger generations were introduced to current political issues and world affairs in a way that suited their age (Berg, in Albrecht and Böning 2005: 13; Uphaus-Wehmeier 1984: 62, 103–10).

How periodicals established themselves according to target groups can be shown by the example of women's magazines, which have become a particular focal point of recent research. In England they emerged as early as 1700. Their initial programme was aimed at giving advice on the conduct of daily life. The first women's periodical worldwide, *The Ladies Mercury* of 1693, promised answers to 'all the most nice and curious questions concerning love, marriage, behaviour, dress, and humour of the female sex, whether virgins, wives, or widows' (Adburgham 1972: 26) and encouraged women to send in questions – a practice later imitated by its successors. Many periodicals established in the eighteenth century tended to add the word 'Female' to their titles in order to pass themselves off as the female counterpart to existing men's periodicals: for example, *Female Tatler* (1709–10), *Female Spectator* (1744–46) and *Female Guardian* (1787).

In England, a number of women were politically active and independent much earlier than in all other parts of Europe. The *Female Tatler* and the *Female Spectator*, for instance, published several political articles (Adburgham 1972: 57). The reputed publisher of the *Female Tatler*, Mary de la Revière Manley, was arrested because of her satirical articles against the Whigs, and subsequently took over the editorial office of the Tory newspaper *The Examiner*. For a short period in 1716, a decidedly political weekly was published specifically for women: *The Charitable Mercury and Female Intelligence. Being a Weekly Collection of All the Material News, Foreign and Domestick. With some notes on the same* (Facsimile in Adburgham 1972: 65; McDowell 1998). Despite being given several prison sentences, its editor Elizabeth Powell could not be discouraged from acting out her journalistic enthusiasm.

Other countries did not act as expeditiously in the question of women's periodicals. In France there was in fact only one long-running journal before 1789, the *Journal des dames* (1759–78), which was issued by a man, but it employed women as well as men (Rattner Gelbart 1987). England's great freedom of press gave them more leeway, and their work as newspaper sellers presumably further stimulated the distribution of papers amongst women (Nevitt, in Raymond 1999: 84–108). Since reports on regional or social events were common in England earlier than on the Continent, women also had better access to the media. Elsewhere, such circumstances did not automatically lead to the establishment of women's magazines, as a glance at the United States proves. Journals for women did not emerge until 1792/93 with *The Lady's Magazine*, in which literature, fashion and advice columns predominated (Aronson 2002: 49).

In the course of the eighteenth century, a variety of women's periodicals emerged in Germany which initially copied their English forerunners: the *Female Tatler* was adapted into the first German women's periodical with the same name (*Vernünftigen Tadlerinnen*, 1725/26), edited by Gottsched; the *Female Spectator* was transformed and translated into *Die Zuschauerin*

(1747); and the English paper *Lady's Museum* was turned into its German equivalent *Museum für Frauenzimmer* (1790). Between 1720 and 1800 at least 115 periodicals designed specifically for women circulated in Germany, most of them appearing after 1780 but being short-lived (Weckel 1998: 26). An important source was moral weekly periodicals, based on English models and published under fictitious names, as demonstrated by titles such as *Die Braut*, *Das Mädchen* and *Die vernünftigen Tadlerinnen*. Magazines targeting women were generally published by men. When women contributed, their writings were usually published anonymously (as was the case with Gottsched and Klopstock's wives). Nonetheless, this role-play was very important in that it provided role models; these pseudonymous publishing personalities who articulated their opinions could inspire women to try out their own authorial, journalistic or editorial talents. Moreover, these magazines proved that there was an undoubted demand for women's journals.

In the German territories, women did not work as publishers until 1779. About sixteen women edited newspapers in the last quarter of the eighteenth century, although much like their male colleagues, many remained anonymous. These women were exceptionally well educated; most were Protestants and half were aristocrats, while the other half came from bourgeois backgrounds. From 1796 onwards, women temporarily disappeared from the publishing business. Ulrike Weckel has argued that professionalisation and commercialisation of the literary trade necessitated well-established names and were thus responsible for this development (Weckel 1998: 198, 307).

Compared to their English precursors, the content of German women's periodicals tended to be less sensationalist and of a more educational and literary nature. Reports on current politics, court cases or atrocities were not included. Only in the wake of the French Revolution were there a few political references and nationalistic tones. By the same token the newspapers were not protofeminist in nature, as their female image instead reflected existing middle-class gender polarity. A few individual articles treated male condescension and bourgeois role models as objects of derision, but generally the paper supported the attitude that women should not neglect their duties as housewives in favour of reading and writing.

Be that as it may, these periodicals represented an important opening for women to gain presence in the media sphere. Letters to the editor were an exchange platform for communication, and the opportunity to submit their own literary work motivated women to write publicly. In addition, they encouraged women to subscribe in their own names and so demonstrate contractual competence. The fact that lady's periodicals were openly available in libraries not only increased their reach; it also demonstrated their acceptance among men (Weckel 1998: 61–67).

Even though the development of the periodical market in Europe differed from country to country, the given examples underline how dynamic, varied and keen to experiment this market proved to be in the course of its progression.

Interpretations, Effects and Usage of Periodicals

Hitherto research on the social and cultural significance of periodicals in the seventeenth century has been scarce. The Strasbourg *Relation* from 1609 assigned the newspaper two functions: on the one hand it was intended to help the ruler to 'govern commendably and strive to preserve his subjects in peace and serenity', on the other hand its aim was to sharpen the critical faculties of the 'private individual' and offer them moral support to achieve 'godliness and the amendment of life and to admonish'. The newspaper was to serve as a path 'to reason, wisdom and experience guided by rectitude' (*Relation* 1609, printed in Blühm and Engelsing 1967: 20–22). Besides the medium's morally instructive function, then, such analyses adumbrated the newspaper's claim to both counsel political authorities as well as to judge them on the basis of its own observations.

Extensive contemporary evaluations of newspapers can be found in the myriad of scholarly papers which were published in the last third of the seventeenth century, such as those written by Ahasver Fritsch ('Gebrauch und Missbrauch der Zeitungen', 1676), Christian Weise (1676), Tobias Peucer ('Über Zeitungsberichte', 1690) and Kaspar Stieler ('Zeitungs Lust und Nutz', 1695). They concordantly emphasised the newspaper's benefit to society (these texts are reprinted in Kurth 1944). Stieler particularly stressed that newspapers should protect against imminent dangers and impart knowledge of the world to the bourgeois class. He recommended all sovereigns to consult newspapers in their decision-making processes, as these were 'impartial, fearless, not ashamed and did not blush' in contrast to human advisers (Stieler 1969: 20). Critics, however, did not vouchsafe these functions to the average reader. The jurist Ahasver Fritsch in particular declared in his polemic pamphlet that the information conveyed through newspapers would not benefit the majority of readers, since in his opinion they could not understand it. On the contrary he claimed that newspapers might cause damage if they were to print false reports in order to 'make the people panic' (printed in Blühm and Engelsing 1967: 52; Kurth 1944).

Another central line of argument in contemporary discourse revolved around the significance of the new medium in the context of individual psychology (also cf. Pompe 2004: 42f.). The *Relation* of 1609, but also Tobias Peucer's dissertation of 1690, located the origins of the newspaper in the inquisitiveness inherent to man. Contemporary critics of the newspaper questioned whether its usage could lead to addiction. Fritsch brought forward the argument that newspapers were read in offices and even during church services as proof of 'newspaper addiction' in society. Inasmuch as this is a classical topos of media criticism, Fritsch also warned that early newspapers were not solely an expression of rationality.

Thirdly, contemporary papers questioned especially whether the information printed in newspapers was actually true. There seems to have been a fairly high level of distrust. Calvinist theologian Erich Behringer warned in 1614 that it was unwise to place trust in newspaper reports (Behringer 2003: 372), and even Christian Weise, who himself defended the usefulness of newspapers, criticised false reporting and admonished readers to be discriminating (printed in Blühm and Engelsing 1967: 56). Most contemporaries also censured the fact that papers voiced their opinions and that their criticism was partisan (Berns 1976: 207; Adrians 1999: 40). This concomitantly underlines the negative image against which early newspaper editors had to struggle.

Researchers attribute the same societal and cultural effects to newspapers as to printing: they contributed to the standardisation of language, the generation and archiving of knowledge, and the establishment of permanent spheres of communication. What is more, they transformed news into a universal currency of social relations (Raymond 2001: 1; Wilke 2008: 40). As diaries and letters indicate, the reading of newspapers had the power to change people's mapping of the world, even as early as the seventeenth century. Occurrences which had previously seemed distant were now becoming an inherent part of people's private thoughts. Periodical reports on distant events which included date and place thus shifted the relation between space and time (see Behringer 1999: 69f., 81).

Similarly, newspapers, periodicals and pamphlets influenced political communication and ruling practice. They published dossiers, documents and the authorities' war commentaries, and achieved increased public legitimacy for their actions through their regular reporting (Repgen 1997: 48f., 83; Haks, in Koopmans 2005: 181). Broadsides remained central to these developments, as the Seven Years' War illustrates. Even absolutist governments adjusted to the expansion of the media and systematically legitimised their doings in the press, be it in the context of declarations of war, responses to reports from abroad or entertaining topics from the court or diplomacy (Gestrich 1994: 12, 17, 26, 85; Schultheiß-Heinz 2004: 64). This even applied to the Tsars in eighteenth-century Russia (Plambeck 1982: 41). Newspapers thus became an integral part of foreign affairs, a state of affairs substantiated by the fact that diplomats and sovereigns officially rejected news from other countries. 'Newspaper diplomacy' did not merely encompass petitions and semi-official newspapers within the borders of a specific country, but also included newspapers printed in foreign languages which were specifically targeted at neighbouring countries.

The increasing demand for newspapers simultaneously highlights the growing desire for political information and thus the politicising of the society. The German newspaper historian Johannes Weber assumes that daily political reporting diluted authoritarian dignity, whether it was news on other territories or the 'secularisation of political percipience', since these fragmented reports undermined the religious legitimacy of power (Weber 1997: 46; and 1999: 43). Above all, newspapers levelled information discrepancies between the different sections like noblemen or townsmen. English newspapers especially tended to politicise. In the 1640s Civil War, they led to the formation of parties, especially with their reports on parliament (Mendle 2001: 57). Verbatim reports from the English Parliament, printed regularly from the 1760s onwards, also changed the role of Parliament, for political addresses now had to be tailored to a broader public. The English press of the eighteenth century did not refer to its readers as subjects but rather as 'the people', 'Englishmen', or 'the public', and this alone already promoted sovereignty of the people. However, it would take until the 1770s before newspapers in England completely took over the pamphlets' commentary function and with it the ability to impact political decisions by means of campaigns (Barker 2000: 127, 145, 170f.). However, even in France and Austria, where the authorities regulated the press stringently, newspapers achieved a 'perforation of the arcane of political leadership' (Arndt 2002: 23).

Since early newspapers reported on war to a large extent, their media effect was discussed within this context. The historian Johannes Burkhardt considered that newspapers exerted a very strong media effect and were guilty of 'warmongering and the prolongation of war' during the Thirty Years' War (Burkhardt 1992: 230). Other authors have tended to ascribe this function to broadsides (Welke and Wilke 1999: 44). In other countries and conflicts, newspapers also almost unanimously called for war (re. England: e.g. Barker 2000: 139). Yet they did not operate simply as an autonomous patriotic authority, but rather in the context of power structures. But even if the authorities could co-determine newspaper contents, this did not automatically guarantee the desired media effect. After the Battle of Dettingen in 1743, for instance, the returning French troops were greeted with derision despite ample propaganda, because other media and rumours spread by word of mouth had given different information (Küster 2004: 258). The reason these media wars had considerable consequences for real wars was that to a certain extent the outcome of battles was negotiated through the media (Schort 2006: 412–16, 475).

For a long time the most influential approach to explain the social effects of periodicals and newspapers in the seventeenth and eighteenth centuries was

Jürgen Habermas's model of the 'bourgeois public sphere'. Even though historians have long criticised and corrected the empirical foundations of this approach, Habermas still provides a perspective for interlinking communication and social history (on criticism: Calhoun 1992; Gestrich, in Zimmermann 2006). Habermas conceives the bourgeois public sphere as a 'sphere of private people come together as a public' (Habermas 1989: 86). In the eighteenth century, this public ostensibly used its own rules to re-form itself from its familial intimacy into an opinion-forming body that could reason in public debate and critically monitor the government. The media are of significance in Habermas's model on a number of levels: along with capitalistic goods traffic and the literary public sphere, he considers them a pivotal prerequisite for the development of the bourgeois public sphere; secondly, they created and shaped spaces in the bourgeois public sphere, such as reading societies and coffee houses which provided newspapers; thirdly, they facilitated the formation of a public which transcended national borders; fourthly, the media stabilised communication among the middle classes; and fifthly, they contributed to structural change and the deterioration of the bourgeois public sphere because the rise of commercial mass media and quasi-monopoly media structures transformed the active public into passive consumers.

The debate on Habermas's model and the research it triggered deliver insights into the connection between media development and formative social processes. Initially, Habermas was criticised for what he marked as the inception of the bourgeois public sphere. Medievalists, for instance, argued that the debates on the Investiture Controversy could also be understood as the formation of a public sphere, because this conflict witnessed a wide-ranging, partisan and topic-based mode of communication which had 'ad hoc character', verbal and written, beyond an institutionalised form of communication (Melve 2007: 643–59). By the same token it was argued that there certainly was an awareness of borders between private and public spaces in the pre-Modern Era, although these spaces were multifunctional (cf. Tlusty, in Rau and Schwerhoff 2004). Within the Holy Roman Empire, religiously segmented public spheres can be detected, particularly in the context of the Reformation. Other authors have placed the formation of the public sphere in the first half of the seventeenth century with the establishment of newspapers and the development of the postal system (Behringer 2003: 673–81), or regarded the eighteenth century as the dawn of a 'public sphere defined by journalism', since journalistic treatment of news and the rational-critical debate had previously been lacking (see Weber, in Kutsch and Weber 2002: 18).

Several points in fact favour the identification of a public sphere in seventeenth-century Germany no later than the establishment of the newspaper market, for a gain in range and reflective quality is evident from around 1700 onwards. After all, newspapers did not refrain from taking a position, and nor did their readers assimilate regular news stories without forming their own opinions. Particularly the juxtaposition of the correspondents' differing interpretations represented an early form of exchange of ideas, which was supplemented by broadsides, books and other media. This was also recognised by contemporaries: as early as 1700, history professor Johann Peter Ludewig, for instance, attributed the task of 'using existent knowledge to form judgements on future matters' to newspapers, as 'this is what learning to think in a rational-critical way means' (quoted from Böning, in Welke and Wilke 2008: 296). Likewise, in 1676, dramatist Christian Weise compared the newspaper reader with the theatregoer who cannot actively intervene in events but 'reason critically on the basis of the action' (printed in Blühm and Engelsing 1967: 56).

For Habermas, however, the starting point for the emergence of a bourgeois public sphere was to be found in early eighteenth-century England. The early establishment of coffee houses, the free press and its self-concept of being a 'Fourth Estate', and the local culture of debate served as evidence for his thesis. Yet this assumption also needs to be modified. On the one hand, the process began even earlier in England and can be dated roughly from the upheavals in the 1640s (Raymond 1999: 109–40). On the other hand, Habermas idealised English circumstances, since in fact the press did not start to develop the potential that Habermas had attributed to it until the last third of the eighteenth century (Barker 2000).

Moreover, the public sphere was not formed in demarcation from the state, as posited by Habermas. It was in fact the case that government officials of all countries interacted within the new medial communication sphere, even in England and the Netherlands (Barker 2000; Popkin 2005: 26). The example of the German *Intelligenzblätter* underlines this as well. In a similar vein, there have been frequent warnings against reducing the public sphere to the bourgeoisie, for the aristocracy and the lower classes also participated: the aristocracy by their membership in reading societies and the lower classes by having newspapers read to them, looking at pictures, joining in protests and participating in tavern discussions. The same was true for women, whom Habermas also failed to consider in his observations. As gender history has consistently criticised, the connection public/male and private/female was an established construct at the time which cannot be adopted as an analytical tool. And as previously illustrated, women did share in the public sphere of the media.

Habermas also initiated very productive research on the locations in which media were collectively discussed and read. This was especially true for reading societies, but also coffee houses and inns. In London alone, there were approximately five hundred coffee houses around 1710, in addition to six thousand pubs. Here, newspapers were freely available, enabling even destitute people to read or be read to. At the same time, coffee-house discussions inspired new media. The early moralistic weeklies in particular announced their intent to print all the news circulating in the coffee houses, even specifying coffee house addresses for reader replies (Winkler 1998: 814–30). Nonetheless, coffee houses did not automatically create a critical public sphere. For in spite of the fact that they began to spring up in Vienna as early as 1683, no comparable critical public sphere existed because absolutism inhibited its development.

For the lower classes, even the locations where newspapers were sold served to facilitate communication, whether it was the post office, newspaper stalls, or the street. In return for a fee, people would read out aloud from newspapers or negotiate a collective newspaper purchase. In rural areas, at least a few reading clubs emerged here and there, initiated by schoolmasters in the late seventeenth century, and in the eighteenth century by pastors as well (Welke, in Dann 1981: 37–40; Winkler 1998: 834).

Over and above these, bourgeois groups created socially restricted spaces for their collective media use. Privately organised lending libraries and reading societies, which have been researched in Germany in a myriad of local studies, were of great significance. These clubs represented associations in which citizens could jointly purchase media such as newspapers, periodicals and books. They rented separate rooms in inns or apartments for general meetings and group readings. Financial reasons, the desire for a large assortment of reading material, and the need for discussion and shared reading experiences led to the formation of such reading communities. They had emerged early in England as well, but their proliferation in Germany was much greater. As with the expansion of periodicals, there were major differences to the rest of Europe, particularly the Eastern regions. Whereas in Bohemia the first reading rooms opened in the 1770s, they did not arrive in the Czech Republic until after 1810, in the context of the Czech national movement (Sÿmeček, in Dann 1981: 232). In Russia, organised reading communities were not able to fully unfold until the end of the reign of Tsar Nikolaus I (1825–1855) due to state repression, although salons already existed (Remnek, in Barker and Burrows 2002: 232). In the subsequent reform period under Alexander II these circles became more widespread. They ranged from groups of friends to salons, and their participants engaged in critical exchanges about the regime (Alexander, in Dann 1981: 239f.).

What conclusions can be drawn about media use and its effects on the basis of reading clubs? In the first place, purchase lists reveal the great significance of periodicals. Besides newspapers, magazines with historical-political, geographical or other popular scientific contents were most notably purchased. It was not unusual for large German reading societies to take out subscriptions to a dozen different newspapers, including some from neighbouring countries such as England, France and Italy. This selection made it possible to critically assess and compare newspaper contents.

Secondly, one of the most important breeding grounds of self-organised civil society emerged from the collective media use practised within reading clubs: creating a charter, making joint decisions and electing officers on the basis of equal votes were ways for club members to practise democratic procedures. Reading societies experimented with methods of self-administration, equality, and democratic negotiations and have thus been considered as a pre-stage of democracy. Thirdly, the social exclusivity of reading societies was important in the light of the cultural and communicative development of the bourgeoisie, in spite of the fact that some members were aristocrats (Puschner, in Sösemann 2002: 202). In a sense, reading societies represented a 'personified enlightenment' and personified bourgeoisie. The lower classes were either excluded from the outset by the charters or the imposition of membership fees. The same initially applied to women, who were considered to interfere with free rational-critical thinking. Hence, reading societies for women emerged as substitutes. In addition, lending libraries gave them access to newspapers, periodicals and books, and from the nineteenth century onwards reading clubs also offered media access to women more frequently.

Although Habermas's book has been refuted on many levels, the productive discussion on his model of the 'bourgeois public sphere' has shown what power the media could possess in the seventeenth and eighteenth century to shape the social and cultural realms of the time. It has also become clear that it was not only those literary periodicals and books beloved of literary critics that were of great importance, nor the pamphlet journalism preferred by historians. It was also to a much greater degree the newspapers that defined the two centuries preceding the French Revolution.

CHAPTER 3

The Media and the Road to Modernity

The Media, Revolutions and Nationalism, 1760–1848

During the major revolutions that took place in the late eighteenth and second half of the nineteenth century, the media experienced a development that was entirely new and downright explosive. They played a central role not only in the American War of Independence and the French Revolution but in the revolutionary upheavals that took place around 1830 and 1848 in Germany and in Western Europe generally. On the one hand the media fostered the dynamics of these movements in multiple ways, while on the other the revolutions transformed the media. A systematic comparative study of this mutual relationship has yet to appear, although some programmatic anthologies do exist (cf. Grampp et al. 2008).

This interactive relationship was already in evidence during the American Revolution, which originated in the protests of the North American colonies against tax increases levied by England. The colonies began by striving for equal representation and ended by gaining their independence. Research has shown that the driving forces behind this movement were, for instance, local committees or patriotic Protestant preachers. However, if one considers what actually triggered the protests, it becomes apparent that the media played a crucial role. Thus the tax on printed matter levied by England with the Stamp Act of 1765 mobilised media protests. The Stamp Act was seen as an attack on North American newspapers and was consequently combated in many ways: newspapers printed petitions and readers' letters voicing their grievances about the tax; they demonstratively refused to pay it, instead using stamps imprinted with a skull; and they organised gatherings, notably the 'Stamp Tax Congress' of 1765 in New York. In fact the newspapers succeeded in stirring up unanimous resistance to this law, which led to its repeal a year later. Thus the media public became aware of their own power (Sloan and Williams 1994: 123–30).

A characteristic of media content was that exaggerated descriptions of individual conflicts were published in order to stir up sentiment. The 'Boston Massacre' of 1770 gives proof of this by its very name. Many newspapers printed melodramatic reports that the British had opened fire on a group of innocent civilians, killing five people. In the same vein, journalists stirred up sentiment by means of symbols. One key symbol of the struggle was a snake set above the slogan 'Join or Die', that first appeared in Benjamin Franklin's *Pennsylvania Gazette* in 1754 and was regularly published in numerous newspapers after 1765 (Frasca 2006: 148f.). The individual segments of the snake symbolised the nine colonies thus called to unite against the French and British lust for power.

In like manner editorial offices formed the nucleus for protests in various revolutionary actions. Thus the famous 'Boston Tea Party', in which Boston burghers disguised as Indians boarded English ships and threw tea overboard to protest against taxes and customs duties, was essentially planned in the editorial rooms of the *Boston Gazette* (Burns 2006: 159–62). Many of America's Founding Fathers had previously been active as journalists or publicists: Benjamin Franklin, for example, was one of the most important newspapermen in the Colonies, and Samuel Adams and Alexander Hamilton also launched newspapers (Frasca 2006). Their work made them famous and facilitated their populist agitation during the war.

Even debates about the Articles of the Constitution were largely carried out in the newspapers. Most notably, the eighty-five newspaper articles that appeared in various New York publications in 1787–88, and are now known as 'The Federalist Papers', were written by the Founding Fathers of the United States. Moreover, newspapers were instrumental in the formation of political parties. Beginning in the 1770s, newspapers aligned themselves more closely with the parties then in process of formation, so that by 1808 three-quarters of all newspapers were affiliated with one party or another (Copeland, in Barker and Burrows 2002: 149). Papers often enjoyed the patronage of 'their' parties in the form of emoluments, appointments or printing privileges, or had actually been founded by the party in question (Burns 2006: 241, 262–92). However, this period was not just a 'dark age of partisan journalism' but rather the manifestation of a productive culture of debate that contributed to the shaping of a nation. It was precisely because of the central role played by the press that freedom of expression in North America was explicitly granted at a very early date. The Virginia Declaration of Rights of 1776 was the first to provide for freedom of the press, basing its arguments on principles of natural and human rights. The Constitution of 1791 went even further by forbidding any law that might restrict it.

Freedom of the press and the debates that took place in the newspapers about the new political system unquestionably boosted circulation, which by

1800 had trebled to about 145,000 copies, with 234 newspapers vying for the readers' favour (Copeland, in Barker and Burrows 2002: 149). Thus it is clear that the American Revolution not only decisively changed the structure of the press but also proved lucrative for publishers.

The French Revolution and the Media in Europe

Researchers have devoted more attention to the role of the media during the French Revolution. Newspapers, magazines and professional journals were certainly of lesser importance in France during the time preceding the Revolution than had been the case in North America. Before 1784 the official French press expressed almost no criticism of the *Ancien Régime* (cf. Censer 1994: 213). Licensing and censorship policies, which had always been strict and were made even more restrictive in the late 1750s and again after 1776, simply left too little leeway for free expression. Nevertheless the role played by newspapers was not wholly without significance. First and foremost they regularly reported on events in North America and thus presented an alternative state model. Affluent Frenchmen could find detailed information, primarily in French-language newspapers published abroad such as the *Gazette des Leyde* which was published in the Netherlands and which also printed the text of the Declaration of Independence (Popkin 1990: 22).

The so-called underground media played a crucial role. In view of censorship restrictions, pamphlets, illustrated flyers or scandal sheets were more suitable instruments for mobilising the populace (Baecque, in Darnton and Roche 1989: 165–76). At their centre was the 'disclosure' of secrets and the 'true' character of the rulers (Engels, in Mauelshagen and Mauer 2000: 185). Pamphlets and suchlike resembled vernacular speech and enjoyed spinning rumours. In the process they were not chary of sexual mockery, and spun stories about the sexual escapades of the King and Queen. These tactics, in conjunction with rationalist, informative writings, served to reduce the almost sacred status of the monarchy (Darnton 1982: 1–40).

At the same time, pamphlets provided a field of endeavour for journalists from those newspapers that had shot up like weeds after the outbreak of the Revolution. The important Revolution-era journalist Louis-Marie Prudhomme was said to have authored fifteen hundred pamphlets during the two years preceding its outbreak before he began publishing the paper *Les Revolutions de Paris* in 1789. The Declaration of the Rights of Man and of the Citizen, declared on 26 August 1789, also established freedom of the press as a human right and ushered in a press boom hitherto without parallel. During the first years of the Revolution, three hundred new newspapers and magazines appeared annually, so that by 1799 about two thousand different ones were published, not counting forty thousand flyers (Reichardt 2008b: 234). The number of pages increased and circulation shot up: the *Gazette Universelle* had a daily circulation of eleven thousand copies, the *Journal du Soir* ten thousand. Now local events completely took over centre stage in place of foreign policy. Contents no longer differentiated between opinion and news. The dividing line between often short-lived newspapers and flyers that sometimes appeared in numbered form was often blurred. They were now sold on the street, where headlines were shouted out or texts read aloud. In like manner clubs of newspaper subscribers sprang up, with articles often being read out at the beginning of meetings. Foreign observers in particular noted with amazement that everyone in Paris was suddenly reading newspapers (Gough 1988: 233).

In order to appeal to the illiterate segments of the populace, pictures were accorded a pivotal role. On the one hand, religious images or statues of monarchs fell victim to iconoclastic destruction, yet on the other, symbols of the new order were displayed, some even designed by artists and paid for by the Committee for Public Safety. The destruction of the Bastille or insulting depictions of clerics or aristocrats were among the predominant motifs (Reichardt, in Dowe 1998: 193–200). In general the media were eclectic, mixing elements of oral communication (songs, dirges, rumours, sermons) with written ones (Reichardt 2008b: 258f.). Thus a multifaceted form of public discourse influenced by the media came into being, something that had already been developing in England over many decades.

The self-concept of these journalists differed markedly from what it had been prior to 1789. They no longer saw themselves as chroniclers but rather as political educators and people's advocates. It was above all the radical journalists who now viewed themselves as judges and investigative champions fighting against corruption and counter-revolutionary forces. As was the case in the United States, journalism provided a springboard to leading positions in politics. Jean Paul Marat (in his paper *L'Ami du peuple*), Camille Desmoulins (*Révolutions de France et de Brabant*), Jacques Pierre Brissot (*Mercure Française* among others) and Jacques-René Hébert (*Le Père Duchesne*) became key figures of the Revolution (Gough 1988: 173, 231). Journalists were drawn from all social classes and sometimes even included aristocrats and clerics (Murray 1991: 187). As in North America, newspapers had the function of shaping political parties. They were not merely the mouthpieces of the clubs but rather their crystallisation point. The press discussed and legitimised decisions. Now that the legislative process had become public, the press acted as its monitor, debating pivotal questions such as whether to execute the King or declare war. Campaigns in the radical media promoted events such as the famous 'March of the Market Wives' to Versailles, thereby according them collective significance. The monarchist press, too, profited from the new freedom and launched protest campaigns in their turn, especially after 1790 (Gough 1988: 233, Murray 1991: 105f.).

Of course the French Revolution bestowed only a brief flowering on the free media market. As early as 1792, a new censorship policy was instituted which suppressed the monarchic press. Furthermore, the Jacobins now gave financial support to their own newspapers, as the monarchists had once done. During the following year, 'counter-revolutionary' writings were declared capital crimes, and numerous editors and journalists fell victim to the guillotine. After Robespierre's execution there was a return to greater freedom of the press, which allowed the political right to maintain some public presence. With the advent of Napoleon Bonaparte, however, there was again a gradual return to censorship. Newspapers once more had to be licensed, and this licensing was supervised by a 'bureau de la presse' subject to the Minister of Police. Moreover, after 1799 the official government organ, *Le Moniteur*, dictated which texts could be published by the few remaining newspapers that were still permitted: four government-funded papers for Paris and only one newspaper for each département (Gough 1988: 229). This fact also illustrates the limited power of the newly media-hungry public: faced with the guillotine and the troops it proved defenceless.

The French Revolution did not change the media landscape in France only. On the contrary, numerous other European countries experienced a similar tension between modernisation and restoration. These effects of the Revolution led to much greater partisanship and political polarisation of newspapers in neighbouring countries, where detailed daily news reports led to a dramatic rise in circulation. This race for news had the effect of promoting a certain degree of professionalism, with the English *Times* in particular gaining in prestige because it had its own journalists working in Paris.

News reports about the American War of Independence had already led to an initial polarisation of the West European populace during the 1770s and 1780s. Thus the 'patriotic revolt' of 1786/87 in the Netherlands was associated with incendiary newspaper articles. Later reports about the French Revolution are thought to have provided the impetus for the Netherlands' version of the French Revolution in the Batavian Republic in 1795 (Broersma, in idem 2005: 233–55). In the years between 1796 and 1799 the effects of the French Revolution in the Italian states were an easing of censorship and marked newspaper expansion, with the media expressing widespread sympathy for the revolutionaries (Hibberd 2008: 17f.). Even in England and Germany, the press at first welcomed the revolutionary coup in France before a conservative journalistic counter movement was launched, with only a few papers that supported the Reign of Terror managing to survive after 1793 (Barker 2000: 176–78).

In consequence of reports about the French Revolution, Germany experienced an increase in local protest movements that adopted symbols popularised by the media – for example, the cockade or the liberty tree (cf. Berding, in Böning 1992: 5–10). Often the daily press simply translated articles from

French newspapers or pamphlets. On occasion they even invoked the struggle for freedom as justification for violence, sophistically rationalised events or blamed the consequences of the Revolution on a failure to implement reforms (Koch, in ibid.: 242). German newspapers thus voiced criticism and took sides. Some addressed themselves specifically to the lower classes by presenting events occurring in France in dialogue form. Even the *Intelligenzblätter* became more political (Böning 1999).

Having first encouraged a flowering of journalistic discourse across Europe, the French Revolution was now to blame for its Europe-wide restriction after the mid-1790s. Primarily responsible for this was the fear of revolt common to all governments. It was hardly surprising that Austria in particular tightened censorship after 1793 and revived the Police Bureau for Press Surveillance at Court. Even reading rooms were forbidden. At the same time, urged by the Imperial Court, Prussia also passed new laws against 'seditious writings'. However, local research has shown that this mainly served to increase self-censorship and did not necessarily result in a significant increase in the number of prison sentences (Reinalter, in Böning 1992: 19; Hagelweide, in ibid.: 252–55). Consequences were much more severe in the regions occupied by Napoleon. In the counties of the Rhine Federation he had most of the newspapers shut down, and the remaining ones often had to be published in two languages. In occupied states like Württemberg, political reports could come only from official sources like *Le Moniteur*. All serious newspapers had to comply with this ruling, and in Baden only a single newspaper was permitted (Schneider 1966: 175f.). The consequences were a deterioration of content as well as a huge decrease in circulation. By 1806 at the latest, licensing and censorship modelled on French practices had led to heavy restrictions in occupied Italy (Smith 1979: 92). The French *Moniteur* thus became the reference point for a new type of centralised media system for large parts of Europe.

Even in the mother countries of press freedom there were certain restrictions. In England the French Revolution led to a general conservative backlash in the 1790s. In its wake the government of William Pitt once more raised taxes on newspapers to prevent the dissemination of radical writings, ruled that mastheads must contain the printers' address, and sponsored papers loyal to the regime (Barker 2000: 69f.). To make matters worse, the number of indictments and prison sentences for journalists increased. Even in the United States, where freedom of the press had just recently been declared, freedom of opinion was restricted in 1798 by penalizing 'false, scandalous, and malicious writing' against the government, the administration and the Congress. This led to about twenty-five arrests before the law was repealed four years later. Ultimately criticism of these restrictions served to strengthen press freedom in the United States during the nineteenth century (Lewis 2008: 21).

At the same time, the Napoleonic Wars enabled techniques of political propaganda to take hold, with Napoleon himself as role model. In Prussia the prime driving force was the reformer, and later Chancellor, Karl August Freiherr von Hardenberg. As early as 1807 he wrote a memorandum in which he demanded that one must 'honour and influence public opinion to a greater degree by means of appropriate publicity, news, praise and blame, etc.' for the purpose of achieving 'an excitation of patriotic enthusiasm' (quoted from Schneider 1966: 178f.). Metternich employed similar tactics in Austria. The ambivalence of this focus on the people is obvious: it was based on authoritarian tactics but enhanced the status of the public as an instance through which governments could strive to implement and legitimise their actions. Thus Hardenberg introduced official government gazettes to publicly justify political measures (Hofmeister-Hunger 1994: 403 and 217). Because governments feared revolt, these official gazettes were distributed free of charge and in large numbers to the lower classes especially – forty thousand copies of the *Schlesische Volkszeitung*, for example – in order to supplant the pamphlets and warn against agitators (Böning, in idem 1992: 502f.). In the war against Napoleon, Austria and Prussia imitated his *Bulletins de la Grande Armée* for the purpose of mobilising the people by means of proclamations, statistics and battle hymns (Hofmeister-Hunger 1994: 265–69).

This propagandist mobilisation against Napoleon corresponded with the consolidation of nationalism. The connection between nationalism and communication was stressed early on by pioneering studies like those of Karl W. Deutsch (1953) and Benedikt Anderson (1993). Nevertheless even recent studies on the history of nationalism rarely take the role of the media into consideration. Anderson viewed newspapers not merely as transmitters of nationalistic pronouncements but rather argued that the consciousness of reading newspapers concurrently with millions of others shaped the national community envisaged in the press (Anderson [1983] 2006: 33). Moreover, the print media were the first mass-produced industrial product to create a common market, promote a common language and publicise maps that shaped the concept of nation states. It was the vital media market that first enabled the formation of a national cultural canon as a well as a patriotism that manifested itself in negative ethnic stereotypes and the rejection of French lifestyle (Waibel 2008: 163–66).

This connection between the media and the development of nations was even reflected in the titles of many newspapers. Thus in North America some early papers were named *Gazette of the United States*, *American Minerva* and *National Gazette*. In Germany, there was a plethora of nationalistic journal names between 1780 and 1815, like *Teutsche Mercur, Deutsche Chronik, Ponoma für Teuschlands Töchter* and *Journal von und für Deutschland*. Furthermore the media continued their mobilisation campaign with pamphlets, caricatures, and patriotic poems and songs, which promoted communication across all social barriers (Hagemann, in Sösemann 2002: 296). Speeches, plays, gymnastics clubs and fêtes did the rest, but these, too, interacted with the print media. It was not until they appeared in print that speeches such as Johann Gottlieb Fichtes 'Reden an die deutsche Nation' or Schleiermacher's sermons became widely known. Nationalistic writers like Ernst Moritz Arndt and August Kotzebue adapted their language to the media with the intent of reaching even the lower classes (ibid.: 283). The burning of French papers and symbols, as at the Wartburgfest in 1817, emphasised this bond between the media and nationalist practice.

In order to drum up support for the war against France, the publication of nationalistic papers was permitted in 1813/14. For the same reason, the Russian army had already abolished censorship in its liberated regions, as had the Prussian command, with a resulting boom in newspapers and historical-political journals (Hagemann, in Sösemann 2002: 286–95). The Prussian government went so far as to promote nationalistic papers like Görres' *Rheinischer Merkur* and sponsor Kleist's *Berliner Abendblätter* and Ernst Moritz Arndt's poems criticising local censorship (Hofmeister-Hunger 1994: 300–309). Some speeches, specifically intended only for the press, were often reprinted – for example Blücher's appeal to 'the people of Saxony' that complemented the Prussian King Friedrich Wilhelm's appeal 'To My People', which appeared in the *Schlesische Privilegierte Zeitung* in March 1813. In this way the configuration of the war led to a new type of communication between rulers and people that served to mutually strengthen nationalist sentiment.

The degree to which media and nationalist movements in Eastern Europe interacted needs to be examined in more detail. It seems to have been the case in Hungary, the Czech Republic and Poland, since newspapers and magazines in the native language made their appearance at precisely this time, as did literary societies (Balogh and Tarnói 2007). The same held true of Greece, where the first newspapers appeared in 1811. Greek-language papers published abroad backed the struggle for independence, which many Central European intellectuals supported ideologically, materially and sometimes even by fighting – like the Swiss Johann Jakob Meyer, who published the *Elleniká Chroniká* in 1824 and then went to Greece to fight against the Ottomans. On the other hand, it was not until the 1860s that Russia permitted the publication of independent papers like *Golos*, which, in spite of censorship, fostered nationalism by such expedients as praising Russia as an enlightened and civilised country in Asia (McReynolds 1991: 45f.; Renner 2000: 378).

In Latin America one can also detect a certain correlation between the establishment of newspapers and national liberation movements. At the beginning of the nineteenth century, newspapers appeared in Mexico that strongly expressed their commitment to the struggle for independence, and this led to the abdication of the Spanish Viceroy in 1822. Similarly, numerous newspapers circulating in Colombia and Bolivia stood up for independence and called for the founding of the Republic of Bolivia in 1825. In Brazil, however, it appeared that only national independence in 1822 led to a certain increase in the number of newspapers, which in turn promoted the formation of republican and monarchist factions (cf. contributions in Wilke 1992–1996). Foreign media reports influenced the fight for independence. In particular, the Haitian Slave Revolution (1791–1804), which led to the founding of this state, became a global media event. Broad reports in North American and European papers debated slavery in this context.

Restoration and the Revolutions around 1830

In Western Europe this brief media flowering was followed by a lengthy phase of restoration during the post-1815 era. This was not an immediate consequence of the Congress of Vienna, since the Viennese federal records promised only 'uniform provisions for freedom of the press' (Wilke 2008: 167). In a similar vein many federal states passed fairly liberal constitutions, and approximately two-thirds contented themselves with post-censorship. It was not until 1819 that the Karlsbad Decrees led to a drastic and uniform restriction of freedom of expression. This epoch was characterised by strict pre- and post-censorship of printed works of up to 320 pages, as well as surveillance by informers. The whole was accompanied by arrests of journalists and scholars who had expressed their opinions openly. As a consequence, newspaper content became less attractive: the number of relevant topics declined, and even a newspaper as important as the *Augsburger Allgemeine Zeitung* took its commentaries mainly from the foreign press (cf. empirically: Blumenauer 2000). In their place the publication of court news and decrees increased, and self-censorship blocked rational argument. There was scarcely any expansion of circulation relative to population growth, despite the fact that technical developments should have led to an increase. The introduction of the high-speed press in 1814 initiated the first definitive changes in printing technology since the days of Gutenberg.

In spite of the repression, censorship was often circumvented. In the German Federation the most important method was to relocate publishing houses to those states in which censorship was more laxly applied, like Bavaria or Saxony. Political articles about foreign countries, especially England and the United States, were a means of indirectly disseminating ideals. Furthermore, there was a kind of 'idea smuggling', done by means such as secret messages hidden within texts, poems and books, as well as in songs, and by symbols and icons on handkerchiefs and medallions (Siemann 1987).

Despite or rather because of repressions there was a revival of protest movements in Western Europe around 1830, and these were often partly initiated by newspapers. The outbreak of the July Revolution in France was mainly due to the 'July Ordinances' issued by King Charles X, which further restricted freedom of the press and the voting census. Journalists initiated a resolution against the Ordinances, and the protest paper posted by forty-four editors from twelve newspapers on 27 July 1830 mobilised the street against the government (Charle 2004: 37–41; Reichardt 2008b: 241). In particular, the newspaper *Le National*, founded in 1830, was one of the most important germinal cells of protest (Church 1983: 74). The paper collected signatures against the Ordinances, and its editor Adolphe Thiers was one of the main activists of this revolution, which indeed succeeded in driving out the royal family and placing the liberal 'Bourgeois King' Louis Philippe on the throne. In the 1830s, Thiers became Minister and Minister President, and in 1871 advanced to become the first President of the Third Republic.

A similar link between the media and revolution was evident in Belgium, which now emerged as an independent state for the first time. After the King of the United Kingdom of the Netherlands reacted autocratically to demands for reform, the Flemish and Walloons in the Catholic south, influenced by the Parisian July Revolution, rebelled in 1830 against the mainly Protestant north. A chief advocate of their reform demands was the newspaper *Courier des Pays-Bas* and its editor Louis de Potter. An anti-clerical journalist, he called for an alliance between the Liberals and the Catholics, who now used nationalistic arguments to protest against the government (Church 1983: 83). The struggle for freedom of the press was another important reason for protests. At least seventy thousand people signed a petition demanding it, while prosecuting journalists like Potter made them martyrs. Both the official publishing house that printed the royalist paper *Le National* and the private residence of its publisher were targets of the first violent protests in 1830. Here, too, the revolution caused many journalists to join the new government.

Of course there were no revolutions in Great Britain, Italy or the German Federation in 1830; nevertheless they too experienced protest movements supported by journalists and the media. Illegal nationalist papers were published in the Italian regions; since the late 1820s Guiseppe Mazzini and others, operating from Marseille, had established programmatic papers supporting his movement 'Young Italy' (Gernert 1990: 51f.; Hibberd 2008: 18f.). In Germany the Paris Revolution revived the nationalist movement and led to turbulent public gatherings in some states. 'Freedom of the press' developed into a key idea of these protests (Koch, in Grampp 2008: 286). The climax of this political activity was the famous Hambacher Fest in 1832. The key figures involved in its preparation were also journalists – most prominently Philipp Siebenpfeiffer, who changed the name of his paper

Rheinbayern to the more programmatic *Deutschland*, and Johann Georg August Wirth, whose paper *Deutsche Tribüne* was subject to continuous censorship but nevertheless continued to appear in spite of numerous lawsuits. In February 1832 they founded the Deutschen Vaterlandsverein zur Unterstützung der freien Presse (German Fatherland Association for the Support of a Free Press) that organised a gathering registered as a folk festival in Hambach. At least thirty thousand participants stood up for freedom of the press, for a German national state, and against arbitrary use of police power. Thus the media became intermeshed with sundry organisations and traditional rituals. The festival was closely monitored by the press, which openly expressed its sympathy in numerous articles. In the short term the forces of repression triumphed; leading journalists were arrested or forced into exile, and press censorship and restrictions in the public sphere actually increased. But at the same time this had the effect of politicising those writers of the 1830s, like Heinrich Heine and Georg Büchner, who are now known as 'Young Germany'. Above all it was a beacon for the nationalist movement and a precursor of the revolution of 1848.

Something very often overlooked is the fact that there was a simultaneous interplay between press and protests in England too. Even here, the fear of revolt current after the defeat of Napoleon led to restrictions of press freedom as well as to higher taxes and sureties for newspapers, and four years later, concurrent with the Karlsbad Resolutions, the 'Six Acts' restricted public communication to an even greater degree. However, English journalists were more courageous than those on the Continent. Around 1815 and 1830 respectively, a radical press with high print runs flourished. It bore belligerent names like *Poor Men's Guardian. Published in Defiance of 'Law', to try the Power of the 'Might' against 'Right'*. Each edition was adorned with a picture of a printing press and the caption 'Knowledge is Power'. Between 1830 and 1836 alone about 550 illegal newspapers came into being, and because they did not bear the revenue stamp, were able to be sold cheaply, thus ensuring high circulation. The radical paper *Weekly Political Register*, published by William Cobett, had a print run of forty thousand copies (Wiener 1969: XVII). These papers exercised moral criticism of the 'Old Corruption' in simple, accusatory language, denounced the exploitation of the populace and injustices in courts of law, and advocated freedom of the press, free suffrage and better working conditions. The *Radical Press* and *Unstamped Press* thus put their imprint on a proto-socialist movement, addressing 'the people' as the true sovereigns of the nation (Conboy 2002: 72).

Furthermore, English journalists encouraged protest gatherings that had a similar exponential effect as the Hambacher Festival. Thus in 1819 a mass gathering of sixty to eighty thousand people in Manchester was organised by the Patriotic Union Society that was sponsored by journalists from the

Manchester Observer. Many editors from the serious London press attended, and then reported in horror on the bloody suppression of the gathering, with fifteen dead and hundreds injured – and especially on the violence against women (Bush 2005: 30–35). This turned the 'Peterloo Massacre', as it was called by the press, into a similarly iconic object of remembrance as the 'Boston Massacre' had been in the American Revolution. In a similar vein, a year later in London, radical journalists incited protests in the 'Queen Caroline Affair' because the future King George IV had succeeded in divorcing his wife. In the protests and reforms of the early 1830s, the *Radical Press* and *Unstamped Press* again played a pivotal role (Barker 2000: 11f.). They also succeeded in getting the hated stamp tax reduced to one penny. In so doing, the *Unstamped Press* in effect abolished itself, paving the way for a flourishing, high-circulation popular press in Great Britain.

Media and the Revolution 1848

This intermeshing of media and revolutions was in evidence all across Europe in 1848. These uprisings, too, had their origin in Paris, spreading from there to the rest of the continent (Dowe et al. 1998). Once more the media influenced the course of revolutions and were themselves in turn transformed by them. In many countries censorship had already been relaxed in the years preceding 1848, so that the media were able to give voice to liberal and nationalist demands and disseminate reports about sundry protest activities. After 1847, liberals in the Kingdom of Sardinia-Piemont flocked around the Turin newspaper *Il Risorgimento*, and in the German Federation around the *Deutsche Zeitung*. This upswing corresponded to technical advances, the high-speed press being used with markedly greater frequency during the 1840s (R. Stöber 2000: 116). Its high purchase price necessitated high, quickly produced print runs, and these were more difficult for the censors to control. This in turn made it possible to distribute thousands of leaflets with the 'Demands of the People' that had been formulated at the Offenburg People's Assembly of 1847 (Siemann 1985: 115).

During the revolution this new technology made possible several print runs per day, which imparted a new dynamism to protests. Important papers, like *La Presse* in Paris – with a circulation of over 70,000 – and the *Kölnische Zeitung*, appeared three times daily in 1848 (Reichardt 2008a: 16, 19). In light of these numbers, their call for the King's abdication carried special weight. By contrast, the telegraph played hardly any role at this time, since most Central European newspapers had been forbidden to use it due to fear of uprisings. The spread of revolution rather tended to be facilitated by the growth of other new vehicles of speedy transmission – the railway, for example, that was built up in Germany after 1835, or the regular use of carrier pigeons, that had long been employed for this purpose by newspapers and news agencies.

After the outbreak of the revolution, freedom of the press and of expression were pivotal demands briefly realised in many countries, even in conservative Austria. Under the influence of events in France, in 1848 the German Bundestag granted each member state the option of establishing freedom of the press (Greiling 2003: 507). Article IV of the constitution passed in 1849 contained the pioneering words: 'Each German has the right to freely express his opinion in word, print and pictorial representation'. Freedom of the press enabled the media to expand throughout Europe with lightning speed. In Paris alone, 450 new, albeit mostly short-lived, periodicals appeared in July 1848 (Reichardt 2008b: 242). In Austria the number of newspapers trebled to 215, while in Germany the number grew to an estimated 1,700 (Siemann 1985: 117). Street sales moreover accorded them a new presence, but the line between pamphlets and short-lived periodicals was often blurred. Seen in this light, we should not associate the revolution of 1848 simply with barricades or new parliaments. Newspaper-reading citizens who debated and discussed issues characterised it to a much greater degree. The revolution moreover abruptly changed the profiles of newspapers and magazines. Semi-official state-financed papers like the Österreichische Beobachter in Vienna and the *Rheinische Beobachter* in Bonn disappeared. Other periodicals sought to mark their transformation by eliminating determiners like 'official' or 'privileged'. It was above all in the provinces that new political papers were born, with hitherto 'neutral' newspapers adopting a political position that they emphasised by using attributes like 'Volk', 'German', 'free' and 'citizen' (Koszyk 1966: 110; Greiling 2003: 506, 514). In France, the names of newspapers often harked back to the slogans of the French Revolution: *La Liberté*, for example.

The year 1848 also saw the unfolding of the partisan press in Central Europe. As had been the case in earlier uprisings in North America and France, newspapers and magazines were not established as mere mouthpieces of existing parties, but both coexisted in a mutual formative process. It was at this time that the four movements that continued to define politics in many countries up to the twentieth century (Conservative, Liberal, Catholic and Socialist) emerged with their own press. Publicists gradually discovered their place in the political landscape during the course of the debate. Newspapers negotiated the policy objectives of their respective party lines on the basis of unfolding current events. In the provinces, too, pub gatherings, the formation of political associations, and the political alignment of local newspapers were intermeshed (Beine 1999).

The leading organ of the constitutional liberals was the *Deutsche Zeitung* (1847–1850) that addressed itself to the bourgeoisie (Hirschhausen 1998);

next in importance was the *National-Zeitung*. The *Deutscher Zuschauer* from Mannheim, however, was more radically liberal. This was a harbinger of the ideological division that would mark the liberal movement far into the twentieth century. Furthermore, as precursors of the Social Democratic movement, papers with low print runs published by workers' organisations began to appear: *Das Volk*, the movement's main organ *Verbrüderung*, and finally the Socialist *Neue Deutsche Zeitung*. Karl Marx, returned from exile, became editor-in-chief and later owner of the *Neue Rheinische Zeitung* (Koch, in Dowe 1998: 797). Newspapers published by workers' organisations appeared in France as well: for example, *Commune de Paris* or *La Vraie République* (Reichardt 2008a: 22).

With the *Neue Preußische Zeitung* – called simply 'Kreuz-Zeitung' because of the Iron Cross in its masthead – the Conservatives founded a newspaper intended by its co-founder Ludwig von Gerlach to serve as a means of consolidating Conservatism and providing a counterweight to the *Deutsche Zeitung* (Bussiek 2002: 63f.). Thus the Conservatives began to combat political reforms by using the techniques of the reformers: freedom of the press with a press of their own, and parliamentarianism with their own coalition. In comparison with the Liberal papers, however, Conservative periodicals and journals were only of secondary importance. The same was true of political Catholicism. After 1815 and especially from the 1840s onwards, the number of Catholic magazines increased. In the German Federation alone, 92 papers appeared before 1847, with Conservative 'ultramontan' ones dominating. Articles in these papers emphatically condemned the revolutions, identifying them with the Reformation that they saw as their root cause (Schneider 1998: 46f., 354–59). The most important Conservative political journal was the *Historisch-politische Blätter für das Katholische Deutschland*, which had been edited by Joseph Görres since 1838. In 1848, political Catholicism organised itself on all levels of the public sphere: as a coalition in the German Parliament in Frankfurt, in assemblies like the first Catholic Diet, in the founding of religious societies, and of course in the new media. The mainly conservative Cologne newspaper *Rheinische Volkshalle* became the leading Catholic organ in that year. Thus there was a growing insight among Catholics that they should engage in debates on the politics of the day to assert their presence in the media and the public sphere.

Satirical journals also flourished in the context of the revolutions of 1848. In Berlin alone about thirty-five appeared in 1848/49 satirical papers with titles like *Der Teufel in Berlin* and *Kladderadatsch* that alluded to the revolt while mocking it at the same time (Koch 1991: 57–130). Now Germany joined ranks with France and England, where high-circulation satirical papers had already established themselves in previous decades, particularly *Le Charivari* after 1832 and *Punch* after 1841. Yet their mockery of the cowardice and ignorance of the citizenry and the incompetence of politicians both old and new also betrayed a sense of powerlessness.

Another new development in 1848 was women's involvement in journalism. Generally speaking, women too participated in political change. They took part in protests and assemblies, distributed printed matter in the streets, or at the very least attended sessions of Parliament as observers.

In 1848 a newspaper called *La Voix des Femmes* appeared that inaugurated the founding of numerous women's associations and held gatherings of the 'Central Committee of the Society of the Voice of Women' in its editorial rooms as well (Koch, in Dowe 1998: 785f.). In Germany at least a few women played a part in political journalism, even editing political newspapers independently. In the *Neue Kölnische Zeitung*, Mathilde Franziska Anneke for example stood up for the establishment of a republic, and when this paper was thereupon forbidden, the *Frauen-Zeitung* published by Louise Otte stepped into its legacy. It printed news and comments on daily political happenings, and demanded equal rights for women (Wischermann, in Blühm and Gebhardt 1987: 351; Freund 2004: 173). Thus the revolution of 1848 marked a milestone in the development of emancipated woman journalists and the public participation of women in politics.

As had been the case in previous revolutions, journalists proved to be political actors and often entered the political arena. In Paris, after Emile Girardin, the publisher of *La Presse* called for the king's abdication, journalists again took up numerous government posts (e.g. Foreign Minister or Minister of War), and sometime later, the editor-in-chief of *Le National* became mayor of Paris. In the National Assembly that framed the Constitution, about 11 per cent of the members were full-time journalists and 10 per cent had journalism as a part-time occupation (Koch, in Dowe 1998: 779).

The revolution of 1848 failed, and with it the short flowering of a diverse and sophisticated media world. Political restoration had many consequences for the media: freedom of the press was abolished, journalists were arrested or forced to emigrate, and the majority of those papers that had just come into being folded or suffered from vastly decreased circulation. The state now used financial incentives to influence the press to an even greater degree than before. Nevertheless there was no going back to former conditions, for governments could no longer act with their old severity without discrediting themselves. Instead of pre-censorship, the government of Germany was now content to practise post-censorship, which in turn made it ever easier to test limits (Requate 1995: 251). Moreover, the media had developed new models in 1848 that either survived covertly or were revived from the 1860s onwards. In this way at least a few satirical journals or party newspapers were able to survive and become reference points for the formation of political societies during the following decade.

Politics and Society in the Age of Magazines and the Popular Press

Many things have been attributed to the waning nineteenth century. It is considered the beginning of 'classical modernity', the 'political mass market' or else the *fin de siècle*, vacillating between euphoric awakening and future angst. The influence of the media on society now played a central role and for this reason the decades following the 1880s have been described as the beginning of a *Sattelzeit* (period of transition) for the mass media, as a way of describing the process of mutual transformation that took place in the media and society (Knoch and Morat 2003: 19f.). New electronic communication (telegraph, telephone), new reproduction media (popular press, magazines) and new technical forms of reprography (photograph, phonograph, and finally film) were the building blocks of this ensemble. The traditional forms of newspapers and periodicals also experienced dynamic changes during this Golden Age of the press. Circulation numbers, variety and frequency of publication rose sharply. In several Western countries circulation numbers of daily papers and periodicals hit six digits or even the million mark, like the Parisian *Petit Journal* in 1890. In a small country like the Netherlands sales rose from ninety thousand in 1865 to approximately one million copies before the First World War. Beginning in the 1860s a significant press market rapidly emerged, even in Russia and Japan.

This boom in newspapers and periodicals went hand in hand with multifarious societal upheavals. A primary precondition for this was nearly universal literacy, the fruit of compulsory schooling first established in Germany, and afterwards also in France and England. Its introduction firstly created an expectation among publishers that they would be able to produce simple mass-circulation papers for millions of new media consumers (Brown 1985: 30; Curran 1978: 57). Secondly, media expansion was closely tied to urbanisation, as large cities were the guarantors of both news topics and sales markets. Thirdly, the reduction of economic restrictions by the state promoted a sudden press boom. For this reason, the discontinuation of stamp taxes (1853–1861) in Great Britain is seen as a central turning point in media history, as it reduced the price of newspapers and thus generated a rapid rise in circulation. This allowed the provincial press to flourish, and Liberal papers like the *Daily Telegraph* were able to break the ascendancy of the Conservative press and the pro-government *Times* (Lee 1976: 69). At the same time the abolition of taxes was based on the belief that financial competition would provide more effective protection from the radical media (Hampton 2004: 33). A similar newspaper expansion followed upon the discontinuation of economic restrictions in the Netherlands in 1869 and in the German Empire after the passing of the Reichspressegesetz (Imperial Press Law) of 1874 (Wetzel 1975: 61, 291;

Kohnen 1995: 111). In Vienna and Austria, however, it was only when the 'newspaper stamp' was discontinued in 1899 that the age of an inexpensive mass-circulation press set in, with the establishment of the *Kronen-Zeitung*, for example.

Fourthly, the press also flourished thanks to the abolition of direct and indirect forms of censorship. A particularly liberal press law was passed by France in 1881, while in England there was a decrease in the number of libel trials, which had until that time functioned as a kind of indirect censorship. In the 1860s censorship was relaxed even in Russia in consequence of the reforms instituted by Tsar Alexander II, which enabled the press to thrive, and in 1905 further easing of restrictions triggered a second wave of new publications (McReynolds 1991: 220). As for Germany, although the Reichspressegesetz of 1874 had for the first time – with the exception of 1848 – granted extensive press freedom, during the following decades the *Kulturkampf* (culture struggle) and the Socialist Laws subjected almost more journalists and newspapers to political persecution than ever before. In Prussia alone there were fourteen hundred trials during the subsequent four years (cf. Wetzel 1975: 159). The Socialist Laws of 1878 even led to a partial return of pre-censorship over the next twelve years, by prophylactically forbidding Social Democratic printed matter. Not until the 1890s did Germany come close to the standard of Western press freedom and experience widespread growth of the mass media, but even so, critical journalists still had to live in fear of prosecution.

Fifthly, the indispensable preconditions for expansion were technical innovations. These included greater ease of distribution (railroad, steam ships), communication (telegraph, telephone, etc.) and production. Since the 1870s the rotary press had increasingly come into use. Autotype facilitated the printing of photographs, and the invention of the typesetting machine combined setting and casting after the 1880s (R. Stöber 2000: 120f.). The high cost of purchasing a rotary press literally forced its owners to produce extremely high print runs in order to amortise their investment.

In spite of national differences, three formats characterised the press boom in Western countries: the daily popular press that avoided partisan alliances; party organs or party-affiliated periodicals; and relatively un-political but richly illustrated weeklies. Nevertheless the lines of demarcation between them were not as clearly drawn as many studies or even contemporaries would have it. The new mass press was given various names: 'Yellow Press' in the United States, 'Popular Press' in England, 'Petit Press' in France and 'Generalanzeiger' in Germany. With all its novelty, of course it had predecessors across borders. Inexpensive mass newspapers with their entertaining and instructive contents had already appeared in the 1830s, most prominently the *Penny Magazine* in 1832, adapted in Germany one year later under the same name *Pfennig-Magazin*. In the 1840s and 1850s these were followed by rapidly growing illustrated family weeklies that tended to avoid politics in the narrower sense. The *Illustrated London News* (1842), the Paris *L'Illustration* (1843) and the Leipzig *Illustrirte Zeitung* (1843) not only appeared at the same time and with similar names, but the German magazine had copied the format and often even used the pictures and articles of the other weeklies as well. Drawings were often based on photographs, as printed photographs were only made possible by technical advances at the beginning of the 1880s, and were not regularly found in illustrated magazines or newspaper supplements until the end of the 1890s. In this respect one can speak of a rapid upsurge of visualisation even before 1900 that familiarised people with distant lands, local court cases, and society personages (Weise 1989).

Some of the key traits of the popular press in the waning nineteenth century – besides high circulation and low cost – were their local frames of reference, their sports reporting, their accounts of sensations (accidents, crimes, etc.) and the large amount of advertising they contained. Nevertheless, national differences and frequent fluid transitions to different formats are unmistakeable. Thus the new mass press was not always apolitical or only interested in the pursuit of sensational news items or topics of local interest. This was particularly true of early American prototypes of this format, and also the Parisian *Petit Journal* that had initially eschewed political themes in order to avoid the press tax (Thogmartin 1998: 63f.). Beginning with the 1860s, many other countries had similar papers, like the *Folkets Dagblad* in Denmark, established in 1863 (Hoyer, in Broersma 2007: 42).

However, researchers have often been too hasty in projecting impressions of today's popular press onto newspapers of that time like the *Daily Mail*, *Pall Mall Gazette* and *BZ am Mittag*. These were not yet dominated by sensationalist headlines, but rather by contemporary domestic and foreign policy, with sports, local news and entertainment gaining in importance. Since these papers were especially well furnished with editors and correspondents, they can also be seen as precursors of today's serious journalism. The Anglo-Saxon 'popular press' in particular set new benchmarks with its critical investigative journalism. Furthermore, all newspapers showed a recognisable trend away from the former dominance of foreign policy articles and towards more reporting on domestic policy, regional news and cultural themes (Wilke 1986). Nevertheless, politics in the narrower sense was seldom found in high-circulation pictorial papers like the *Illustrated London News*, the *Gartenlaube* or the *Berliner Illustrirte Zeitung*, which primarily collected interesting, curious and entertaining topics from all over the world. Yet here too, lines were blurred: for example, the illustrated weekly *Reynolds's Newspaper* continually seized upon both the spectacular and the political.

By the same token, the new mass press was not always neutral. Papers of this kind often began with the avowed intention of remaining aloof from single parties so as to be able to address a broad readership. In actual fact they often strayed from this course and followed the political persuasions of their owners. In this way the initially apolitical *Petit Journal* moved into the Nationalist-Conservative camp after a change of ownership. Just as the papers of the major British editor Lord Northcliffe, such as the *Daily Mail*, favoured the Conservatives, the German *Berliner Lokalanzeiger* and the illustrated *Die Woche*, from the publishing house Scherl, also took a conservative course and supported the Kaiser. Here again the boundary with the party-affiliated press was blurred, although the popular press retained greater political flexibility.

The boundaries between financing and marketing were likewise fluid. The assumption that it was primarily the new mass press that was financed by advertising does not stand up to general scrutiny. In Great Britain, where classifieds were already more entrenched, advertisements accounted for more than half the space in classical newspapers like *The Times* and the *Manchester Guardian*, and consistently adorned their front pages (Brown 1985: 16). Similarly, the advertising columns of Germany's party and opinion press were often even more extensive than those in the popular Berlin papers, taking up more than half the space (Requate 1995: 363f.). The notion of the popular press as a 'centre of corruption' was rather an offspring of contemporary cultural criticism. Indeed, the French partisan press in particular was especially vulnerable to corrupt influence because it used hardly any advertising to finance itself.

The popular press likewise professionalised the job of journalist, which until the 1850s had served mainly as a transitional or second job for writers, professors and politicians. It was not until the last third of the nineteenth century that journalism became a permanent full-time profession worldwide. As is always the case with new professions, journalists now began organising themselves in groups that could give voice to their interests (Requate 1995: 222–42). By 1900, journalism was developing culturally into a field that embodied the ambivalence of modernity like hardly any other. A mixture of social advancement and job insecurity, a new sense of power and gnawing self-doubt, elitist consciousness and popular culture characterised both journalism and the *fin de siècle*.

Studies distinguish between two separate journalistic templates that remained the defining models until the end of the twentieth century: on the one hand the news-oriented investigative Anglo-Saxon journalism, and on the other the opinion-oriented, party-affiliated journalism of the European continent (Requate 1995; Esser 1998). These two journalistic cultures have been somewhat sweepingly described by German scholars as 'track hounds and Missionaries' (Renate Köcher) or 'News and Views'. In Anglo-Saxon countries journalists have, since the 1850s, proclaimed the press to be a 'Fourth Force' next to politics. Anglo-Saxon newspapers, publishers and journalists continued to favour certain parties, it is true, yet the profession enjoyed greater independence than on the Continent. Consequently, the post-1880s British press saw itself less as an 'educational agent' than as an advocate of the reader – a 'representative medium' (Hampton 2004: 52). The parliamentary system, ample press freedom and stronger market orientation all favoured this development.

The 1880s also marked the appearance in the English-speaking world of reporters who were increasingly conducting independent inquiries, holding interviews and doing on-the-spot investigations to uncover abuses and to push for policy reforms. The first interview is often attributed to the *New York Herald* in 1859, but it took two decades before this form of dialogue became established in the Anglo-Saxon world (Hoyer, in Broersma 2007: 36). To gather information for their disclosures, disguised journalists smuggled themselves into factories, madhouses or brothels. In England this procedure, pioneered by William Thomas Stead, was known as the 'New Journalism', and in the United States as 'Muckraking' (Wiener 1988). In the countries of Continental Europe, independent reporting and the separation of opinion and news began later because of the stronger ties between newspapers and political parties. Here journalists tended to see themselves as cultural and political educators. The ideal was not so much fact-based, well-researched news as well-formulated argument (Høyer and Pöttker 2005; Bösch, in Zimmermann 2006). Consequently German newspapers daily seized upon political commentaries of their competitors for the purpose of emending them.

Nevertheless, Anglo-Saxon journalism and its Continental counterpart moved closer to each other around 1900, when various forms of investigative journalism increased in Continental Europe as well. For example, in the Netherlands the young reporter Marie Joseph Brusse wrote a number of socially critical articles beginning in 1898, for which he disguised himself as a sailor and a tramp in order to pursue his investigation (Wijfjes, in Broersma 2007: 72). Although in Germany new formats such as interviews developed slowly only after the turn of the century, reporters were already travelling to the scenes of events to do their own research (Bösch 2009: 472). And even in 1890s' Russia, reports of this kind appeared in an attempt to alter politics and society (McReynolds 1991: 164f.). On a less positive note, British journalism tended towards greater partisanship in the period around 1900, whereas the liberal German popular papers like the *B.Z. am Mittag* came very close indeed to Anglo-Saxon standards.

Although Anglo-Saxon journalists enjoyed a better reputation than their colleagues on the Continent, there were few differences in social standing and income. Both British and German journalists from the major newspapers had university degrees as a rule, and in Germany as well as Britain editors could at least look forward to earning a good salary (Brown 1985: 76, 210f.; Requate 1995: 143f., 218; Retallack 1993: 188–200). However, getting journalistic training on a professional footing progressed slowly. The Ecole Supérieure de Journalisme in Paris was a first important step in 1899. In other countries, like Germany, attempts to establish schools of journalism at universities or business colleges came to grief, because of the resistance of colleges as well as the self-image of the journalist, who considered education and writing talent as sufficient qualification. Even in the United States, initially not a single university was willing to accept a donation from the publisher Joseph Pulitzer to finance a department of journalism. Not until 1912 did New York's Columbia University finally accept Pulitzer's offer, after the University of Missouri had established one of the world's first degree courses in journalism.

Recent studies have revealed the social and cultural significance of the press boom – for example its connection with urbanisation. The more locally focused popular press helped numerous new citizens of large cities to orientate themselves, made the metropolis accessible to them and developed its image. Its attractions, its job market and its crime were interactively presented. As Peter Fritsche has demonstrated in regard to the Berlin press of 1900, the media defined how people viewed the city and acted in it, perhaps by encouraging the reader to keep his eyes open for anything newsworthy (Fritzsche 1996: 16). Conversely, newsworthy attractions often arose because the media drew attention to them. It was not unusual for city newspapers to initiate these attractions themselves. The Ullstein Verlag in Berlin, for example, organised an automobile race and a '*B.Z.*-Air Race', and then provided running reports on them. By the same token it encouraged its readers to send in their own photos of the city, and this as early as 1900. In Austria the Viennese press organised treasure hunts, and the French magazine *L'Auto* initiated the annual bicycle race, the Tour de France, in 1903 and immediately trebled its circulation (Charle 2004: 197f.).

At the same time the newspapers influenced the daily rhythm of a city. Two or three daily editions (morning, noon and evening) set the pace for news in cities like Berlin and Cologne. In Great Britain there was one daytime edition, but the rise of evening papers compensated this. New means of travel, like bus, train and tramway, made newspaper reading an omnipresent practice by which people could incidentally demonstrate their political leanings. Likewise, headlines became an acoustical component of the city. German travellers in New York, London and Paris were constantly aware of the news criers. In Berlin, where street sales had long been forbidden the better to control subscription sales, the first newspaper vendors appeared in 1904. The *BZ am Mittag* in particular embodied the 'pace of Berlin'. This popular organ published stock indices during the midday break, as soon as the market had closed, as well as international news of that morning. This hectic pace of the press led to its being considered both expression and cause of rampant nervousness, and typesetters were viewed as probable candidates for mental hospitals (Radkau 1998: 242).

Like the news criers, the great newspaper offices were landmarks of the metropolis, uniting editorial offices and production under one roof. Newspaper districts like Fleet Street in London and Koch Straße in Berlin apparently presented a mighty counterpoint to government districts. People often gathered in front of the big news buildings, eager to get the first copies as quickly as possible because they were interested in the classified ads. But there were also many visitors to the editorial rooms, since newspaper office hours were published in the masthead. People came to report news, display artworks and seek advice.

Pioneering studies have shown that this interaction between the press and the citizens was also helpful in the fight against crime. The young popular press publicised spectacular murders that shook the city and sometimes the entire world. The new mass publication *The Star* became hugely successful with its articles about Jack the Ripper's murders of prostitutes. Its critical reporting in turn had repercussions for the police investigation, finally contributing to the resignation of the Chief of Police. With their endless reports about such murders, newspapers also shaped people's views of society. They uncovered urban poverty and prostitution, and offered interpretations – from the Marxist class struggle to feminist points (Walkowitz 1994: 191–220; Curtis 2001; Hett 2004: 57). Police and newspapers enlisted readers' aid in the pursuit of criminals by asking them to help to find witnesses and perpetrators (Müller 2005). News reports about spectacular trials furnished new insights into the underworld and questioned the legitimacy of judicial actions. As Benjamin Hett has argued, two-class justice disappeared in the light of public scrutiny (Hett 2004: 222).

Press photographs often bolstered this socially critical reading of the metropolis. The very first printed photos in newspaper history, published by Stephen H. Horgan in the *New York Daily Graphic* in 1880, depicted slum housing in New York. The documentary photos of Jacob A. Riis that appeared in newspapers in 1888/89 served to enduringly raise New Yorkers' awareness of the slums in their own city (Emery and Emery 1988: 225). While investigating, journalists acted as 'urban spectators', exploring the metropolis as if it were a 'dark continent' (Walkowitz 1994: 33). The reporters from the *Berliner Illustrirten Zeitung* visited unusual locations like prisons, the 'madhouse' and warming halls, or simply wrote about 'Berlin by Night'. The British star journalist William Thomas Stead conversed incognito with pimps and prostitutes in London's East End in 1885 to better enable him to describe their lives. He even personally initiated the purported purchase of a thirteen-year-old girl. His investigative report about 'The Maiden Tribute of Modern Babylon' in the *Pall Mall Gazette* strongly influenced the notion that in the midst of London even children were sold as 'white slaves'. This triggered mass protests numbering 150,000 demonstrators, generated a flood of signed petitions, and finally achieved the goal towards which Stead had been working: the age of consent was raised (Schults 1972: 128–68).

These arresting modern developments, for which the popular press had paved the way, also included the 'New Woman'. As Jane L. Chapman argued, popular papers like the French *Le Petit Journal* and the British *Daily Mail* presented not only conservative representations, but also a 'a form of female empowerment' (Chapman 2013: 196). By 1900, the most important popular journal *Berliner Illustrirte Zeitung* regularly printed pictures of prominent women who were moving into male-dominated fields. These pictures, which circulated worldwide, showed female surgeons and policewomen from the United States, female 'city fathers' from Norway, women election campaigners and suffragettes from England, women lawyers from Paris, and the first 'female university professor'. Although these photo essays reached millions of readers and were certainly very important for women's liberation, they have often been neglected in the field of gender studies. The women's movement that established itself in the United States in the mid-nineteenth century and gained a tentative foothold in Europe during the following decades relied on new media of its own as well, which had emancipatory content quite different from that of women's magazines in the eighteenth century. This already applied to *The Lily*, founded after a women's congress held in New York in 1849 and boasting six thousand subscribers. It was even truer of other magazines that followed, such as *The Woman's Journal* of the American Woman Suffrage Association. From 1858 until 1864 *The English Woman's Journal* served as the most important forum for the early feminist movement in England. In Germany, Louise Otto, chairwoman of the Allgemeine Deutsche Frauenverein, published the magazine *Neue Bahnen* from 1865 until 1895. The Social Democrats published *Die Gleichheit* (The Equality) as part of their programme, and Helene Lang *Die Frau* (The Woman) as a new voice of middle-class women. In so doing they attempted to shed light on the contemporary political situation, voiced criticism of specific laws, and provided a platform for the exchange of controversial opinions. The debates in middle-class papers usually skirted the issue of male–female differences, whereas *Die Frau* expressly underlined them. In contrast, the Social Democratic organ *Gleichheit* concerned itself primarily with the balance between work and capital, and integrated women into the social context (Kinnebrock 1999: 157).

The English women's movement reached a broad public because it made use of spectacular actions geared towards the media: English women fought against prostitution and the forcible physical examination of prostitutes, with proto-feminists like Josephine Butler organising campaigns in the 1870s after several scandalous incidents; the suffragettes who fought for women's rights in the years around 1900 held demonstrations aimed at the media and committed selective acts of vandalism in order to draw attention to their cause (Chapman 2013: 117–41).

In general, the popular press helped to enhance the importance of women since publishers now discovered them as an important target group for the new sales market. This was true not only for fashion magazines and home companions explicitly directed at women (like *Die Modewelt* after 1865, and successful family journals like the *Gartenlaube*). In England, new papers like *The Star* and the *Daily Mail* introduced regular women's pages, and numerous illustrations were included as a means of attracting female readers. In addition to advice and articles about everyday life and fashion, they printed many reports about modern women who could be seen as emancipatory role models. These 'women's pages' also served as an incentive to read the rest of the daily paper with its political content. In 1903 the publisher Lord Northcliffe even brought out a penny paper for women – the *Daily Mirror*, 'written by gentlewomen for gentlewomen' (Lee 1976: 82). However, it only achieved a real breakthrough when it addressed both sexes with the headline: 'A paper for men and women'.

Although women were still underrepresented among journalists, their numbers were already increasing significantly, and in the United States the proportion of women was up to an estimated 7 per cent by 1900. In fact as early as 1879 every eighth Congressional reporter in Washington was a woman (Emery and Emery 1988: 215; Chambers et al. 2004: 15). In England in 1911 nearly 4 per cent of newspaper owners and publishers and 15 per cent of all writers were women (incl. Schriftsteller, Lee 1976: 73). For this reason the 'Society of Women Writers and Journalists' had been established in England in 1894, and books on journalism for women appeared on the market. Even in Russia female journalists gained prominence at several newspapers (McReynolds 1991: 150f.). Although female editors long remained a minority in Western countries, journalism gave women access to an academically and politically informed occupation and allowed them to participate in public life. This was pioneered first in the United States and then in England, where at an early stage individual women were able to move into top positions in the field of political journalism, either as foreign correspondents (Margaret Fuller/*New York Tribune* 1846) or editorial writers (Harriet Martineau/*Daily News* since 1852) (Emery and Emery 1988: 132f.; Chambers et al. 2004: 18f.).

From the 1880s, a few female journalists even made a name for themselves by performing spectacular stunts that turned them into role models. Nellie Bly travelled solo around the world in seventy-nine days for Pulitzer's *New York World* in 1889. Two years before, on an assignment for the same paper, she had disguised herself so she could be admitted to a New York 'madhouse' and report on abuses there, an action that subsequently led to reforms. Ida

Tarbell's spectacular articles denouncing Rockefeller's oil trust and damaging his reputation also had momentous consequences because they showed how he had systematically ruined smaller businessmen.

During the Boer War there were even three British women who exerted a definitive influence on both the interpretation and the course of the war: Flora Shaw, the foreign correspondent of *The Times*, defended the government position, in close alignment with Colonial Minister Joseph Chamberlain; Sarah Wilson provided the *Daily Mail* with exciting impressions from the front lines; and the reports of the nurse Emily Hobhouse pilloried the British 'concentration camps'. Thus female journalists not only demonstrated that women were tough and resilient but also that they had the ability to influence politics and society.

Mass Press and Politics

Politics, too, was transformed by mediaisation in the waning nineteenth century. This was true not only of political institutions and political spheres but of political communication as a whole. This is most evident in the case of rulers. Although royal houses suffered losses of political power during the late nineteenth century, there was a simultaneous increase of their public presence in everyday life, which served to cement their social position. Queen Victoria was in fact known as the 'First Media Monarch' (Plunkett 2002). The German Kaiser Wilhelm II was not only titled as a 'Media Monarch' but as 'First Film Star' as well, whose ostentatious self-staging, magnificent uniforms and journeys were extremely media-friendly (Loiperdinger 1993; Windt, Luh and Dilba 2005). This popular staging of monarchs was a consequence of the illustrated press and the popular mass media, which often printed daily bulletins about the royal family. Although the media actively sought the proximity of the monarchs, the monarchs themselves also consciously and deliberately bowed to the logics of the media. Consequently, the royals deliberately published family pictures that corresponded to the cosy middle-class paradigms in illustrated reviews – for example, Queen Victoria as 'mother' and Kaiser Wilhelm I as 'spa guest' (Plunkett 2002: 148; Geisthövel, in Knoch and Morat 2003). This promoted their 'civic publicness', and it was to a great extent the photos of the royals that ushered in the triumph of public photography. The media encouraged rulers to make spectacular public appearances – like Queen Victoria's Diamond Jubilee in 1897, or the commemoration of the one-hundredth birthday of Kaiser Wilhelm I. Yet at the same time the omnipresence of the media endangered the monarch's position. In Great Britain, King Edward VII (1901–1910) felt this while still Prince of Wales, when his love affairs and gambling caused scandals that plunged the monarchy into a deep crisis (Bösch 2009: 373–93). The German Kaiser Wilhelm II was able to mesmerise his hearers during his public appearances, but newspaper articles about his aggressive rhetoric increasingly led to outrage across all party divides, as did his 'Hun Speech' in the year 1900, that encouraged German soldiers to slaughter Chinese (Bösch 2009: 393–420). The Kaiser likewise failed at the new interview format. His *Daily Telegraph* Affair' in 1908 revealed how the Kaiser's haughty and contradictory utterances in interviews led to criticism and international crises.

These interviews with the Kaiser occurred at a time of changing foreign policy in the media age. Governments now tried to shape their foreign policies more directly by making well-chosen statements to the media (Bösch and Hoeres 2013). Paid journalists in the latter days of the German Federation and the Age of Bismarck had already been employed for this purpose (Kohnen 1995: 160). Reichskanzler Bülow (1900–1909), no less than the Kaiser, banked on interviews with the foreign press, although these were not yet common in Germany. As the German historian Dominik Geppert has recently demonstrated, the conflicts played out in the media sometimes influenced or substituted government action in German–British relations. As unofficial emissaries, the media intervened in foreign policy and deliberately cemented stereotypes. At the same time they attempted to promote an easing of tensions by sending journalists from Britain and Germany to interview the other country's politicians (Geppert 2007: 351–86, 422f.).

The innumerable scandals in these decades, which were brought up in every Western country, coincided with the development of the popular press, too. Both media and public were outraged by cases of corruption, abuse of power by the military and deviant sexual behaviour by politicians. This often led to political crises that discredited the reputations of the elite. One has but to recall the Panama and Dreyfus Affairs in France, the Cleveland Street and Parnell Scandal in England, and the Eulenberg Affair in Germany to prove the newfound might of the popular press. As 'Fourth Power' it now applied moral standards as a means of monitoring politics and demanding political reform. However, these scandals might also be set in motion by some politicians themselves who opted for a media-friendly type of communication in this new political arena (Bösch 2009).

Not much research has been done to date on the extent to which the media not only favoured political leaders but also strengthened the position of parliaments, for party-affiliated as well as non-party papers published regular and detailed reports on parliamentary debates and printed long texts of speeches. This publicity moved members of parliament into the political spotlight, and their verbal slugfests were often followed with as much enthusiasm as boxing matches (Bösch 2004). Media presence in the parliaments also created an immense crush in the public galleries (Biefang 2009: 145).

Demarcation lines between politics and journalism continued to be quite fluid. The enhanced position of the media actually strengthened journalistic presence in politics. Even in Great Britain, where journalism had freed itself from party ties at a very early date, the number of journalists with seats in the House of Commons grew, and by 1906 they were the third largest vocational group, especially among Liberals and Irish Nationalists (Lee 1976: 199, 294). In France, where the relationship between political parties and journalists was particularly close, about one-third of all delegates during the Third Republic had journalistic experience. In Germany, where journalists were not held in very high esteem, this applied to barely 10 per cent of Reichstag delegates during the time of the German Empire, and most of those were Social Democrats (Requate 1995: 90, 291). But leading politicians from other parties also had journalistic backgrounds – like Eugen Richter (Liberal), Matthias Erzberger (Centre) and Wilhelm von Hammerstein (Conservative). This was another factor that facilitated the adaptation of media communication within politics.

Nevertheless, heads of large publishing houses during these decades seldom held leading positions in politics, although their journalistic power increased tremendously at the end of the nineteenth century. In the United States, especially in New York, publishers like Joseph Pulitzer and William R. Hearst owned the papers with the biggest circulation. In London, Cyril Pearson of the Morning Leader Group, and even more prominently Lord Northcliffe, controlled over two-thirds of total circulation (Lee 1976: 293). In Germany this concentration in the hands of a few was evident both in Berlin, whose newspaper market was controlled by Ullstein, Mosse and Scherl, as well as in other good-sized cities, where the 'Gazette King' August Huck owned about a dozen papers. The big German publishers exerted their political influence mainly through the ideological tenor of their newspapers, whether liberally inclined (Mosse, Ullstein) or conservative (Scherl). Not until the Weimar Republic did a German media mogul and party leader come to prominence in the person of Alfred Hugenberg, who in 1928 took over the leadership of the conservative DNVP. In other countries the desire for political power manifested itself earlier. In the United States, William R. Hearst not only had himself voted into Congress but also tried to get the Democratic nomination for President, albeit without success. In like manner, Lord Northcliffe ran on the Conservative ticket in the 1890s and bought up a newspaper in his election district expressly in order to support his campaign. Only after they had failed in their political ambitions did these publishers restrict themselves to exerting political influence primarily through their contacts and their publications.

Faced with this challenge, many governments changed their manner of dealing with the press. Repression increasingly gave way to attempts at influencing journalists through informal contacts. Files in Great Britain document written correspondence and personal meetings between politicians and journalists, and many publishers were given titles (Brown 1985: 193). In France and Germany, journalistic bribery can be documented up to the late nineteenth century. Under Bismarck the government paid numerous journalists and pro-government newspapers honoraria out of the so-called 'Reptile Fund' taken from the confiscated fortune of the Guelph family (Wetzel 1975; Kohnen 1995: 159). Bismarck's successors endowed individual journalists with considerable sums of money as well. The government also subsidised WTB, the leading news agency, and issued a news summary called 'Provinzial Correspondenz' for the provincial press at a moderate price.

The Viennese government pursued a similar strategy with its Österreichische Correspondenz, granting it privileged access to telegraph messages (Kohnen 1995: 154; G. Stöber 2000: 60–63). In view of the new popular press, however, these hidden payments became less important. They were also getting too risky, after scandals attending the systematic bribing of journalists in France, Italy and Germany during the 1880s were disclosed to the public (Hibberd 2008: 27; Bösch 2009: 343–61).

Future researchers would do well to examine more closely the way governments adapted their communication styles to the specific logics of the media. From the 1880s, leading members of the British parliament developed an organised form of 'lobby journalism', whereby chosen journalists could obtain sensitive information (Sparrow 2003). The German chancellor Bismarck had already cultivated close informal contacts with individual journalists, and even after his resignation attempted to carry on with politics by means of 'discreet indiscretions' leaked to the press. After 1900 the Chancellor Bernhard von Bülow stopped prosecuting the press and instead opted for active dialogue. Like many of his ministers of state, he deliberately gave the illustrated journals access to his private life, permitting them to photograph him during his holidays with his wife and his dogs. His press secretary Otto Hammann consequently became one of his closest associates. In the same way other members of the Reichstag regularly granted off-the-record talks to journalists of like persuasion in order to feed them information about their positions. On the other hand the government had little success in its attempts to build up a coordinated public relations sector; only the ministries of Foreign Affairs and the Navy were reasonably successful (Jungblut 1994).

It would also be advisable to examine more closely the interaction between media and political parties. Since most parties, with the exception of the Social Democrats, initially had no detailed party manifestos, their near- and middle-term guidelines were developed by the newspapers affiliated with them. By the same token the parties of that time (again excepting the Social Democrats) were still without stable organisational or membership structures. For this reason, party-affiliated newspapers formed the connecting link with the party base whose very formation as such was often the result of reading the same papers. In France especially, the newspapers thus became a kind of party substitute, but in Germany, too, they served to unite like-minded people in various regions of the country (Requate 1995: 394). Because the political orientation of the newspapers displayed in coffee houses and pubs determined the clientele, they indirectly had the effect of creating gathering places for those of similar worldviews. The newspapers on display in these locales often triggered political debates (Bösch 2004).

This booming Central European party press was neither an anachronism nor a new form of journalistic dependence. On the contrary, parties were modern democratic organisations, and for journalists, party affiliation often meant independence from the government. Thanks to the party press, several competing organs could coexist even where supernumerary newspapers were not profitable. This ushered in a change in the political power balance of the media market. Thus the Liberal press was dominant in Great Britain during the Liberal governments of the 1860s to 1880s, and later the Conservatives dominated the media and voting market (Lee 1976: 158, 179). In a similar way the Social Democratic press in Germany expanded rapidly after 1890 with a concurrent increase of the votes of their party, SPD. Studies in Norway also show that during the late nineteenth century both the Liberal and Conservative press held sway in their respective voter strongholds (Høyer, in Høyer and Pöttker 2005: 77). Nevertheless, one should not unthinkingly equate voters with newspaper readers. In actual fact, the circulation of the SPD press before the First World War was less than the number of SPD voters; among the Liberals, this situation was reversed (circulation data according to R. Stöber 2000: 213 and 222). Consequently it is reasonable to infer that many Social Democrats read Liberal newspapers, especially during the 1890s.

The media thus had a twofold effect on social and political milieus. Such milieus developed in many Central European countries at the end of the nineteenth century in the wake of culture struggles and the persecution of Socialists. On the one hand the party press promoted a fragmentation in separate social environments: Social Democrats, Catholics, Liberals and Conservatives not only tended to move within their own organisations, pubs and political parties, but the fact that they got their information from disparate media sources magnified the differences in their worldviews. Events occurring in other social spheres were often ignored or derided. On the other hand the news organs, particularly the Liberal ones, built bridges to other spheres. Even in the Conservative *Kreuz-Zeitung* one could sometimes read the text of SPD Reichstag speeches, albeit in condensed form and garnished with negative commentary.

There is still a great need for research, especially in Germany. In contrast to England and the United States, practically no reliable, substantiated, source-based studies about the great publishers and journalists exist (anecdotal: Mendelssohn [1959] 1982; about Theodor Wolff: Sösemann 2000; mainly up to 1890: Requate 1995). Notwithstanding this unsatisfactory state of affairs, the self-concepts of these men, their contacts with editorial departments, their attitudes towards politics, and innovations in the Anglo-Saxon world all need to be examined. Likewise, there are hardly any studies dealing with the new popular press that emerged during the decades before and after 1900. Not even the contents of the biggest papers (*Berliner Morgenpost, BZ am Mittag, Berliner Lokal-Anzeiger, Berliner Illustrirte Zeitung*) have been methodically evaluated, with the consequence that extremely sweeping judgements about them continue to circulate. Possible aspects of such studies might be the extent to which these papers changed ideas about politics, sports, and the relationship between the sexes. At least some party organs like the so-called '*Kreuz-Zeitung*' have already been researched (Bussiek 2002).

Another area that should be addressed is the German provincial media, because they were truly characteristic of the country. Here one should examine and compare the extent to which the provincial press merely accepted the official state news bulletins and followed the lead of the big newspapers, but also how they established relationships to their environments. What role did they play in shaping social grouping, political parties and local power structures; how did they organise job markets, influence local purchasing behaviour and free-time activities, and the relationship between rural and urban spheres? Previous studies have shown that farmworkers read newspapers in part because of their classified ads, which therefore provide valuable source material on the life of rural workers. Their preferred reading was generally local or religious weeklies provided by the local gentry (Schulz 2005: 148f., 257). Finally, there has been very little research done on the relationship that existed among representatives of the international popular press, although a closer analysis of adaptations and specifically national traditions could reveal quite a bit about the cultural peculiarities of individual countries.

Globalisation, Colonialism and Media Transformation

The nineteenth century experienced an accelerated 'transformation of the world' (Osterhammel 2009). In its course, the second half of the century witnessed the beginning of a phase of rapid globalisation. This was characterised by global consolidation and integration, an increase in trans-border interactions and cultural contacts, and increased cooperation and standardisation – but, at the same time, growing cultural differentiation. In like manner globalisation was partially responsible for the development of a new worldview that moved time and space closer together.

Telegraphy

Previous studies on world history and globalisation have stressed media change as an important driving force in this process, frequently pointing to the role played by the telegraph, news agencies and the popular press. However, these have generally not gone beyond a few introductory remarks, while historical accounts have concentrated on themes like the global economy, colonialism and cultural exchange (see, e.g., Wendt 2007; briefly on the media: Osterhammel 2009: 63–83). Future research would do well to incorporate the respective mechanics of the new global media into world history in general.

Doubtless studies of the telegraph as a medium and motor of globalisation can be approached in very different ways. Seen from the vantage point of both scientific and technical history, this already applies to its inception during the 1830s, in which researchers from different countries participated. While visiting a Heidelberg professor, William Fothergill Cooke, the British inventor of the telegraph, saw a needle telegraph developed by a Russian; together with the British electro-physicist Charles Wheatstone he refined, patented and tested it in a trial run. The electromagnetic telegraph of the American Samuel B. Morse and the facsimile telegraph of the Scotsman Alexander Bain followed a few years later. After 1850, intense work began on a worldwide cable system, which in spite of immense costs and many setbacks, was spurred on by grand visions and expectations of profit. The first cable was laid from London to Paris in 1851, out as far as the Crimea four years later, and, after many reversals, across the Atlantic in 1866. Starting in the 1870s, telegraph cables from Europe extended as far as Rio de Janeiro, Cape Town, Australia, Calcutta and Peking, so that a global media network can be said to have existed since that time (cf. Wobring 2005). Economic interest in South Africa was the primary reason for including Africa in the global network during the 1880s. Another factor was that the telegraph promoted global accords. Thus in 1865 the World Telegraph Accord in Paris made the Morse code a single, cross-boundary world 'language' for this new medium, and established international conventions that standardised the transmission of telegraph signals. Henceforth the International Telegraph Union (ITU) coordinated communications and held annual meetings.

As early as the nineteenth century, telegraphy served to promote the awareness that the world and its cultures could cooperate in an innovative way. Samuel Morse had already prophesied that telegraphy would 'make one neighbourhood of the whole country'. After the telegraph connections between England and France were in place, *Punch* saw the two countries as 'The New Siamese Twins' (quoted in Read 1999: 13). The transatlantic cable was compared to an umbilical cord that would unite Great Britain and the

United States as never before. Because of its network character, telegraphy was declared the 'Victorian Internet' (Standage 1998). Yet notwithstanding its immensely greater speed, caution should be exercised in making such comparisons: telegraphy at that time was extremely expensive, and available only to the upper classes on a regular basis. Furthermore, it took several hours to send messages over longer distances and several days to the Far East, as transmission through a succession of relay stations was very time consuming. In any case, short messages sent by telegraph were no substitute for written correspondence.

Newer studies wrestle with the question of whether telegraphy was propelled more by nationalistic imperialism or the global economy. Doubtless the possession of high-speed telegraph lines provided an information advantage for trade and imperial conquests (acc. to Hills 2002). Great Britain in particular used the telegraph to secure global dominance and owned approximately 68 per cent of the world's cables in 1900; the United States had close to 20 per cent, but Germany only 2 per cent, albeit with an upward tendency (Wobring 2005: 183f.). It took decades before the United States was able to catch up with Great Britain by expanding its transatlantic cable system (Hugill 1999: 230).

On the other hand, Dwayne Winseck and Robert M. Pike have recently argued that global telegraphy was overwhelmingly based on economically motivated international cooperation (Winseck and Pike 2007). They perceive it more as a force of internationalisation than a struggle for information control. Big cable firms like the French Atlantic Cable Company, the Indo-European Telegraph Company and the Western and Brazilian Telegraph Company were in fact financed by capital from several cooperating nations. Persian and Ottoman firms were even involved in the construction of the telegraph network between England and India. At the same time, the various national telegraph companies were major international players, as Microsoft and Bertelsmann are in today's phase of globalisation. John Pender, who established most of the British – and thus worldwide – cable companies, is accordingly considered the Bill Gates of the late nineteenth century.

At the same time, it is evident that the various states increasingly attempted to place the media under state and therefore national control. It may not come as a surprise that in authoritarian governments like Germany telegraphy was put under the auspices of the postal service so that telegrams could be monitored. But even England increasingly turned to the buying-up of private cables from 1868 onwards, and two years later purchased the underwater cable to Germany from Reuters (Read 1999: 51). During the heyday of imperialism between the 1890s and 1910, state control of the cable networks was especially intense, even in Japan and the United

States, and was organised on the principles of private enterprise. The work of Winseck and Pike counters this with the argument that only 20 per cent of the network lay in the hands of the state, and therefore political interests could only partially circumvent economic ones (Winseck and Pike 2007: 226).

More importantly, telegraphy was unquestionably used as an instrument of military control. Hence the expansion of the telegraph line from Great Britain to India came as an immediate reaction to the Sepoy Uprising of 1857/58, as a means of expediting the deployment of troops in case of unrest. This was the reason why the Chinese resisted telegraph cables, whereupon the cable companies laid them surreptitiously and then with cunning and a good deal of diplomatic pressure confronted the Chinese with a fait accompli after 1870 (Baark 1997: 87). Here again, the Boxer Rebellion gave impetus to an expansion of the cable system as a safeguard of Western influence (Winseck and Pike 2007: 140). Yet at the same time the telegraphic stream of information in colonial regions promoted intra-national communication, patriotic sentiments on the part of the natives and subsequent movements towards independence – particularly in India (ibid.: 343f.; on China: Baark 1997: 194). Furthermore, telegraphy changed the role of diplomacy in general. As David Paul Nickles has argued, telegraphy reduced the power of foreign diplomats and opened up new possibilities for negotiations between governments, which could help to avoid the escalation of conflicts – like the possible entry of Britain into the American Civil War (Nickles 2003).

The effects of telegraphy on society can be traced in many other areas. They are most evident in the financial sphere. Prior to the advent of telegraphy, regular trans-border communication using carrier pigeons had expedited the flow of information between the big stock exchanges. Now the telegraph accelerated the emergence of a global economy by interlinking the exchanges and facilitating trans-border contracts. By the same token it strengthened the concentration of business in particular exchanges. While the stock markets in New York, Boston and Philadelphia had been of roughly similar size during the 1840s, the dominance of Wall Street grew with the introduction of the telegraph (Baark 1997: 53). As early as the 1860s the first tickers clicked out stock prices on tickertape. This networking of the markets of course also heightened the vulnerability of the global market. Thus the first world financial crisis occurred in 1857, shortly after the introduction of telegraphy, and it would be well to examine more closely the extent to which this speedy communication triggered panicky chain reactions following the failed speculation of an American bank.

Moreover, telegraphy transformed the inherent content of communication and the press. This was true not only because of the increasingly rapid availability of the latest news. Media experts argue that telegraphic transmission caused the newspapers to focus on events, a development that favoured a truncated headline-like concentration on bare facts – 'News' instead of 'Views', in fact. Finally, transmission was extremely expensive, so it had to be limited to key data. This led the culture critic Neil Postman to the conclusion that telegraphy accelerated the growth of irrelevant and incoherent exchanges, since it gave precedence to acoustical, sensational and unusual information in place of considered analysis of content such as that found in books or written correspondence (Postman [1985] 2005: 65–76.). Telegraphy was indeed responsible for the fact that the popular press covered their front pages with short, unconnected bulletins intended to stress the paper's global currentness. However, the oft-repeated assumption that the amount of foreign news increased because of telegraphy is certainly not accurate for Central Europe, since its ratio tended to decline in the context of nation building, press freedom and the development of parliamentary systems (Wilke 1984: 152).

News Agencies

Telegraphy did promote the rise of globally operating news agencies. Whereas only a few big newspapers had previously been able to afford foreign correspondents, the wire services now made it possible to telegraph news from all parts of the world into the European provinces. This in turn led to a rapid rise in the status and consequent growth of the provincial press after the 1870s. Beginning in the mid-nineteenth century, the British Reuters Agency, the French Havas and the German Wolff's Telegrafisches Bureau (WTB) developed into the world's biggest wire services and were soon joined by the American Associated Press (AP). After the 1860s, Reuters in particular had offices at its command worldwide, from Australia to Bombay to Cape Town. Examples of how Reuters expedited news transmission even before the establishment of the global cable network are legendary: for example in 1862 by means of a regular courier service from Peking to Siberia so as to take advantage of the just-completed telegraph, or even before the Atlantic cable was laid by means of an ingenious system of ship traffic between telegraph stations that enabled Reuters to be the first to report the assassination of Lincoln to the London public (Read 1999: 38).

These wire service bureaus stood simultaneously for global cooperation and the politics of national interest. Their trans-border cooperation was sealed in 1870 by secret cartel agreements between Reuters, Havas and WTB. In 1893 the Associated Press (AP), which had previously cooperated with Reuters, joined them. In this way a small number of news agencies divided up among themselves the job of transmitting news worldwide so as to forestall ruinous competition. They agreed to share information, with one agency generally being responsible for a specific region. In this system Reuters (which covered primarily the British Empire from Canada through East Africa and Asia to Australia) and Havas (primarily South America, West Africa and the Western Mediterranean) were clearly dominant; the German WTB tried to cover Northern Europe and parts of Central and Eastern Europe. The agencies also agreed on cooperation in several regions, such as the Habsburg Empire. For the Germans even this position as junior partner brought many advantages: they could reduce the costs of news gathering, rid themselves of competitors because they had exclusive rights and, most importantly, protect their own ascendancy (Basse 1991: 48f.). They also hoped for an opportunity to expand further eastwards.

The power of the wire service agencies was rooted not only in the fact that they had access to news from other parts of the world; they also had fairly exclusive transmission rights. That economic interests superseded political ones is shown by the longevity of the cartel, which continued to exist into the 1930s. The breadth of its clientele precluded one-sided and judgemental reporting. Even during the patriotically charged Boer War, Reuters also broadcast reports from the Boer perspective (Potter 2003: 44). Other agencies such as the Russian ones had hardly any chance in the global market because they were considered unreliable, and so WTB could function as the most important dispatcher of news from Moscow and St Petersburg (Rantanen 1990: 169–72).

Yet even in the global news agencies there were increased attempts by the state to exercise control as a means of protecting national interests. This was especially true of WTB. Under Bismarck in 1865 the Prussian state gained extensive influence, and then in 1880 the German Empire used covert subsidies to do the same. In return, WTB sent news articles to various government departments before publication, pledging itself to broadcast in detail the pronouncements of the chancellor and state secretaries. News items that might give cause for concern were to be submitted to the Foreign Office for an advance check (Basse 1991: 31f., 61–63; G. Stöber 2000: 58). In this way WTB's trans-border communication was simultaneously part and parcel of national policy.

The rise in state influence can be documented not only in France, where the Havas successor *Agence France-Presse* even today exists largely on state commissions because the French government sits in the board of this public organisation and is the primary client. Tendencies in this direction were also evident in Great Britain for a long time. Hence Donald Read's standard work on Reuters labels the agency 'a semi-official institution of the Empire' during the late nineteenth century. His pointed conclusion is that not until the Suez Crisis of the 1950s did Reuters develop into a supra-national agency and stop reporting news primarily from the British perspective (Read 1999: 474).

Regional studies of media communication in the Empire have come to the same conclusion. In the case of India, Chandrika Kaul has demonstrated that news articles from Reuters were often semi-official and avoided touchy subjects because of the agency's close ties with the Indian Office (Kaul 2003: 46f.).

The telegraph and the wire services fostered the emergence of newspapers not only in the provinces but also in many parts of the non-European world. In Asia, South America and Africa they provided easier access to global news. After Reuters made Shanghai the base for its Far Eastern news service in 1871, many foreign papers sprang up in the cities of China (Wagner 1995). Conversely, the rise of a powerful press in New Zealand, Australia and Argentina made them attractive new markets for news agencies and telegraph companies (Winseck and Pike 2008: 11).

The Boom of the Press in East Asia and the Colonies

Although countries such as China and Japan had a long-established culture of writing and printing, yet it was not until the nineteenth century that they adapted Western-style periodicals, and in quite disparate ways. No other country in the world experienced a transformation of its media with such lightning speed as Japan, which today has the highest newspaper density in the world. One could point out that within a few decades Japan passed through the entire development formerly experienced by the West, and managed to integrate its own traditions as well. The fact that Japan had been extremely isolated before the middle of the nineteenth century makes this even more astounding.

The rapid expansion of modern media in Japan can be explained by the favourable conditions there. Literacy was quite high even before the school reform act in 1872, but especially after it: not only the urban bourgeoisie and landowners could read, but also some of the small farmers, with differences within the provinces (Rubinger 2007: 162–80). Also a well-established market for books and commercial lending libraries existed. There had also been a kind of precursor of the newspaper, the so-called *kawaraban*, a single-page gazette that reported on important events. When Japan ended its isolation in 1853–54, there were already five hundred different *kawarabans* in existence, with a circulation of approximately one million (Huffman 1997: 22). As Japan was strongly urbanised, especially in Edo (later Tokyo), it already possessed an existing market of publishers, distributors and readers.

The establishment of this new market occurred within the framework of countless reforms during the Meiji Period (1868–1912), when Japan experienced a fundamental transformation in many facets of its society and often modelled itself on the West. As James Huffman has argued, the media played a defining role in these changes (Huffman 1997: 2). After Western merchants had established the first newspapers, numerous Japanese newspapers and magazines appeared during the 1860s and broadened people's awareness of the outside world, for example the *Magazine of the Western World* (after 1867). Japanese travel to the United States and Europe also increased knowledge of the Western press. As early as the 1870s the media had begun to bring politics into the public sphere and promote societal debate. This new press landscape in Japan revealed parallels to Germany. On the one hand there were party-affiliated 'big newspapers' (*o-shimbun*) for the elites, which focused on politics and political positioning rather than on commercial interests. On the other hand there was a popular press of 'small newspapers' (*ko-shimbun*) with simplified script, which concentrated more on societal news (Huffman 1997: 41, 69–73; Nojiri 1991: 35f.). In the 1870s, bonding and censorship gave rise to prosecution, with 144 journalists being incarcerated between 1875 and 1877 alone. But in fact the political leadership focused more on financial but often covert support for the press (Huffman 1997: 53–57, 374).

The Japanese press finally came close to Anglo-Saxon standards around 1900. Relaxation of censorship and the wars against China in 1895 and Russia in 1903/05 forced the pace of this change because the numerous Japanese correspondents professionalised their journalistic work and made it more news-oriented. The wars also promoted an increase in circulation and strengthened the influence of a few powerful publishers. Furthermore, it fostered the rise of populist nationalism that pushed for imperialistic expansion while blocking out Japanese war crimes. Larger newspapers now attained circulations of over ninety thousand copies (Nojiri 1991: 35; Huffman 1997: 387).

This turn towards Anglo-Saxon 'new journalism' was evident not only in its focus on facts, sensationalism and classified advertisements but in its confident journalistic self-image and modus operandi. Several journalists now made names for themselves as advocates of the lower classes, publishing reports condemning the exploitation of mineworkers, prostitutes and rickshaw drivers. Some individual campaigns against forced prostitution in particular, were very similar to W.T. Stead's world-famous articles that had appeared in London (Huffman 1997: 247–59). Beyond that, apolitical popular papers enjoyed huge circulation, just as they did in the West. The magazine *Woman's World* with its four hundred thousand copies (1909) had the highest circulation, and the children's magazine *The King* set a record in 1925 when it reached a circulation of 1.5 million (Nojiri 1991: 28).

A process of media modernisation such as Japan's was in no wise a matter of course, even for a country with a long written tradition. This also holds true for China, which had a well-established book market and a newspaper-like tradition of Court news. Moreover, beginning in the 1840s, missionaries and traders had introduced independent newspapers to the port cities where they had contracts. Early Chinese publishing houses developed out of the Chinese editions of the *Hong Kong Daily Press* (1858–1919) and *North China Herald* (1861–1872). Starting in the 1870s, several papers reached a circulation of several thousand but there was no boom as there was in Japan. Because of the ambiguous legal situation, newspapers existed mainly outside Chinese sovereign territory, such as in Hong Kong and the contract ports.

Nevertheless recent studies show that the new press system was not entirely without influence on Chinese development. From the 1890s onwards newspapers appeared in the Chinese hinterland, and a so-called reform press representing different political principles developed (Vittinghoff 2002a). The brief phase of reform in 1898 was followed by a period of harsh intervention in press matters, yet nevertheless the number of newspapers rose during the following years. Here, impelled by their self-image, the flagships of the Chinese press sought an alignment with British journalistic principles: newspapers presented diverse viewpoints, yet various journalists banded together in order to present a united front for more press freedom, and this led to the formation of the first journalistic unions in China (Vittinghoff 2002b: 106). In 1908 a press law was passed based on the Japanese model.

How necessary a long tradition of written culture was for the establishment of the press becomes unmistakeably clear if one looks at Africa. Because of low literacy and a strong oral tradition, Africa has still not developed a strong press. Although twelve times as many people live in Africa today as in Germany, there are only half as many newspapers. Consequently the history of the mass media in nineteenth-century Africa must be considered primarily as a part of colonial history, since colonists' newspapers were dominant and written in their own languages – with the exception of a few papers published by missionaries and a very few by Africans.

In the sub-Saharan regions, media developments were very diverse and characterised by their respective colonial configurations. Evidence shows that the first newspapers appeared in Egypt, Sierra Leone and South Africa around 1800. The colonial press developed most rapidly over the following century in British-dominated regions and South Africa, as the British granted greater freedom and supported the establishment of local newspapers. In this way papers such as the *Royal Gazette* and the *Sierra Leone Advertiser* (1801) appeared in West Africa as early as 1800. Distinctly slower on the other hand was the spread of the media in the French territories, which preferred to market French newspapers. In the German colonies created after 1884 the colonial press likewise emerged slowly and haltingly. It was not until the turn of the century that a total of eleven non-official newspapers appeared: five in South West Africa, three in East Africa, and only one in Togo and Cameroon where, as in the South Seas, official gazettes with advertisements and an editorial section dominated (Osterhaus 1990: 46).

Although newspapers in all the African colonies had low circulation, their significance should not be underrated. On the whole they were a force for establishing a sense of community. In all of the colonies, newspapers were more than mere mouthpieces of colonial administrations, which they often criticised in the name of settlers, the local business community and local organisations and interest groups with whom they had close ties (Osterhaus 1990: 148–54; Pöppinghege 2001: 158, 161). Accordingly the newspapers sometimes campaigned for settlers' rights in order to 'activate, to check or to promote certain developments' (Osterhaus 1990: 474). Often newspapers were indeed able to influence events and thus participate in the administrative process: whether in decisions relating to personnel, the infrastructure (such as the resumption of railway construction in East Africa) or the expansion of racialist ordinances, especially in South West Africa. It was precisely these demands for stricter measures against the natives that demonstrate how the establishment of the 'Fourth Power' did not necessarily lead to a more liberal order.

Parallel to this development, the first newspapers published by Africans appeared during the nineteenth century. These, too, were at first primarily English-language papers. The first founders of these papers were former slaves with close ties to early African-American emancipation movements in the United States. According to some studies, the former slave Charles L. Force printed the *Liberia Herald* in Monrovia in 1826 as the first paper produced by an African, with a manually operated printing press he had brought from the United States (Bourgault 1995: 154). Since no documented evidence for this exists, the first African newspaper has recently been dated at 1830 and credited to John B. Russwurm, who had published *Freedom's Journal*, the first newspaper by an African-American, three years before in the United States (Burrowes 2004: 49, note 2).

There was also the odd African-language paper, originally edited by missionaries but later developed into a mouthpiece of the natives – like the *Imvo Zabantsundu* ('Native Opinion') in South Africa. By printing in native languages, the missionaries raised the status of Africans to that of an autonomous readership. Furthermore, working for the press as well as doing translation work was an important road to social advancement.

The Gold Coast and Sierra Leone evolved into germinal cells of African journalism. Titles like *African Interpreter and Advocate* (after 1867) and *West African Liberator* stressed the aspiration of these journals to articulate and translate the natives' interests. In Gambia as well, complaints against colonial masters led to the establishment of an African newspaper that vied with a paper founded by an English businessman who considered *The Times* too critical of colonial conditions (Grey-Johnson, in Wittmann and Beck 2004: 18f.). These newspapers cultivated the English language among the African elites and were thus not without significance in spite of their marginal circulation and the prevalent illiteracy. For on the one hand each copy was often read out and translated, and on the other, these papers sent signals to the colonial masters. Campaigns launched by African newspapers clearly had at least partial effects; in the 1890s, for example, they were able to slow down land appropriation. Whether these African newspapers were instrumental in the development of 'pan-African solidarity' against colonial intervention is questionable. It was more often the case that African newspapers supported military interventions against neighbouring tribes (according to Osterhaus 1990: 280f., 477).

The role that new media like the telegraph, wire services and the popular press played within the context of globalisation and colonialism in the years around 1900 is best illustrated by a glance at the wars of that period. During the Spanish–American War in Cuba (1898), the Boer War in South Africa (1899–1902) and the Russo-Japanese War (1904/05), foreign journalists arrived to write on-the-spot reports, take pictures for the international press and make the first film from a war zone (Paul 2004: 76–83). An estimated three to five hundred journalists had already come to Cuba. This enabled much of the world to follow events with an immediacy never before possible. Furthermore this new concentration on distant countries was a factor that contributed to a sudden change in the global status of the warring parties. American publishers like Pulitzer and Hearst supported the war against Spain in Cuba, and the United States appeared as an expansive superpower after her victory; and pictures of railroads, telegraphs and armoured battleships in the Russo-Japanese War made Japan appear as a modern power (Gerbig-Fabel 2008).

Admittedly, the part played by early-day war correspondents and their significance for the formation of transnational critical journalism has often been exaggerated. The Crimean War has often been seen as its starting point, when *The Times* and its war correspondent William Howard Russell, in their role as 'Fourth Power', brought down the government by their critical reporting. In actual fact this is based on a myth created by journalists themselves, as *The Times* proved extremely loyal to the government (Daniel, in Daniel 2006: 62). By the same token, photographs played hardly any public role in this war, despite statements to the contrary in the sources. Journalists from all nations were indeed active during the Boer War, but while critical reporting had long been firmly entrenched in London, British journalists in South Africa hardly ever wrote about the brutality of 'their' troops. The critical articles in the *Manchester Guardian* about the concentration camps in South Africa were based on reports by the nurse Emily Hobhouse (Krebs 1999: 32–54). Nevertheless, emotional debates about the Boer War that took place in large parts of the world and put governments in the diplomatic hot seat were manifestations of the media's new global character (Geppert 2007: 125–76).

Many global occurrences in media history during recent years are still in need of study. Systematically integrating an analysis of media development into other fields of research would be the most useful approach. In the case of economic history, for example, one could examine the effects that innovations like new telegraph lines, and up-to-the-minute stock prices in the newspapers, have had on commerce. By the same token students of colonial history should try to discover the significance of the media for both day-to-day and administrative activity in the colonies. There is also very little known about the origin and progression of trans-border news. To what extent were the agencies really responsible for a worldwide homogenisation of news? It is likely that news items were often chosen selectively and adapted to fit into respective cultural contexts. International analyses of trans-border reporting by wire services and newspapers would be very useful in shedding light on this question and on the work of foreign correspondents.

CHAPTER 4

Modernity, World Wars and Dictatorships

Film and Media Culture before and during the First World War

Around 1900, the media market experienced a radical expansion involving in particular the proliferation of gramophones, telephones and private cameras, as well as the emergence of film and wireless telegraphy, the latter leading to the invention of radio in the 1920s. The interplay of these new media, which concomitantly changed the old media, may be justly considered a 'media revolution 1900' (Käuser 2005). Moreover, the new media were an integral part of the nascent popular 'mass culture' which arose simultaneously: department stores, zoos, music and sporting events, as well as cinemas, made it possible to share in spectacular amusements and exotic impressions, apparently without regard to class barriers (Maase 1997). Of course, the synchronous emergence of the pejorative term 'mass' indicates that this leisure culture in fact bred bourgeois demarcations.

As a number of studies have stressed, the development of these new media corresponded to the simultaneous modification of visible reality. What concurrent inventions like the bouillon cube or the X-ray had in common with film was the fact that they broke down traditional perceptions and experiences, re-staging them as products (Engell 1995: 22). Media scientist Friedrich A. Kittler also saw parallels to contemporary scientific studies such as 'psychophysics' in particular, which performed experimental analyses of human perception (Kittler 1995: 280). Hence he spoke of a new 'system of notation 1900', which captured the body in media terms and marked the beginning of 'technological data storage'. Kittler alleged that both film and gramophone had caused the monopoly of writing to collapse, winning over the imagination and relegating books to a restricted space (ibid.: 313). In view of the immensely high circulation figures of newspapers, magazines and books in the twentieth century, this must be seen as only partially justified.

At the same time, film and media studies embedded the new media into ongoing development processes. With virtually no exception, histories of film commenced with older image projections such as the magic lantern, the camera obscura, panoramas, still picture sequences and flick books (cf. e.g. Wyver 1989: 5–14). For film did not merely trigger an advance in visualisation, but was rather the result of the popular visual culture of the nineteenth century. For one, it evolved from the visual attractions of [country] fairs and folk culture which had shaped its early popular reception. The great demand for moving images thus secured the position of the cinema, which automatised and standardised older visual forms of attraction, transforming them into a new product (Bakker 2008: 404). On the other hand, scientific interest also constituted a starting point. Rapid sequences of still pictures were to compensate for the insufficiencies of the human eye. Specific images such as a running horse's legs (Eadweard Muybridge), flying birds (Etienne-Jules Marey) or missile impacts (Ernst Mach) led to an improvement in shutter speed and the invention of the motion picture reel, which formed the basis of film technology.

In the 1890s inventors from several countries developed filming apparatus almost simultaneously. This is further proof of the great desire for moving images, and explains the rapid success of the new medium. As early as 1891, U.S. inventor Thomas Edison developed the kinetograph for picture-taking as well as the kinetoscope for exhibiting motion pictures. The latter was designed as a peephole viewer in which a person had to insert a coin before watching a film, which shows how open the initial use of film was. From 1894 he was able to earn money from his invention in major American and West European cities. Yet although Edison developed the 35 mm film format with perforations on both sides, the French brothers Lumière are credited with being the groundbreaking inventors of film. They adopted Edison's film format, but in 1895 they created an apparatus which enabled the recording and copying as well as the playing of films, which were projected onto a light-coloured surface. In late 1895 the two brothers showed their films publicly in Paris for the first time and charged an admissions fee. Their creation was also technically superior to other continental filming devices developed in the same year, such as the bioscope introduced by the brothers Skladanowsky in 1895, and a projector of the British inventors Robert W. Paul and Birt Acres. The Lumières were clever businessmen as well. They marketed their creation worldwide, not only by selling their apparatus but also by hiring cameramen in their names who would show their movies to audiences across the globe and concomitantly film exotic impressions of foreign countries to show at future destinations. Thus in 1896 the brief success of Edison's filming machine ended.

Early film thus had a transnational historical dimension in a twofold sense. For one, its rapid spread made it a worldwide attraction: from cities like Buenos Aires, St Petersburg, Cairo, Bombay and Shanghai, to countries such as Mexico, Japan and Australia, it was possible from 1896 to attend frequent film screenings, often presented by the Lumières' assistants (Vasey, in Nowell-Smith 1996: 53; Abel 2005: 38, 216). Secondly, films from distant countries would publicise spectacular events and (stereotypical) everyday scenes. Until the First World War, the distribution of films remained on the international level. Thanks to the Lumières and large film companies such as Gaumont, Eclair and Pathé, which took over the Lumières' rights in 1897, France was the leading country in the film industry. Hence just under half of all films available in Germany before the First World War came from French production companies or distributors, whereas a mere 13 per cent were from domestic production companies, another 13 per cent from the United States, 8 per cent from Italy and another 6 per cent from Great Britain (Birett 1991: XV). In the United States, on the other hand, almost half of all films on the market before 1909 were European (Bakker 2005: 313), which meant that, through movies, it was the great Western countries that had the power of visually propagating their interpretations of the world. Until 1911 only one Japanese film was verifiably shown in Germany, compared to approximately fifty films *about* Japan, which were produced primarily in France (list in Birett 1991: 327f.).

With regard to content, it has become common in film historiography to distinguish the 'Cinema of Attractions' before 1906 from the subsequent era of silent films, which lasted into the late 1920s. When considering the change in programming contents, economic structures and screening locations, the years 1913/14 mark an important turning point of 'Early Cinema'. Silent films and talkies were characterised by film theorists as autonomous media to be distinguished from one another: silent film as the first kind of motion picture medium, and sound film as the first audiovisual medium to be technologically reproduced (see Müller 2003: 385–89). On the basis of programme guides, Herbert Birett counted close to seventeen thousand films for the period between 1895 and 1911 for Germany alone; however the number is assumed to be twice as high (Birett 1991: XVII). Their contents point to the context in which they developed and their intermediality, i.e. the mass press (current and historical events, everyday occurrences, national culture and landscapes and the like), funfair attractions and music halls (comedy, exoticism, acrobatics and the like), and fictional literature and theatre, as several short movies were already portraying adventure, love and crime stories. Films with longer narratives and of a more clearly defined genre emerged only after 1907 – succeeding the first film crisis and the structural change it triggered.

By portraying both everyday scenes and special events, early films offer good, though seldom utilised, sources for historians. The Lumières' films, for example, showed sundry cities from New York to Rome focusing on crowds gathered at intersections and famous places. Likewise, they showed festivals and uniformed parades. By frequently showing street cars and trains, urban traffic, factories, ship christenings and world fairs, early film recordings presented a staging of modernity. In this manner, film fashioned the new era of technology and that of the 'masses' both on screen and in the auditorium. Although films often had local or national frames of reference, they were also meant for international distribution and therefore helped to shape regional and national identities as well as global awareness.

Part of this modernity was also the oft-quoted 'invention of tradition' – the cementing of supposedly ancient traditions, to which film contributed. Films depicting the coronation ceremony of Tsar Nicholas II (1896), the grandiose processions of Queen Victoria's 'Diamond Jubilee' (1897), and the baroque self-aggrandisement of the German Emperor Wilhelm II, recorded in 1895 by the British film pioneer Birt Acres at the 'Opening of the Kiel Canal', circulated worldwide. His pompous public appearances and extensive travels made Wilhelm II the most frequently filmed German of his time, with thirty-four films in 1895–96, and he was even called the 'first German film star' (Loiperdinger 1997). John Thompson spoke of a 'mediazation of tradition' (Thompson 1995: 180) – that is, a shaping of media-oriented tradition.

Of no less relevance was the subject of war in 'visual news reporting'. Nowadays, numerous early war films are accessible online and free of charge. They portray troops marching off amidst the cheers of spectators, military equipment and the traversing of enemy territory, but hardly any actual battles. In light of the cameras' weight and their unsatisfactory lenses, such filming was near to impossible. Ostensible battle scenes were virtually always re-enactments aimed at discrediting the enemy and glorifying the prowess of the home troops. Overall the boundaries between fictional re-enactment and documentation were fluid. Naval disasters and current events in the neighbourhood were staged in the same way as the film clips showing deceased public figures such as Bismarck.

In recent years, screening locations and viewer behaviour have also been studied (cf. for instance with literary examples: Paech and Paech 2000). The screening locations of the 'Early Cinema' differed considerably from those of today, as movie theatres built especially for viewing purposes were not widespread in Europe until the 1910s. Early films were shown at market places, festivals or club meetings, in marquees, halls or the open air, as well as in fixed public places such as pubs. There tended to be at least some national differences: in Germany films were often shown in music halls and cheap cellar pubs; the French used cafés; in England music halls were common; Shanghai used tea houses; and in Japan, traditional theatres served as viewing locations. Audience conduct varied accordingly: while formal applause was customary in music halls, pub atmospheres were livelier. From 1896, cinematograph theatres emerged, particularly in the United States and France. Especially from an international perspective, no linear development from the funfair film to cinema can be made out (Brandt 1994: 89).

The cinema of silent film was actually far from soundless. Background music was quite common and, depending on entry fee and establishment, ranged from out-of-tune pianos to the orchestras that were characteristic of picture palaces. Sound machines and film commentators also accompanied the action and were particularly common in the early phases of the established cinema. Most notably, the audience would often give vent to its feelings in a lively manner and thus co-determine a film's interpretation. Films in general were aimed at eliciting a range of emotions from the audience. Advertisements promised laughter, love and chills as well as patriotic elation, and the darkened room made it easier to express feelings openly. The rumour that an early recording of an approaching train by the Lumières caused panic among its viewers is an idle legend circulated out of business interest (Loiperdinger 1996). However, its propagation points to the emotional effect intended by film, which was to literally move its audience.

Although hardly examined as yet, viewer behaviour offers an intriguing cultural and socio-historical field of research for historians in particular. Early films seem to have supported patriotic collectivisation to a large extent. Whenever home troops or the monarch appeared on screen, German audiences would leap from their seats, shout 'bravo' or sing. In similar fashion, they would react with jeers at the sight of foreign powers: for example, clips of Englishmen in the Boer Wars, which nationalistic societies tried to turn to their advantage. The German Fleet Association thus proclaimed that the patriotic hymns accompanying their naval films could stir up even those with little enthusiasm for the navy (Bösch, in Bösch and Borutta 2006: 220f.).

There is little reliable research on the social composition of audiences. Yet certain differences are apparent in international comparisons. In the early days of film, American and British theatregoers tended to belong to the lower or lower-middle classes. In Japan, films were aimed towards the wealthier classes quite early on, as they were embedded in the culture of theatre (Sklar 2002; Abel 2005: 45–47). For a long time, analyses of German audiences were restricted to contemporary discussions and an early dissertation on cinema audiences by Emilie Altenloh (1914), according to which women, workers and young people represented the largest proportion of theatregoers. However, the basis of Altenloh's work is empirically insufficient and thus cannot be regarded as representative (Filk and Ruchatz 2007). The ostensible 'cinema addiction' of women, children and the 'masses' was rather the result of moral apprehensions and middle-class barriers. The patriotic use of films in bourgeois fellowships in itself indicates that men from the lower-middle and middle classes were indeed among the audiences (Müller 2003: 194–201). What is more, film producers were bourgeois also, and consequently so were the perspectives from which they filmed. Nonetheless, the early cinema changed public structures: on the one hand it allowed women to participate in a new public space, and on the other hand it facilitated encounters between different social and political milieus – at least to a larger extent than reading communities, exhibitions or the theatre had done.

Middle-class anxiety about the new media is evidenced by the moral protest movements which occurred in the late nineteenth century in many Western countries. They were directed against music halls, the theatre, 'penny dreadfuls' and film. For the most part conservative and initiated chiefly by teachers and pastors, these groups proffered hardly verifiable individual cases to support their claims that the new media demoralised children and women, were an inducement to crime, and produced restive and listless teenage characters. The labour movement also directed itself against 'trashy' films and cheap novels. They disapproved of the reactionary, militaristic and unrealistic quality of films, considering that they diverted attention away from actual social problems (Maase 2001).

In the years around 1906, film experienced a crisis. Sales stagnated or caved in because short films were no longer regarded as the new attraction, and the middle classes tended to keep their distance. A phase of fundamental restructuring followed, often referred to as the 'bourgeoisification' (*Verbürgerlichung*) of film. In fact, the film industry adapted to the bourgeois conventions of theatre to a great extent in order to retain affluent customers. In the cities, numerous cinemas and picture palaces were now established, some of which were magnificently furnished and had tiers similar to those in opera houses. This encouraged social demarcations in terms of seating arrangements, differing admission fees and dress codes. Moreover, assigned seating disciplined the audience and the dark space thus became more respectable. Narrative film now took over the screen as dramatic story material arranged into acts gradually replaced the 'cinema of attraction'. Film editing, montages, and the use of intertitles furthered the development of longer narratives. In order to improve the reputation of cinema, film producers additionally tried to attract famous stage actors as a means of improving the repute of the cinema. Promotion of stars was also in the theatrical tradition. All this effectively led to a rapid expansion of cinema and a quick rise in viewing figures.

With fictional, feature-length films came different genres. The latter can be understood as a means of refined targeting and a way of managing expectations and audience reception. Different countries preferred different genres, and this in turn shaped both their self-perception and how they were perceived by others. The Americans, for instance, produced westerns and slapstick movies, whereas Italy became known for its historical dramas and epics after

La Presa di Roma was released in 1905. Denmark and Sweden gained fame for their melodramatic and erotic films, while France was celebrated for its experimental and fantastical works. George Méliès in particular utilised film to play with the audience's perception, and dealt with science fiction, as shown for example by *A Trip to the Moon* (for global comparison, see Nowell-Smith 1996). Early German films are hard to characterise. Loyalty and duty, innocence and rescue, as well as transformation, for instance, have been considered typical motifs (Haucke 2005: 21–38).

The establishment of film also professionalised state control. Initially it was conducted like theatre censorship without separate censorship laws. During screenings, the local police would check film contents and viewer reactions. Censorship was thus subjective and depended on regional differences. A film that was prohibited in one place might be permitted in a neighbouring town. Audiences also had the power to effect film bans through their behaviour. Loud and vehement protests at the pictures, for instance, could entail a ban, for disturbance of the public peace (Loiperdinger 2003: 73). In many countries, such local censorship was more stringently coordinated after 1910, corresponding to a change in film distribution, which was no longer marked by sales but rather by film rentals. After 1911, Prussia began to standardise age limits, censorship regulations and film editing. Two years on, Italy followed suit by establishing a national censorship body (Hibberd 2008: 30). Though administered by the film industry, even Great Britain and the United States introduced pre-censorship during this time. After several U.S. states adopted state censorship, however, the Supreme Court demonstrated its support in 1915: due to the commercial nature and precarious effects of film, it did not regard the medium as part of the legally protected freedom of press. Moral rather than political concerns primarily led to censorial control in anglophone countries (Maltby, in Nowell-Smith 1996: 235). Regardless, the practice of censoring impacted both contents and self-censorship.

The Media and the First World War

The First World War shook up the previously established media culture. Conversely, the significance of the mass media market at the war's outbreak was widely discussed in contemporary research. More recent work based on documentary material confutes the assumption that the media fomented war. The English press, for example, was not consistently antagonistic towards Germany before 1914. Liberal papers in particular deliberately refrained from criticism in order to promote de-escalation. Even Wilhelm II was seldom lampooned before the outbreak of the war (Reinermann 2001: 414; Schramm 2007: 498f.). By the same token, although the leading German newspapers increasingly dwelt on the possibility of war, the majority militated against it. Their incrementally consistent fatalism, however, reinforced the impression that there was no alternative to the impending war. Politicians and the military must have been affected by this as well, for they referred to the press in many instances (Rosenberger 1998: 324). Furthermore, the German elite regarded the reluctance of the British public as a sign that England would keep out of the war, and from this they construed that the war would pose less of a risk.

For a short period, the World War caused an enormous surge in demand for the press, which was met by dint of special editions. But in the medium term, it retarded the otherwise flourishing print landscape. The drop in advertisements, shortage of paper and staff, and a sales slump which occurred due to the absence of soldiers resulted in a decline in scope, circulation and the number of newspapers published in Germany of around a fifth. In regard to contents, newspapers were initially in agreement in supporting the war. Even at its outbreak, the middle-class media endorsed the conception of a general pro-war sentiment. Images from Berlin and university towns signalled an enthusiasm for war which in effect hardly existed, particularly in rural areas and amongst labourers.

The great majority of the media in each country supported the war. However, the degree of support varied according to political lines. In Germany, Social Democratic media in particular differed profoundly in their agendas. On the day the war broke out, the major Social Democratic paper *Vorwärts* was still encouraging counter-demonstrations. Shortly afterwards, the SPD papers collectively aligned with their parliamentary caucus in the Reichstag, which had agreed to war loans and thus to war itself. *Vorwärts* articles expressing criticism of war even led to the dismissal of some editors by the party in 1916 (Danker et al. 2003: 62f., 68). Especially the left-wing *Leipziger Volkszeitung* maintained a critical stance during the course of the conflict and published a manifesto written by opponents of war on 19 June 1915. The press thus played its part in dividing the SPD, with twenty local SPD newspapers going over to the USPD, particularly in Thuringia and Saxony. In the case of the liberal press, and the renowned *Berliner Tageblatt* under Theodor Wolff in particular, prohibitions were often imposed when the paper began to voice frequent criticism of the war in 1916 (Sösemann 2000: 150f.).

The bourgeois press, however, supported the war for the most part with patriotic fervour. It lauded the nation's successes, or, in case of failure, evaded the issue by engrossing itself in the technological detail surrounding the subject of air–sea battles. In like manner, papers defamed opponents of war and romanticised combat. A quarter of the images printed in German and French pictorials depicted the soldiers' everyday activities in their encampments (washing, sewing, singing) and touristy impressions, whereas combat operations made up just a few per cent. A myriad of simple soldiers began to send in their travelogues as 'amateur journalists'. Death was completely blanked out and only revealed indirectly in print media through images of memorials and destroyed hostile technical equipment, though at least dead horses were pictured, albeit very seldom (Eisermann 2000: 135–38). The French media, however, regularly published images of ruins and demolished churches for the purpose of pillorying the Germans as uncultivated barbarians.

The war also brought about a change in the film market. After the medium had enjoyed a period of international success, despite French predominance, films produced in enemy countries were now banned. In Germany this led to a sudden lack of films, in spite of people's eagerness for recent images from the front line. Such speedily produced reality films announced footage of battle scenes at the outset, but were hardly ever able to fulfil their promise. As far as re-enactments of war scenes are concerned, which continued to be shown in cinemas, soldiers were quick to see through them and reacted with laughter. Starting in 1916, a change regarding the degree of realism depicted in film finally occurred (international comparison: Oppelt 2002).

Emotionalised feature films were an inherent part of war propaganda. British, French, Russian and American movies would often represent the Germans as barbarians guilty of raping women and killing children in Belgium (Dibbets and Hogenkamp 1995: 40). In England most notably, close cooperation between the government and the film industry led to intensive and successful film-making. Subsequent to their films about the 'Huns', the British also heralded a more realistic approach: *The Battle of the Somme* from 1916 was a shockingly realistic film which, by arousing empathy, succeeded in committing almost 20 million viewers to war within six weeks, despite previous reservations on the part of the government (Reeves 1997: 15). The United States made war participation palatable using a movie entitled *The Battle Cry of Peace* (1915), which featured inebriated attackers wearing *Pickelhauben* and fictitious scenarios of New York air bombings. After America's war entry a multitude of films followed, drawing particular attention to the threat that German soldiers posed to women. German films, on the contrary, were less disparaging of their opponents, but instead embedded the issue of war in love stories, which served to propagandise a collective that transcended social class during the war. First and foremost, however, the film industry placed their trust in diversionary entertainment, as a means of preventing defeatism.

The introduction of censorship regulations was common to all countries, even though such monitoring proved less rigid in Great Britain than in Germany and France. None of the warring parties, including liberal pre-1915 Britain, allowed their journalists to report from the front line. In Germany, freedom of press was rescinded by an emergency decree as well as a 26-point plan specifying bans on reporting concerning not only military matters (such as troop movements), but also information on the economy, the supply situation and inappropriate advertisements. Highly detailed additions were made in the course of the following years, leading to a censorship book in 1917 (printed in Fischer 1973: 194–215). Although prison sentences and newspaper bans were occasionally imposed, punishments usually consisted of confiscations or mere reprimands. Newspapers from neutral countries, however, made military reports from opponents of war available. In order not to deviate entirely from accounts written by front-line soldiers, the *Oberste Heeresleitung* (OHL, Supreme Army Command) committed them to more realistic reporting in 1917.

Also characteristic of the First World War was the state's active propaganda. The French war ministry made the Bureau de Presse central to propagandistic purposes and roped in the Havas agency. The War Propaganda Bureau in Great Britain came into existence immediately after the war's outbreak, initiating approximately 2.5 million publications before mid-1915. Its cooperation with the film industry stimulated film production, and in November 1915 the first cameramen were sent to the Western Front, while major publishers such as Lord Beaverbrock and Lord Northcliffe assumed the leadership of state propaganda (Thompson 1999).

The German *Heeresleitung* (army command), in contrast, had neither prepared an individual media policy, nor was willing to make active use of the new media in any comparable fashion until 1916. Faith in a quick victory, scepticism towards the media, and the 'Spirit of 1914' were the reasons for such apprehension. Initially, the military command tended to rely on censorship and on 'old media' such as placards and official newspaper articles, maintaining a reactive attitude towards foreign propaganda. Compared to the Western Allies, the OHL did little to standardise its propagandistic work, so that by the end of the war a total of twenty-two press offices were under its management. In 1916, 'modernists' more guided by economic advertising and the Western Allies, finally gained an upper hand in the OHL, despite continuing difficulties in realising their ideas (Creutz 1996; Schmidt 2006: 140).

Still, even in Germany some innovations did appear in the field of media policy during the First World War. These comprised the daily press conferences held by the OHL as well as the 'Zentralstelle für Heimatdienste' (central office for homeland services), designed to provide neutral countries with newspapers, photographs and films, and the 'Kriegspresseamt' (the army's public relations office), founded in 1915. Around three thousand 'press instructions' reveal the attempt to covertly control publication (Wilke 2007: 51–57, 104). Although little is known about how far such rules were put into practice, they stood for an intensive and new type of information exchange between the state and the media. Another important innovation was the foundation of the 'Bild- und Filmamt' (Bufa; photo and film bureau) in January 1917, whose purpose was to prepare and organise film and picture propaganda for the government and the military. Despite the fact that the Bufa lacked both professionalism and basic influence, it signified a novel cooperation between the film industry, the economy and the state. In late 1917, this indirectly led to the foundation of the large film studio 'Universum-Film AG' (Ufa), in which film companies, banks, and – covertly – government invested in order to represent German interests with the help of film. In this way, the OHL hoped to gain influence over Northern, Eastern, and Southern Europe (Kreimeier 1992: 20–23).

It is difficult, however, to establish how successful this endeavour was, and many studies on propaganda significantly omit this aspect (see e.g. Schmidt 2006). Immediately after the end of the war, the idea quickly spread in Germany that the Allies had won the war by their modern use of the media, which had mobilised their populace more effectively. Especially in Great Britain and the United States, propaganda may indeed offer an explanation as to why innumerable men enthusiastically went to war. The fact that many Germans were completely taken aback by the country's swift capitulation in the autumn of 1918, thoroughly convinced that the Democrats should be taking the blame, also points to the fundamental impact of the media whose reports on the impending defeat were not publicised until early October 1918 (Welch 2000: 243). Hence the media contributed indirectly to the strain under which the first German democracy was now placed. At the same time one must keep in mind that acceptance and interpretation of media contents is shaped by established cultural dispositions, and even towards the end of the war they were influenced by the people's belief in German superiority.

Golden Years? Media and 'Mass Culture' of the 1920s

The media culture of the 1920s differed in many respects from the pre-war period. The greatest change was wrought by the establishment of radio. The idea of simultaneously speaking to many people by radio and also telephone had already been tested in numerous countries before the war. Countries like Hungary and Italy had already broadcast musical events to registered listeners via telephone. The main foundation for the radio was wireless telegraphy. Nevertheless, radio was also an offspring of the war, where hundreds of thousands of soldiers had gained experience in wireless transmission. Since early radio was technically quite complicated still, these ham operators formed basic listener groups in many Western countries when the war was over, from Germany to British India (Pinkerton 2008: 169f.).

Radio, too, expanded rapidly in many parts of the world. During the first half of the 1920s, radio stations came into being in North America and Western Europe, and also in many South American and East European countries, and Japan. In the second half of the 1920s, radio stations were already broadcasting in India (Shrivastava 2005: 12), Turkey and Morocco. However, organisation, content and social significance of radio differed considerably. In North and South America, commercial channels appeared from the beginning, with little state interference. The United States played a pioneering role and had exceptional transmitting power. Since the existing infrastructure was already privately organised (telegraphy, telephone and railroad, among others), private corporations – such as early radio manufacturers – now established the first transmitting stations in 1920 and produced their own programmes to help to sell their radios. By the end of 1922 the Department of Commerce had already licensed over six hundred stations, with department stores, newspapers, universities and religious groups having their own stations; nevertheless, commercial channels predominated (Hilmes 2004: 44). As might be expected, by 1925 over five million radio sets had been sold. From the mid-1920s, however, the involvement of large corporations increased markedly, with powerful nationwide networks like ABC, CBS and NBC appearing next to the local stations. Since these North American stations were financed by advertising, they broadcast listener-oriented entertainment like popular music, quiz shows, radio plays and advice programmes.

The development in many South American countries was similar to that in the United States, although the number of radios here was much smaller. In Mexico, Argentina and Brazil, commercial channels were also established by radio manufacturers and other corporations (like the cigarette industry). In 1925 Argentina already had twenty-five radio stations and thus considerably more than Germany (Meinecke, in Wilke 1992 Vol. 1: 46f.).

By contrast, state control played a much greater role in Europe. Government interventions during the First World War probably served to reinforce the state's claim. Contributing factors were also the Russian Revolution in 1917 and subsequent uprisings in Europe, which roused the fear that Communists might come to power with the help of radio. Consequently radio came very late to countries that exercised strong control: 1923 to Germany, 1925 to Japan. Anti-American sentiments additionally slowed down its development.

Beyond the American continent, radio was organised in a great variety of ways during the 1920s. A few countries like Spain, Portugal and Italy had commercial channels; others like France had both commercial and state-affiliated ones, while countries like Japan and Germany had only state-affiliated channels. Other countries like Britain granted pioneering private organisations a monopoly. Thus as early as 1927 the previously commercial BBC became a public enterprise without competitors, hoping to resist the Americanisation and 'American Chaos' with 'British quality' (Hilmes 2012: 81). Radio in the Netherlands was structured very much like the press, which was supported by the various religious groups in the country. In the same way the political culture of individual countries defined the scope and reach of the stations. While in Great Britain the BBC was intended to promote national integration from a central location in London, the cultural federalism of the Weimar Republic produced a decentralised system of regional channels. The nine regional companies were public limited companies, but the Post Office owned 51 per cent of their respective shares, and this also applied to the Deutsche Reichsfunkgesellschaft (German Radio Corporation) that maintained the Deutsche Welle (Germany's international broadcaster) (Dussel 1999: 30–39). Both the state's belief in its right to control the media as well as the bourgeois fear of unfettered media development led to this model. The Germans even rejected the term 'radio' and pointedly spoke of *Rundfunk*, as a means of stressing the principle of 'one to many' and distancing themselves from the United States. In addition, the International Broadcasting Union (IBU), founded in 1925, regulated European frequency issues across borders but also organised an international exchange of concert broadcasts (Eugster 1983: 29–56).

Hardly any radio programmes of the 1920s have come down to us. For this reason content analyses are based mainly on programme manuscripts and radio guides. State-affiliated or public channels like those in Germany, Japan and Great Britain mainly pursued the goal of educating their public via bourgeois culture. This included lectures, classical music, literary radio plays and information, although the second half of the 1920s already witnessed an increase in sports reporting, light operettas and comedy. In Germany about half of the programming consisted of spoken or musical programmes. Out of respect for the churches, the Sunday programming was more serious and included religious ceremonies. For this reason British listeners sometimes tuned in to foreign channels like 'Radio Normandie' and 'Radio Luxembourg' on Sundays (Fortner 2005: 51), which had already had an English and a Dutch programme since 1933. At night especially, listeners would go in pursuit of foreign channels because, after the regional channels had shut down, reception was less hampered by static interference (Leonhard 1997: 368).

Tellingly, the stations had hardly any clear ideas about listening habits (Briggs 1995: 295; Führer 1996: 771). Initial surveys found that in Germany entertainment, light music, news and time signals were especially popular. Research on listening habits only began around 1930 in the United States as a means of targeting different listener groups more effectively. Due to the strong role of advertising, audience measurement developed quickly. The use of telephone recalls was replaced by coincidental interviews (Buzzard 2012: 11–15). The non-commercial BBC did not produce its first listener surveys until after 1936, thus documenting its lack of interest in the public's wishes (Scannell and Cardiff 1991: 375).

Many observers feared that radio and records would lead to the demise of live music at dances and concerts. However, the opposite became true. Also the record industry experienced a development complementary to that of radio. After the sale of gramophones and records had taken off in 1900 or thereabouts, it reached an initial high point in the 1920s. Records fostered a nationalisation of taste, too, although they were far less prevalent than the mass media of radio and cinema. Since they were still very expensive, only 3 per cent of all working-class households spent money on records or musical instruments, according to a 1937 study (Ross 2008: 45–50, 130).

Initially, politics and political debates were seldom broadcast on radio – either in solid democracies like Great Britain and Switzerland, or in countries with authoritarian traditions like Germany and Japan (on the BBC: Scannell and Cardiff 1991 Vol. 1: 28–38; on Japan: White 2005: 81f.; cf. Lersch, in Lersch and Schanze 2004: 39). Even news reports were rare on German radio during the 1920s, and were never aired at prime time. Moreover, they were produced by a central, state-controlled station, the later 'Drahtlose Dienst AG' (called Dradag, 'Wireless Service plc'), although not every regional channel took them over without alterations (acc. to Heitger 2003: 254f.). This omission of politics aimed to achieve non-partisan unity. In point of fact, the Weimar Republic thus succeeded in keeping extremist parties out of radio. Yet a culture of political debate and a more open information policy would probably have been better able to stabilise the republic – especially since radio could more easily address people with disparate backgrounds.

In the industrialised countries of the West, radio had developed into a mass medium by the end of the 1920s. In 1929 there were about three million registered listeners in Germany, as well as numerous 'illegal listeners'. Nevertheless recent studies have discovered that radio surmounted class divisions to only a small extent in Germany. High purchase costs, high radio fees and culture-oriented content resulted in disproportionate radio use by middle and upper income groups (Führer 1996: 724; Dussel 1999: 72). By the same token, many countries strove to unite city and country by means of radio, which nevertheless remained city based, at least initially. The fact that electrification still left much to be desired goes far towards explaining this. In Germany only half of all households had electricity.

Around 1930, state control of radio rose internationally, going hand in hand with politicisation. The radio historian Edgar Lersch has come to the conclusion that Germany did not go a separate way in respect of state radio control, but rather that radio had been everywhere 'instrumentalised as an element of national integration' in the wake of the world economic crisis (Lersch, in Lersch and Schanze 2004: 44). One can recognise at least some tendencies in this direction, even though radio cultures remained diverse. Thus in the United States the Federal Radio Commission, founded in 1927 under the Radio Act, promoted nationwide stations and curtailed the licensing of smaller stations; in France the state took over the commercial channel

'Radio Paris' in 1933, and in Argentina radio was put under the auspices of the Naval Ministry in 1929 and the allocation of licenses more strictly monitored. Yet in Germany this upheaval was especially drastic: here radio was nationalised in 1932 under Chancellor von Papen, and in the same year the cabinet was allotted one hour of broadcast time between 6.30 and 7.30 P.M. with the 'Hour of the Government'. During his short term of office, Chancellor Franz von Papen spoke on radio eighteen times but not once in the Reichstag (Lerg 1980: 453). Thus the way was paved for state radio propaganda, even before the National Socialist (NS) takeover.

German Films and the Rise of Hollywood

The film industry also evinced great changes during the 1920s, including the triumph of the American cinema. After international sales of European films had already suffered during the war, the European film industry now completely broke down due to lack of capital. This meant that European producers had no financial resources to make lavish films at precisely the time of the movie boom that had begun after 1910 (Bakker 2005: 313, 342f.). Now the United States could chalk up successes because its smaller production companies had combined to form a few large, wealthy studios. There were many other reasons for Hollywood's success: a large domestic market and films made to please the public's taste, with directors and actors who had immigrated thus making it easier to adapt to diverse markets. In the same manner the deliberate promotion of stars and the construction of genres and trademarks fostered the success of Hollywood, which sold itself as a name brand (Cousins 2006: 42f.). While the proportion of American films rose significantly on the European market, the share of European films shown in the United States since 1915 declined to less than 7 per cent. The big French film companies Pathé and Gaumont sold their international business and concentrated entirely on the domestic market, and the same holds true for Denmark. Others, like Éclair and Cecil Hepworth in Great Britain, went bankrupt, as did a large segment of the Italian film studios that had previously been strong exporters. Yet American film studios based in New York and Florida were also among the losers.

However, Hollywood could not reach every country. Japan was one of the nations with a remarkable independent film tradition where Hollywood could hardly succeed. In 1926 a cinema attendance of 150 million was counted in Japan, and ten years later this had risen to over 230 million (Miyao 2013: 97, note 60). However, 90 per cent of the films were domestic productions, making Japan an important producer of films. In the Soviet Union, about one million people visited the cinema each day in the 1920s (Youngblood 1992: 25). In the early 1920s, the majority of those films came abroad, and

80 per cent of the imported films were German. Hollywood had a brief success in the mid-1920s, but then all foreign films disappeared (Kenez 2001: 63–65).

In Europe, Germany was the country most able to compete with Hollywood, and now it became the biggest film-maker on the continent. This was partly due to postwar inflation, which reduced the price of German film exports, but made the German market unattractive for foreign film companies. Another factor was that Germany profited from the concentration of capital that occurred in 1917 with the establishment of the Ufa, which developed into Europe's biggest film corporation (Kreimeier 1992). By setting quotas for films, the state also helped Germany to maintain a market share of 40 per cent, even into the mid-1920s. Yet this success had a shaky foundation: the debts of German film companies and also the Ufa were increasing steadily, and after the financial disaster of Fritz Lang's *Metropolis*, the Ufa was sold to the Conservative politician and media mogul Alfred Hugenberg and therefore came into the Nationalists' sphere of influence (Kreimeier 1992: 158–73). The establishment of the talkies, which occurred quite suddenly in Germany in 1929, again slowed down the triumph of Hollywood and led to a certain renationalisation of film, especially in Germany. Films with dubbing met with little approval, as voice synchronisation was considered artificial. Initial experiments with movies filmed in several languages also had scant success. In any case, the economic crisis caused the number of cinemagoers to drop significantly in 1932 (Müller 2003: 299–308; Ross 2006: 177).

For this reason, the 1920s are considered the Golden Age of German cinema. There is no doubt that the films that are best known internationally were made at this time. Precisely during the early Weimar Republic, when there was little censorship, expressionistic art films were made, such as *The Cabinet of Dr Caligari* (1920) and *Nosferatu – A Symphony of Horror* (1921). Yet if one looks at the number of cinemagoers, a different picture of Weimar film culture emerges. In its early phases, adventure and detective films produced as cliffhangers were the most popular, also melodramas with long-suffering women (Kaes, in Jacobson, Kaes and Prinzler 2004: 39f.). During the late Weimar Republic the cinema also experienced a political turnabout. As the quantitative analyses of Helmut Kortes have shown, the already small proportion of socially critical films dropped swiftly after 1931, while cheerful and nationalistic films met with great public success (Korte 1998: 423). In any case, oft-quoted socialistic films like *Kühle Wampe* were much less popular than patriotic historical movies like *Fridericus Rex*. Historical films actually accounted for over a quarter of the successful films at the end of the Weimar Republic (ibid.: 160), a state of affairs that documents the escapism of the time.

Yet not only the viewer, but also the state determined film content. Since movies were considered to exert an especially powerful influence, most countries now began to practise censorship based on moral and ideological criteria. In Germany this intervention was regulated by the Reichslichtspielgesetz (Reich Cinema Law) of 1920, with supervisory centres in Berlin and Munich scrutinising films before release. What had previously been the responsibility of the police was now taken over by censorship boards, whose members were made up of welfare and youth agency workers and people who came from the film trade or were knowledgeable about movies. Having judged how the films might influence the youth, what impressions they might create in other countries and how they might affect social class structures, the boards prescribed appropriate cuts, prohibitions or age limits. Although political censorship was not intended, the claim that a film endangered security provided an opening. The state likewise intervened by means of quotas. In 1928 the German government restricted the number of imported films to 260, and a bit later French films were limited to only 120. In 1927 the British introduced a 'screen quota' requiring that at least 7.5 per cent of films were to be domestic productions. In fact this protectionism did lead to a rise in home-grown productions, a trend that was further increased by the talkies.

Between 1910 and 1930 the number of cinemas and cinemagoers grew continuously. Contemporaries were already seeking to explain this by a greater need for amusement in times of want. In 1928 there were 5,267 cinemas in Germany with 1.87 million seats, which was twice as many as ten years before. It is estimated that the weekly number of cinemagoers at the end of the 1920s came to approximately 6 million. Thus it appeared that cinema had created a mass culture spanning all class divides. Yet in fact it remained disparate (Führer 1996; Ross 2006 and 2008). Cinema attendance was greatest mainly in cities with middle-class culture. The working-class cities of the Ruhr region had much lower attendance figures than did the neighbouring middle-class city of Düsseldorf. It was particularly because cinemas had been turned into 'movie palaces' that the core audience stemmed disproportionately from higher income groups – and did not consist mainly of 'little shopgirls', as has often been claimed on the basis of Siegfried Kracauer's essays. The economic crisis and the talkies reinforced this trend. In spite of the mass public, different social classes met in cinemas only rarely. While workers still preferred the inexpensive suburban cinemas, the middle classes attended the movie palaces in city centres. Furthermore, labourers and bourgeois groups tended to watch different types of films, even when they went to similar cinemas: the upper-middle class literary films and expensive American or German blockbusters, and the working class adventure films or American westerns; the lower-middle class preferred mainly German films (Ross 2008: 157).

In the big cities at least, it often came to political disputes either in cinemas, in front of them, and in public. Especially in Germany there were many deliberate protest demonstrations in cinemas, which can be described as 'cinemaclasms' (Nowak, in Bösch and Schmidt 2010). As with protests in theatres, movies that were considered morally reprehensible or unpatriotic were disrupted. Especially foreign films dealing with the First World War were attacked – like *All Quiet on the Western Front*, in which disturbance Josef Goebbels and his Nazi party became famous (Jelavich 2006: 160–74). Not even the talkies were able to silence the audience straight away.

The struggle for interpretation was also waged in the major newspapers, which had included regular film reviews since the 1920s. Thus Siegfried Kracauer of the *Frankfurter Zeitung*, one of the most important film critics of the time, saw film critics as 'social critics', whose job it was to expose and shatter 'the ideologies hidden in ordinary films' (Kracauer [1932] 1974: 11). Weimar Republic critics also wrote brilliant groundbreaking essays on the significance of film. Many of them linked film with the change in psychological dispositions. One of these was Béla Balázs, who viewed film as a historic break because it had initiated a turn towards the visual – a new language of gestures and thus international communication that 'led to a common psyche of the white man' (Balázs [1924] 2001: 16f., 22). Especially influential was Siegfried Kracauer's interpretation of film as a daydream that showed society as it wished to see itself. His later work, *From Caligari to Hitler*, accordingly attempted 'to uncover deep psychological dispositions that prevailed in Germany from 1918 to 1933' by examining films (Kracauer [1947] 1979: 7). It was above all the writings of Walter Benjamin that developed into seminal texts of modern cultural media studies. Using examples from reproducible artworks like movies and photographs, he postulated a perceptive change in the modern age, characterised by the loss of aura and tradition, fragmented perception and homogeneous forms of experience (Benjamin [1936] 2008). No less groundbreaking were Erwin Panowskys concurrent analyses that ascribe a 'dynamisation of space' and a 'spacialisation of time' to film (Schöttker 1999: 65–107).

Politics and Entertainment in the Mass Press

Compared to cinema and radio, the third great mass medium, the press, seemed little changed from the pre-war period. In most Western countries the developments of the late nineteenth century continued and reached their peak. For instance, the concentration of ownership and the rise of press barons increased; like Lord Beaverbrook and Lord Rothermere in Britain and Jean Prouvost in France, Germany was dominated by the media mogul Alfred Hugenberg. He had started his career as director of the Krupp plc, and rose to become the owner of the biggest German media empire. Since Hugenberg was both a member of the Reichstag and, from 1928, chairman of the major conservative party (the DNVP) as well, he represented a new and far-reaching union of politics and the media. The structure of his media empire has been well researched (Holzbach 1981; Gossel 2009), but the contents and effects of his media per se have not been studied in such detail. The press division of the 'Hugenberg System' had a fivefold foundation: its own advertising agencies, for example the Ala (Allgemeine Anzeigen GmbH); its news agency Telegrafen-Union; the Scherl publishing house (which Hugenberg purchased) as well as other newspapers; the *Materndienst* (matrix service) of the 'Wipro' (economic base for the provincial press), which provided about three hundred provincial publishers with paper-maché matrices of articles from various political persuasions; and the Vera-Verlagsanstalt Ltd., which offered financial assistance to newspapers. Hugenberg's companies took advantage of the economic weaknesses of smaller papers in order to exert political influence. In addition to Conservative manuscripts he also sold matrices from centrist and non-partisan sources, in order to unite the entire 'bourgeois camp' under his roof and maximise his profits. His own right-wing party profited from his media empire, but so also did the Nazis.

Also tabloid journalism increased its circulation in many Western countries. In the United States, where tabloid journalism had indeed been established since the 1880s, the year 1926 is considered the 'climax year of the war of the tabloids', that battled for circulation records with sensational photos and stories, especially in New York (Emery and Emery 1988: 326). In Germany, a real sensational press finally came up in these years. Although the party-affiliated press continued to be characteristic of Germany and France, it began to lose importance after the mid-1920s. In Berlin the circulation of party organs sank by about 20 per cent during the second half of the 1920s, while that of the tabloids trebled (Charle 2004: 247–66; Fulda 2009: 22f.). Simultaneously the dividing lines between popular and party press became blurred in Germany.

The circulation of German newspapers, which had dropped during the war, climbed back up to their previous numbers, reaching an estimated 18 million copies by 1932, despite the economic crisis; however, two-thirds of these newspapers had small print runs of under five thousand (Dussel 2004: 129). Job advertisements, increased reading time and withdrawal into private life contributed to this stability during the crisis as much as changes in press content. While other countries were dominated by the press of their capitals, in Germany a truly national press market was still evident only in periodicals and hardly at all in the daily newspapers, with the exception of a few small, supra-regional party organs. And most journalists continued to see themselves as educators and not so much as neutral informers.

This was also true for the popular press. After the liberal *BIZ* (*Berliner Illustrierte Zeitung*) had established itself as Germany's most popular illustrated magazine, the Communists founded the *AIZ* (*Arbeiter Illustrierte Zeitung*), which attained the proud circulation of half a million copies towards the end of the Weimar Republic. Like the *BIZ*, it printed exciting, richly illustrated reports, albeit with the difference that here prominence was given to the oppression of the workers and the achievements of the Soviet Union (Willmann 1974). In the same way, tabloids like Hugenberg's *Berliner Lokal-Anzeiger* campaigned for the Conservatives by spreading scandals about the Democrats and explicitly exhorting readers to vote for the DNVP. Furthermore, many seemingly apolitical provincial papers were party affiliated. This provincial press still needs to be researched, although a few beginnings have been made (Meier 1999). As case studies based on themes, photos and opinions have shown, these papers did indeed align themselves with parties, generally tending to favour the bourgeois ones (Fulda 2009: 107–30). So it came about that newspapers in one and the same town conveyed very diverse news perspectives on any given day, and this they achieved with omissions, opinionated pronouncements and hierarchical classifications (e.g. Führer 2008: 299–306).

Thus the question of how important the press was for political culture and the failure of democracy arises – particularly in connection with the Weimar Republic. Media often supported political participation, but the expansion of media was no guarantee for a democratisation of societies (Bösch and Frei 2006). Without doubt the German press of the 1920s fostered political polarisation and made compromise between politicians more difficult. Indeed, the latter tended to be more willing to compromise than the press, which nevertheless influenced politicians' perception and distorted their view of public opinion (Fulda 2009: 211). However, the political orientation of the newspapers influenced the voting behaviour of their readers only indirectly. Thus the proportion of Social Democratic newspapers was only 3–4 per cent, although the Social Democrats were elected by about a quarter of the voters. Conversely, the Liberal parties broke down almost completely, even in major cities like Hamburg and Berlin, in spite of the fact that powerful liberal newspapers dominated these cities (Dussel 2004: 140; Führer 2008: 318f.). Obviously many Social Democrats read the leftist-liberal press because SPD newspapers did not have sports pages, miscellaneous news items or gripping photographs. By the same token, the rise of the NSDAP cannot be attributed to its newspapers, whose circulation was only 500,000 to 700,000; yet the party received over a third of all votes. In actual fact, the National Socialists profited from the political climate created by the Conservative press, whose daily circulation had grown to between three and four million.

In this context one may ask whether the Weimar Democrats did too little to curb the media. In actual fact, there was no lack of commitment on the part of the government, which on the one hand actively censored non-democratic print media. In contrast to the Imperial Constitution of 1871, article 118 of the Constitution of Weimar guaranteed freedom of opinion and forbade censorship, yet by means of the 'Law for the Protection of the Republic' and the emergency decree of Article 48, many newspapers were banned, particularly during the years of crisis in 1922/23 and 1931/32, and 294 were forbidden in 1932 alone. These bans affected extreme right-wing papers, leftist intellectual satires and especially the Communist press (Petersen 1995). In the same vein, the 'Law for the Protection of Youth from Trashy and Indecent Writings', passed in 1926, provided a useful censorship tool – even against penny magazines.

On the other hand the Weimar governments actively engaged in media politics. Press bureaus were expanded and centralised, and were headed by a chief press officer. The government still had the semi-official news agency WTB at its disposal, which supplied it with information from abroad and disseminated official pronouncements. In the same way, communication with journalists was intensified and became freer. Now representatives of the government answered journalists' invitations to appear at the Berlin press conference where they could explain their policies. Thus it is clear that the Weimar Republic did not fail because it had no means of suppressing radical voices; on the contrary, it intervened innumerable times in film, radio and press. What was lacking in politics was the mutual exchange of divergent opinions.

Fascist Dictatorships and the Second World War

In many countries the political upheavals of the 1930s and 1940s led to fundamental restructuring of media landscapes. Dictatorships and authoritarian regimes changed media structures as much as propaganda battles and wartime occupation did. This caused the media to come under the primacy of politics, although politics also submitted to media logics. However, no detailed comparative studies on this development exist as yet (see, for Germany's sidelong glances at Spain and Italy: Zimmermann 2007).

Researchers soon gave great attention to Nazi propaganda. The first reason for this was that for a long time the support for National Socialism was attributed to the seductive power of propaganda. The seemingly modern, subtle and all-encompassing propaganda machine of Josef Goebbels thus relieved Germans of their responsibility. Yet this manipulation of the masses, emphasised by many contemporaries and historians, was simultaneously a concept created by propagandistic pictures of crowds. Yet recent studies have shown up the limits of this apparently perfect propaganda, its lack of coordination and its politics of the un-political. The same is true of Fascist Italy, where the propaganda system was often brought to grief by its own pretensions and just as often relied on improvisation (Galassi 2008). It has also been argued that the term propaganda should no longer be used as an analytical concept, since as a source term it suggests a one-sided wielding of influence and thus masks communicative interactions (Mühlenfeld 2009: 528).

The media in dictatorships like those of Germany, Italy and Spain took a different development in the 1930s and consequently are discussed separately here. However, the outbreak of the Second World War changed the media in many other Western countries, too. Like during the First World War, the role of governmental influence, propaganda and censorship increased.

Press and Fascist Dictatorships

If one first regards the initial phase of Western dictatorships in the light of media history, several smooth transitions become apparent. Even in Germany, where political restructuring has been particularly rapid and radical since 1933, a number of developments had already begun in the years before. For example the nationalisation and politicisation of radio started in 1932, and the crisis in the Liberal press was around 1930, together with the nationalistic changes that took place in the management structures of many companies. For example, Hans Fritsche, head of the broadcasting department and the most important radio commentator in the Third Reich, had become editor-in-chief of the radio news agency in 1932. In the same way all three Fascist dictatorships in Italy, Spain and Germany allowed the temporary continuation of the bourgeois press when they had first come into power, albeit under control. The concomitant continuity of personnel among bourgeois journalists who were not ostracised either as 'Marxists' or Jews (in Germany) underscores a high degree of self-adaptation (cf. Lorenzen 1978: 180; Frei and Schmitz 1999: 22–26; Galassi 2008: 204).

Nevertheless the year 1933 marked an important turning point in German media policy. This applied particularly to the banning of the 'leftist' press. In Germany, two hundred SPD newspapers and thirty-five KPD journals fell victim to this ban and were barely able to survive in exile (Danker et al. 2003: 116–30). The papers of the big Jewish publishers, most prominently Ullstein and Mosse, kept their names after being forcibly sold, in order to imply continuity. Similarly the 1926 assassination attempts on Mussolini gave Italy an excuse to forbid the anti-Fascist press, and Spain silenced it as from 1939. There were hardly any legal regulations for the censorship practised in all these regimes. On the whole they relied less on daily blue-pencilling than on pre-selection of journalists by professional associations. Italy had already introduced them in 1926; and in Germany, the Reichskulturkammer (Reich cultural association) was created in 1933. Anyone who was unable to join on the grounds of political or racial criteria was de facto banned from the profession. Thus an estimated eighth of all radio employees lost their jobs in 1933, particularly those with managerial functions (the example of Cologne here used as basis for projection: Diller 1980: 127). Yet even in the case of broadcasting one cannot speak of an encompassing personnel policy of the Nazis, or one that was methodically controlled (Münkel, in Marßolek and Saldern 1998, Vol. 1: 125).

In each dictatorship the press was gradually centralised. In Italy the number of newspapers had already shrunk by 75 per cent by 1934. Parallels to the European dictatorships were also evident in imperialistic Japan, which reduced the number of its newspapers to only one per region as of 1942; this formed the basis for the fact that some Japanese papers now have the highest circulation numbers in the world (Saito, in Gunaratne 2000: 563). In Germany, press concentration accelerated with the so-called 'Amman Decree' of 1935, which set itself against 'unhealthy competition', the 'scandal-mongering press' and religious newspapers in the name of an ideology of ethnic community, and in a short time caused the demise of about five to six hundred newspapers. Secret purchases through straw men promoted their concentration within the National Socialist Eher Verlag and destroyed the press diversity that had existed in Germany for hundreds of years. After 1935 it was especially the Catholic centrist-affiliated press that was the first to lose its independence, and this often by means of covert buyouts. The extent to which changes of ownership corresponded to changes in media content needs to be studied in more depth. Not until the Second World War did the National Socialists attempt a comprehensive suppression of the bourgeois press. Both political and financial motives played a deciding role because it meant tremendous gains for the NSDAP, whose newspapers like the *Völkische Beobachter* then reached a circulation of 1.2 million in 1941. Towards the end of the war the NSDAP Eher Verlag controlled over 82 per cent of the market. In total, the German newspaper landscape had declined to a quarter of its original size: 350 party organs compared to 650 private newspapers, mainly small local ones (Frei and Schmitz 1999: 37f.). It is striking that even in democratic countries like the United States press concentration increased in the 1930s. What dictators had enforced out of political considerations had at least partially also become a trend, incidentally induced by financial considerations in the wake of the worldwide economic depression.

Every dictatorship controlled the media through its propaganda ministries. They prescribed media content through state-controlled news agencies, daily press conferences and innumerable directives. For the National Socialist regime, fifteen thousand directives have been documented for the years up to 1939 alone and an estimated sixty thousand afterwards (Bohrmann and

Toepser-Ziegert 1984–2001). In Italy the number of '*disposizioni*' reached its apex at around four thousand in 1938/39 (Galassi 2008: 433f.). These directives instructed journalists about contents, the positioning of articles and even prohibitions (Wilke 2007). For instance, according to notes made secretly, the press directive for the *Kristallnacht* (Night of Broken Glass, 10 October 1938) demanded: 'Reports should not be given much prominence; no headlines on the front page. No pictures to be published as yet. Collected reports from the Reich are not to be compiled, but it may be reported that similar actions have been carried out in the Reich. Reports on individuals are to be avoided. More detailed reports on local events are permitted …' (Bohrmann and Toepser-Ziegert 1999, Vol. 6.3: 1060f.). In so doing the regime largely focused on how Germany would appear to other countries (Pöttker 2006: 171). Very little research has been done on the extent to which such communications were actually implemented. A case study of two Mannheim newspapers has discovered discrepancies in only 5 per cent of cases, and these were not greater in the bourgeois newspaper than in the local NSDAP organ (Dussel 2010: 558).

The press directives simultaneously presented a dilemma that even Goebbels often deplored: on the one hand he wished for an interesting and compelling press; on the other hand the controls guaranteed unimaginative uniformity. For this reason Goebbels founded the weekly *Das Reich* in 1940, a journal meant to be an intellectual figurehead for both inside and outside Germany to give the best writers more freedom. Conversely, both Italy and Germany failed in their attempts at creating a new type of professional journalist faithful to the system by building schools of journalism. The Italians had already closed theirs in 1933; the German 'Reichspresseschule' was shut down in 1939, albeit after 750 trainees had absolved it and left with good job opportunities. In both dictatorships, factors that contributed to the closings were controversial financing, chaotic administration structures and the perception that these schools did not produce good journalists (Müsse 1995; Galassi 2008: 384–89). Only in the Spanish dictatorship did journalistic training by the state become permanently established after the Press Law of 1938 made it compulsory (Lorenzen 1978: 200f.).

Political radicalisation stemmed not only from the authorities, even in the case of media policy. Occasionally Goebbels and Mussolini's 'Ministrero della Cultura Popolare' curbed journalistic utterances that were too extreme in order to safeguard the media's credibility and appeal (Zimmermann 2007: 107). Both regimes banked on politics of the apolitical, which was probably particularly effective in sustaining these dictatorships. Especially high-circulation papers like the *Berliner Illustrierte Zeitung* regularly printed entertaining pictorial articles about the political elites, the spirit of optimism and the ostensibly modern achievements of the dictatorships. For this reason the photo historian Rolf Sachsse viewed state-directed propaganda photography as a 'medium that trained people to turn a blind eye', which served to create positive identification patterns and covered up 'negative' memories like war crimes (Sachsse 2003: 14–18). Magazines even printed pictorial reports about concentration camps and ghettos but played them down completely by staging them as 'reformatory camps' (Knoch 2001: 76–88). The heroicised picture world of the magazines also played a prominent role during the Second World War, visualising soldiers as 'well-trained craftsmen of war' and battles as sports events. On the other hand, not only in Germany but in democratic countries like the United States, one generally saw only enemy corpses in the media, with America demonstrating a discriminatory attitude by showing mainly the bodies of Japanese. Only as of 1943 did the United States allow a few faceless pictures of its own casualties to appear in the press, precisely because the Allies now knew that their side would win (Paul 2004: 237–40, 252f.).

The Nazis tried to learn from the First World War and the poor German propaganda. They now created a modern international magazine as a means of improving their reputation in occupied and 'friendly' territories: as of 1940 the magazine *Signal* appeared, distributed by the Wehrmacht under participation of the Foreign Office and the Propaganda Ministry and published abroad in approximately two dozen languages, with up to 2.4 million copies (Rutz 2007). *Signal* was quite subtle in its use of modern journalistic tools to promote National Socialism. Modelled on the American *Life* magazine, it printed reports with excellent colour photographs showing heroic soldiers, idyllic family life and pretty women. In order to gain a wide readership abroad, the ideological tone of the articles was kept deliberately low key.

In what measure individual press organs offered resistance is debatable (most recent: Studt 2007; Heidenreich and Neitzel 2010). There was probably greater leeway in the Spanish dictatorship, where at least the renowned daily *ABC* was able to express monarchic viewpoints (Lorenzen 1978: 154). A subject of debate for Germany has been the degree to which the former liberal *Frankfurter Zeitung* possessed and utilised certain freedoms since it was a respected flagship abroad. In any case, it hired leftist-liberal journalists who had been fired by other papers, and even employed Jewish editors under the guise of salesmen. Its wary distancing from the regime was usually expressed in subjunctives and quotes, avoidance of Nazi vocabulary and uncensored reports taken from local newspapers (quite one-sided: Gillessen 1987: 200–229). Yet such small, carefully shared-out latitudes simultaneously served to stabilise the regime, especially as the *Frankfurter Zeitung* contained articles that supported the system (Sösemann 2007: 34f.). Forms of resistance can also be discerned in several discriminating Catholic organs like the magazine *Hochland* and the Catholic diocesan press, whose circulation rose at the end of the 1930s – despite or perhaps because of its 'theologising'. Nevertheless these papers, too, were intended to provide outlets.

Radio as a Medium of Propaganda

The extent to which media politics and propaganda reacted to public moods can also be seen in broadcasting. Radio was often seen as the most important for the daily propaganda of the Nazis. At the beginning of the 1930s, very diverse regimes discovered the possibilities of using radio as a political mouthpiece: as of 1933 in the United States, President Roosevelt had regularly advocated his policies in his 'Fireside Chats' (Craig 2000), in Great Britain ministers of state and party speakers were given programmes (Scannell and Cardiff 1991: 51), and in Brazil the autocratic President Getúlio Vargas used radio to cement his power. The fact that the Nazi party leadership regularly aired political speeches and ceremonies on radio after 1933 thus corresponded to a general politicisation of this medium. The communication structure of the radio, whereby one person 'speaks' to the masses, was particularly suited to the Nazis' blueprint for society. Yet even in democratic countries, radio enabled heads of state to appear as charismatic and exceptional personalities. In the United States, for example, listeners reacted to Franklin D. Roosevelt's speeches by sending him admiring letters (Craig 2000: 154f.).

Hitler's major speeches were extensively broadcast, with cinemas, theatres and concert halls even being cleared for collective listening so as to make hearing him a great experience. However, because of their length and syntax, Hitler's speeches were less suited to radio than, for example, those of President Roosevelt. The latter were more professional and probably more successful, since they were personal, brief, easy to understand and delivered in a warm voice, and had probably reached 30 million people even before the war began (Craig 2000: 195; Führer 2008: 97f.).

In the same period, the Nazi regime began cutting down on its open propaganda. In order to fulfil listeners' wishes, it reduced the proportion of textual broadcasts and consequently of party speeches and the cultural lectures beloved of the educated bourgeoisie. On the other hand entertaining programmes with light music increased. Next to music that was considered typically German, even Germanised forms of tango, swing and jazz – although jazz was officially opposed as 'nigger music' (Dussel 1999: 92–94). In this way National Socialism proved to be a dictatorship of moods, in which radio was to serve as a popular diversion – garnished with a few explicitly ideological programmes. After setbacks in the war began to mount after 1942, Goebbels intensified the entertaining programmes as a means of distraction. In 1944, 82 per cent of programming consisted of music, by which radio intimated normality in a lifeworld that had been destroyed (Dussel and Lersch 1999: 122). This was a general international trend, too. Even the cultivated BBC yielded to listeners' wishes when the war began, and integrated the working class and popular music into the world of radio. At the same time the BBC improved its domestic reputation during the war because it cheered people on during the Blitz, encouraging them to stand fast and fight. Meanwhile, American critics and institutions like the Rockefeller Foundation supported educational public service broadcasting like in Britain. Transnational adaptions increased, as did governmental influence, even in democratic countries (Hilmes 2012: 23).

However, radio broadcasting and propaganda remained less developed in Southern Europe. In many respects there were clear differences in radio programming in Italy and Spain. Under Mussolini, the ratio of politics and direct propaganda rose as of the 1930s, and cultural programming was not reduced as much as it was in Germany. This may explain why radio was less widespread in Fascist Italy and contributed less towards stabilising the system. Franquist programming in Spain was even less attractive, although commercial broadcasters were still allowed here and only a small, primarily urban middle class were able to receive the broadcasts (Zimmermann 2007: 148–59). For this reason, although airings in cafés, schools and public squares increased the number of listeners, one cannot generally conclude that radio played a key role in establishing right-wing dictatorships.

National Socialist orientation towards the public was also evident in how radio was organised. The Nazi Party did indeed centralise it because regional stations lost their shares to the Reichs- Rundfunk-Gesellschaft, but protests of listeners and local party elites were able to prevent the standardisation of radio programming until the war broke out (Dussel 2000: 83–87). In the Second World War the regime then stopped making these allowances for the medium, installing standardised programming in 1940, with only a few small regional segments permitted during the forenoon hours. This also meant the loss of previously widespread broadcasting in local dialects and made a more standardised language accessible to Germans (Führer 2008: 89f.).

In Germany the National Socialists propagated radio listening as a practical form of ethnic community, which was shaped by the concurrent reception of the same broadcasts. The expansion of programming for diverse social groups, such as farmers and young people, was intended to heighten social integration. The most popular radio broadcasts, for instance 'Das Wunschkonzert' (request concert), insinuated that it was an apparently non-political, plebiscitary entertainment; sometimes several thousand musical requests per airing were sent in, with messages for other listeners. The pieces were selected in such a way as to appeal to all social groups and musical tastes, in part with personal input from Goebbels. When the programme was renamed 'Wunschkonzert für die Wehrmacht' (request concert for the Wehrmacht) in 1939, and thus became a symbol of the bonds between homeland and front, it embodied the idea of ethnic community in wartime (Koch 2003: 172–206).

Accordingly, the National Socialists strove for blanket radio expansion. The construction of the inexpensive 'Volksempfänger' (people's radio) was largely responsible for the fact that by 1938 the number of radios had doubled to 9 million and peaked at 16 million in 1943. Although this was a commercial success compared to the failed 'Volks-productions' (like the Volkswagen), it is not proof of the stellar modernity of National Socialism. Listener density in the United States remained unrivalled, and in France and Norway the number of listeners rose even more at this time (Frei and Schmitz 1999: 84; König 2004: 84). In 1941/42, Sweden and Denmark had the highest listener density in Europe, followed by Germany and Great Britain. In general, a north–south divide continued to exist for radio. In Italy the number of radios only reached 1.8 million by 1942, despite enormous efforts to promote their spread. In addition, although these dictatorships fostered broadcasting that addressed all social groupings, one can hardly speak of this as 'modern', since it was enforced through violence and prohibitions; freedom to choose from a variety of media offerings in the manner of a modern, functionally differentiated society did not really occur (König 2004: 255; Ross 2008: 386). Nazi media were a part of modernity, but in its pathological and illiberal form.

Inland radio programming was especially easy to control in dictatorships. Yet at the same time, radio was able to evade controls as no other medium because people could listen to broadcasts from abroad, despite the fact that reception quality on simple radio sets like the Volksempfänger was poor (König 2004: 39f.). Even before the war many foreign stations had emerged for the dissemination of ideologies, like Radio Moscow in 1929, or the stabilisation of colonial empires, like 'BBC World' in 1932. Parallel to its politics of appeasement, Great Britain had already established a German-language channel in 1938 in order to influence German sentiment against war. During the Second World War an actual battle developed among numerous foreign stations. The Germans broadcast foreign-language programmes just as the Americans did in 1942 when they set up the 'Voice of America' (VOA) as a foreign broadcaster after their entry into the war. According to Nazi court files, Germans listened mainly to the BBC and the Swiss national channel 'Beromünster' (Hensle 2003: 321). Yet initially the German-language propaganda channel for England was quite successful: in a survey taken at the beginning of 1940, a quarter of Britons admitted to having listened to 'Lord Haw-Haw' on the previous day, as the speaker William Joyce was mockingly called because of his upper-class accent. His popularity can be explained by curiosity, derision and a desire for information (Williams 2010: 127).

Nevertheless, the German-language channels of the BBC and VOA were more influential. They not only promised more objective information about the course of war, German losses and casualties, and the political situation, but also lured listeners with modern music, satire and other forms of entertainment. The presence of German speakers, in particular prominent figures like Thomas Mann, served to increase listeners' trust in the imparted information.

Yet as a rule, German emigrants did not have leading functions in these stations, as there was considerable mistrust. Next to this 'white propaganda', that came recognisably from foreign sources, a 'black propaganda' made the rounds. The latter left its origins unclear and intimated that resistance groups were broadcasting within the country. The intention was to undermine the security of those in power, although the tone was sharper and contents less trustworthy.

How much the regime feared these 'enemy broadcasters' was demonstrated by a plethora of reactions. At the beginning of the war the 'Verordnung über außerordentliche Rundfunkmaßnahmen' (ruling on extraordinary broadcast measures) had already prohibited listening to foreign channels. The Nazi regime tried out jammers, albeit with little success, and intentionally broadcast Western types of music to retain its own listeners. In occupied territories like the Netherlands, the Germans even deliberately confiscated radios. After the war, many Germans boasted that they had secretly listened to foreign programmes at peril of their lives, which was often stylised as resistance. Contrary to a widely believed myth, however, listening to foreign channels was not punishable by death but merely imprisonment. Of course, if this was connected to other accusations, it might indeed have ended in a sentence of execution (Hensle 2003: 139).

'Hostile propaganda' also caused a change in the media policies of Western democracies. State influence increased dramatically. At war's end, the British 'Ministry of Information' was an administration with 3,000 employees, and the American 'United States Office of War Information' (OWI) even had 14,400 employees. In Great Britain, censorship was only permitted in case of articles endangering Britain's war interests, but the Churchill government put pressure especially on leftist-liberal newspapers, and supervised BBC and wire service reports in order to strengthen endurance and staying power (Williams 2010: 134, 140). By means of popular media appeals, the home country also became part of the front in Great Britain.

The effect of Allied radio propaganda on the Germans is difficult to assess. On the whole, one can say that it was considerable, although it did not trigger widespread resistance. Reports gave information about the Allied advance and thus, in contrast to the First World War, reduced the belief in victory at an early stage, which in turn fostered rejection of the regime. In Germany the frequently satirical reports about Nazi elites probably increased scorn for the regime. The fact that numerous German cities surrendered without a fight was also due to the precise information the Germans had about the enemy's advances. In occupied areas like France and the Netherlands these programmes were often an important bridge to exiled organisations that formed the resistance. In this way Charles de Gaulle was regularly able to mobilise the resistance against the German occupiers in the programme 'Ici Londres', after his famous radio speech of 18 June 1940. German-language stations from abroad also informed about Nazi atrocities. German-language BBC programmes already began very detailed reporting on the Holocaust in June 1942, and even daily in the week before Christmas 1942. These programmes were in turn taken up by other stations, like the Dutch 'Radio Oranje', among others (Longerich 2006: 438).

Film and Propaganda

Research has given particular attention to movies and newsreels during the Nazi era. While historians soon examined the organisation of film policy, media historians concentrated on writing numerous movie analyses based on aesthetics and content (Segeberg 2004, among others). In general one can recognise structural similarities to Nazi press and radio policy. What characterised the cinema during National Socialism were not such well-known propaganda films as 'Triumph of the Will', 'Jud Süss' and 'The Eternal Jew', although research has focused on these until the present day, and they could sometimes indeed be very successful, as was the case with 'Jud Süss'. But of the more than a thousand films produced between 1933 and 1945, the ratio of apparently non-political films dominated – and this is especially true in regard to the numbers of cinemagoers. Close to half were comedies and a good quarter were melodramas, whereas directly propagandistic movies accounted for between 10 and 25 per cent of all productions, depending on the counting (Welch 2001: 36).

Explicit propaganda movies appeared most frequently in the wake of general NS radicalisation around 1937 and again in 1940/41, while the proportion of comedies further increased especially after the defeat at Stalingrad in 1943, which demonstrates that cinema functioned as a means of distraction. The war film genre also played merely a subordinate role. Explicit propaganda movies were likewise relatively rare in the Fascist dictatorships of Italy and Spain. Here, too, comedies and melodramas were dominant. Spanish comedies were reputed to contain double entendre, which fostered subversive hilarity (Marsh 2006: 39f.; Zimmermann 2007: 210–13). It is noticeable that many propaganda films made use of historical subject matter as a means of conveying their ideas with more subtlety and universality. The stories of great men like Robert Koch, Carl Peters and Andreas Schlüter, and historical conflicts and battles such as Patriots, Jud Süß and Kolberg were among these. This historically founded propaganda could also be found in Italy and Great Britain (Fox 2007: 223–43). Nazi propaganda movies were definitely not very aesthetically innovative, Leni Riefenstahl's works notwithstanding. A comparison with earlier Weimar film-making makes this clear.

Problematic and much discussed is how to differentiate between films that were apolitical and those that were political and propagandistic. Initially only a small segment of movies was considered propagandistic, but since the 1970s all the films of that time have increasingly been seen in this light, as comedies also helped to stabilise dictatorships. Even though transitions between tendentious movies and entertaining ones were very fluid, it is necessary to gauge contents of specific films to determine which values and norms they implicitly conveyed. The distinction between 'Fascist films' and 'films made under Fascist regimes' shows that the regime formed the framework in both cases (Witte 1998: 29).

A glance at Nazi film policy makes clear how closely movies were bound up with the National Socialist regime. It was similar to the policy applied to the press but much more extensive in that it could exercise greater control. Here, too, compulsory membership in the Reichsfilmkammer selected film-makers according to political and racialist criteria, and this led to the emigration of approximately fifteen hundred actors and directors, some of whom were very prominent. The tightening of censorship at first mainly affected movies made before 1933, while new films were controlled by an increase in prior vetting. Subsidies provided through the newly established Filmkreditbank (bank for film loans) were a part of this, since every script had to be approved by the Reichsfilmdramaturgen (specialist in dramaturgy), who was answerable to the Propaganda Minister. Nevertheless many censorship cases affecting even propaganda films cropped up, especially during the war; this was because people involved fell from favour (as with *Titanic*, 1943), because high-ranking officers complained (*Große Freiheit Nr. 7*, 1943), because of political features (*Das Leben kann so schön sein*, 1938), and because the political situation had changed (*Besatzung Dora*, 1943). The authorities also exerted influence by covertly buying up production firms, which helped to centralise the movie business. As early as 1937, the Ufa, Tobis and Terra dominated nearly the entire film market, with Hugenberg, once allied with Hitler, losing his UFA shares majority to the Reich in the same year (Kreimeier 1992: 221–29). This became the nucleus of Ltd (UFI), which consolidated the whole of Germany's film production. Thus resistance could best be expressed in movies through aesthetic opposition, ambivalent innuendo and omission of any and all contentual links to the regime.

Protectionist policies, the transition to talkies and the growing number of cinemagoers all strengthened the domestic film industry. Nevertheless, during the 1930s a good 20 per cent of all movies shown in Nazi Germany still came from the United States and a further 20 per cent from other countries, especially Austria (Spieker 1999: 337). Out of economic considerations, Hollywood adapted itself to the German market by eschewing recognisably Jewish characters. Additionally, German cuts and dubbing changed U.S. films even more. The withdrawal from the German market occurred rather on the basis of economics, as censorship, quota regulations and the currency differential harboured financial risks (ibid.: 331–34). Leading National Socialists valued American films as community-building models. Of course, these were successful primarily in the cities, since cinemagoers in rural areas and working-class neighbourhoods preferred German films (Führer in Führer and Ross 2008: 98–108). Only when it became clear that German films could not compete internationally were stronger restrictions on U.S. productions enforced at the end of the 1930s, and in 1940 they were completely prohibited. There were similar tendencies in Italy and Spain, where Hollywood had celebrated even greater triumphs into the 1930s, after which a renationalisation of cinema was enforced. Subsidies, quotas and the promotion of young talents strengthened the domestic movie industry, in Italy especially.

War and occupation gave the German film industry access to new, often enforced markets in both allied and occupied territories. The National Socialists used movies in their attempts to broadcast their ideology into occupied countries, which had hardly any means of defending against this (Kreimeier 1992: 331–41). Yet the export of films met with only moderate success: in nearly every country viewers preferred their own movies and newsreels (Vande Winkel and Welch 2007). Only in Italy were some German films marketed on the basis of an agreement, and Germany became the main country of export for Italian productions, but further plans for cooperation in the 'German–Italian Film Union' came to nothing. Among neutral countries it was especially Switzerland that showed German newsreels and movies, in part because they produced too few of their own. Yet the hoped-for film hegemony of Germany as the 'Hollywood of Europe' was certainly not achieved.

A pivotal role in propaganda was played by the newsreels, which had been shown before the main feature since the 1910s and are very accessible sources today (circa 6,000 newsreels at: www.wochenschau-archiv.de). Because of their propagandistic potential, documentaries preceding the main film were compulsory in Italy as of 1926, the more so as newspapers and radio reached only small segments of the population. Germany followed suit in 1938 with mandatory newsreels as well, which, like pictorials, contained glorified depictions of the party elite, the vaunted modernisation of the country, and entertainment news on sports, daily life and fashion (Bartels 2004: 279f.). Pride of place was given to musically enhanced visual impressions, with hardly any factual information being communicated by the speaker. Besides the German newsreels from Ufa, Bavaria/Tobis and Deulig, the American FOX newsreel also maintained a presence in the 1930s. As had been the case with the motion picture, this was purchased at the cost of accommodation. All newsreels were finally centralised in 1940 in the 'Deutsche Wochenschau' (ibid.: 162). FOX newsreels and the

'Actualitades Ufa' also appeared in Franco's Spain until the domestic newsreel 'NO-DO' prevailed in 1941.

Second World War newsreels are considered virtuoso propaganda and have frequently been analysed. Their dramatic images of combat were the achievement of propaganda units, *Propaganda-Kompanien* (PK), formed as early as 1938, each including over 250 newspaper journalists, photojournalists, film journalists, and radio reporters, as well as a total of around 300 film journalists. These propaganda units, whose numbers reached fifteen thousand men in 1942, were part of the combat troops and thus not independent journalists. They were allowed a fair amount of freedom to film at the front, and their job was to try to capture battle scenes which looked as authentic as possible. They sent their film material to Berlin, where selection, recompilation and often dubbing were undertaken under the surveillance of the Ministry of Propaganda – sometimes on approval by Goebbels himself.

As quantitative analyses have shown, reports on the German troops now made up half of the newsreels (Bartels 2004: 427). With their rapid, sometimes abrupt transitions (hard cuts) and contrasts as well as alternating long shots and close-ups, the images resembled Riefenstahl's aesthetics. Without reference to place, they portrayed advancing soldiers, modern technology, and the romance of a soldier's life within short anecdotal narratives. Especially in the first few years of the war, they not only constituted a link between home and the front, but more often than not were the real cinema attraction. Instances of defeat were mentioned indirectly at best, which undermined the reports' credibility, particularly in the case of Stalingrad. Whereas initially German casualties were for the most part omitted, towards the end of the war newsreels graphically showed violence directed against German women, who even related their experiences of being raped by Soviet soldiers. Such reporting was intended to stir up fears and rally the populace for the 'Volkssturm'.

As was the case in the West in the 1930s, the era of National Socialism also experienced a general cinema boom. In 1936/37, the number of theatregoers once more reached the previous high of 1928. The viewers' social spectrum also became broader: the lower classes were now spending twice as much on films than they had ten years previously. Moreover, the NSDAP introduced film into small villages where the medium had hardly been heard of before. Since socialistic films were prohibited, film theatres often brought together different social classes by force of circumstance. The Hollywood-like promotion of film stars probably also furthered this surmounting of social borders between the viewers of successful films. Nonetheless, socio-cultural distinctions were still evident in the cinema of the 1930s (Ross 2006: 185–93).

Even in dictatorships, viewer behaviour co-determined how films were interpreted. Reports on Germany by both SD informers and the exiled SPD frequently documented audience reactions: patriotic scenes or advancing soldiers were occasionally applauded and cheered; yet moments of resistance are also recorded, such as giggles at the sight of Nazi minister Hermann Göring or, in another instance, the silence in the audience that followed upon on-screen applause for Hitler. After the outbreak of the war, some reports noted 'loud laughter' at staged scenes, and signs of boredom at newsreel repeats (Stahr 2001: 168–82).

On the whole, however, media propaganda met with acceptance, as shown by the viewing figures of a number of high-grossing propaganda films as well as the high circulation of NSDAP newspapers. Yet one cannot necessarily deduce a direct influence from the numbers of viewers and readers. After all, the NS dictatorship neither succeeded in arousing widespread enthusiasm for the outbreak of the war in 1939, nor was it able to prevent the change in sentiment that occurred in 1943. The strongest impact of NS propaganda was doubtless generated in the mid-1930s when political, social and economic successes were implied, and around 1940 in justifying the wars of aggression. Its long-term effects became evident in the decades after 1945, in which images and clichés of NS propaganda continued to circulate, such as the notion that National Socialism was responsible for eliminating laziness, corruption and criminality, and that it systematically tackled problems. The fact that historical films and documentaries once more showed this film and photo material after 1945 enabled these ideas to be passed on, leading some to speak of the 'belated triumph of Joseph Goebbels' (see Paul 2004: 247).

CHAPTER 5

The Media during the Cold War

Media and Socialism in the GDR

After 1945 the media in nearly every country that had been involved in the Second World War experienced a transformation. This was especially noticeable in Soviet-dominated Eastern Europe and explains why media experts speak of an autonomous socialistic media model (cf. Thomaß 2007: 33f.). In contrast to the right-wing dictatorships of the twentieth century, the socialistic media system was not merely controlled and directed by the State, but owned almost exclusively either by the State or the Communist Party. This applied to radio, news agencies, cinema and press – with a few exceptions like church publications and the Samizdat, that is, media banned by the State and so disseminated clandestinely.

The Soviet Union was the model that the Central and East European public were forced to emulate when they reorganised their public spheres. Compared to the Fascist dictatorships, Soviet Communism at first relied very little on modern mass media. After the Revolution of 1917 almost everything was in short supply: paper, experienced journalists and a literate populace. For this reason the high circulation numbers of popular newspapers that had initially been distributed to the country free of charge (like *Bednota*) tumbled drastically during the 1920s when they had to be purchased. In 1924 the circulation of 2.5 million copies was still significantly less than before the Revolution, amounting to only one-eighth of the numbers in Germany (Lenoe 2004: 16). The enormous circulation for which the party organ *Pravda* was famous only set in during the 1950s. Radio and television, however, expanded a little later: radio became a real mass medium in 1960s and television in the 1970s (Roth-Ey 2011: 11).

As far as content was concerned, the Communist media gave priority to indoctrination of the public rather than information. Numerous censorship and regulatory measures that were increasingly adopted around 1930 demonstrate the permanent state of dissatisfaction under which party leaders laboured, but also their great faith in media propaganda, which they hoped would transform both the people and the productivity of the country. In the 1930s they also largely failed to make good their plan of reaching the illiterate rural populace via radio. Any lasting achievements must be credited to the cinema of the 1920s. The government sponsored propaganda films as well as art films, hoping that their emotional appeal would win the allegiance of the barely literate public. Nevertheless, under Stalin, even semi-official masterpieces like *October* (1927/28), Eisenstein's film about the Revolution, were censored. For although censorship was officially non-existent in the Soviet Union, in actual fact the number of censors climbed to an estimated seventy thousand by the 1970s and 1980s (Lauk, in Høyer and Pöttker 2005: 173). In addition to pre- and post-censorship, procedural censorship of past publications was introduced in the 1930s. Now media documents were continuously subject to alteration in both text and visuals, with pictures often being retouched (Waschik 2010: 12).

Nevertheless, recent research has made clear that in spite of manifold efforts at control, the Soviet press was not as monolithic as had long been assumed (Aumente et al. 1999: 18). Although where important political themes were concerned, newspapers followed the required party line and lauded the nation's achievements, they still retained their individual profiles. This was partly a result of political design but also had much to do with the editorial staff itself. By the same token, intra-party power struggles were carried out in the press (Lenoe 2004: 182–211). Besides propagating the Communist ideology, the media's main role was to promote unity and identity in a nation comprised of heterogeneous republics with dozens of languages. For this reason Russian was the language of the most important newspapers and television stations. From the 1970s onwards the Russian-language press was actually expanded due to fear of secessionist nationalism.

After 1945 the Soviet Union handed media operations over to the occupied East European states. Since these systems were also part of the state apparatus, their development largely depended on the prevailing political course of the Soviet Union. Until 1947 the Soviets had granted East European countries some latitude as a means of gaining their trust, but this phase was soon followed by one of enforced political conformity and personnel purges. After the 1960s one can, in a somewhat generalised way, detect a slight drift towards a modicum of government-channelled freedom that increased slightly in the 1980s. As Kristin Roth-Ey argued, 'the Soviet culture formation was a most successful failure': it failed in the Cold War competition, but its films and television programmes were greatly popular (Roth-Ey 2011: 23, 130, 221).

Expressions like 'Communist Media System' admittedly obscure the differences that existed in Eastern Europe. The Yugoslavian media enjoyed an especially high level of freedom that even extended to cooperation with the West: there were numerous joint film productions, for example, and Yugoslavia was the only Communist country to become a member of the 'European Broadcasting Union' (EBU). Beginning in the 1960s, Yugoslavia consequently took part in the Eurovision Song Contest and presented itself with Mediterranean flair. Some leeway for development was also in evidence in Poland, which had a prominent church press (albeit accounting for only 1 per cent of circulation) and a significant underground press with a self-image that drew on experiences during the German occupation and often formed the backbone of the opposition movement, especially after 1979. Even after martial law was imposed in 1981, an estimated eight hundred illegal publications remained in existence (Paczkowski 1997: 26). This contrasted strongly with those Communist countries that granted no leeway and had not even tapped into modern media development. Thus there was no television in Albania as late as the 1980s, and Romania had only one television station with very truncated air times, and practically no underground press. In fact, any critical information about the regime that the Romanians received, like that leading to the fall of the dictator Nicolae Ceaucescu in 1989, came from the freer Hungarian radio.

The East European media systems were linked by firm cooperation. As in Western Europe, the broadcasting field was the province of a transnational organisation called OIRT (Organisation Internationale de Radiodiffusion et de Télévision) and Intervision, which fostered the exchange of technical information and programming. They were an arena for the circulation of news, sport and culture. Their common framework was dictated mainly by the Soviet news agency TASS, which prescribed a general agenda especially for international news. While the Soviet television imported only 5 per cent of its programme, the proportion of foreign programmes in the rest of Eastern Europe ranged from 17 per cent in Poland to 45 per cent in Bulgaria in the early 1970s – especially from the Soviet Union (Mihelj, in Imre et al. 2013: 15). Nevertheless, the Soviet Union never managed to achieve the same dominance or presence in East European cinema and television as the United States in the West.

With respect to television, shared programming was not restricted to East European contributions in any case but included Western programmes in equal measure. This meant that in 1968 a good 42 per cent of 'foreign' programmes in the GDR came from 'capitalistic' countries, with the Socialist Intervision acquiring over a thousand Eurovision programmes per year during the 1970s, but only a few hundred programmes per year making the journey from Eastern to Western Europe (Eugster 1983: 185f., 231; Heimann, in Lindenberger 2006: 254). This exchange pointed up some striking differences: in Poland and Yugoslavia, American series like *Sesame Street* were already being aired during the 1970s, whereas they were banned as 'imperialistic' in the Soviet Union (Eugster 1983: 172, 186). Intervision even regularly broadcast Western news reports, especially after 1976. Most prominently, Czechoslovakia and Poland acquired a great deal of Western material (Mihelj, in Imre et al. 2013: 17), and since 1981 nearly all Socialist countries have aired Western films in equally large measure. In post-invasion Czechoslovakia, light entertainment programmes increased in an attempt to win the support of the people and prevent more of them watching Western programmes (Bren 2010: 121, 202). Television built visual bridges between East and West, and it would be well to examine more closely the social consequences of this phenomenon.

However, written media also crossed the borders between East and West. Uncensored underground 'tamizat' texts, as mentioned earlier, were transferred and translated from East to West. These were not only political transmissions, but also cultural exchanges (including art, photos and videos), which contributed to the rise in relevant intellectual debate (Kind-Kovács and Labov 2013: 11–15). Sometimes such illegal publications were printed in Western media or broadcasted in the East by Radio Free Europe.

The most extensive research on Communist media has been done on the GDR (focusing on the dominance of the SED: Holzweißig 2002; on content and appropriation: Zahlmann 2010). Here the radical changes in media politics that aimed to secure the dominance of the KPD (German Communist Party) and the communist successor party SED (German Unity Party). These were already being rigorously enforced in the immediate aftermath of 1945. In the field of journalism, publishers were forcibly dispossessed, long-established newspapers rich in tradition were silenced, and the local papers that had been so characteristic of Germany were shut down, yet SOZ (Soviet Occupied Zone) and 'administrative' area newspapers were subsidised. Be that as it may, the SOZ brought back some earlier German traditions. The party-affiliated press structure so typical for Germany was revived: each party was allotted one leading newspaper and several regional ones. The papers affiliated with the KPD and SED respectively were increasingly favoured with larger paper supplies and higher print runs, while others soon felt the effects of censorship and repression. Another German tradition revived after 1947 was the nationalisation of radio, with the SED carrying out a radical personnel purge on the basis of political criteria. In similar fashion the Soviet administration and the SED took over the Ufa, changed its name to DEFA (Deutsche Film-Aktiengesellschaft) and created a nationalised system of film production.

As problematic as a comparison between National Socialism and the GDR may be in many respects, it would be rewarding to do more research in the field of media production in view of the fact that both dictatorships developed similar media policies on an institutional level, although they often applied them differently (Classen 2007). With the 'Department of

Agitation and Propaganda in the Central Committee of the SED', a government agency once more controlled censorship and opinion-making. As had been the case with National Socialism, dissatisfaction with their own propaganda and monitoring apparatus led to constant restructuring (Holzweißig 2002: 1–31). Directives given to the press also tied in with pre-1945 practice. In the GDR there was a renewal of verbose and occasionally grotesquely detailed guidelines issued for newspapers, and at the same time complaints about the papers' conformity. No reports are on record about journalists protesting against these directives (cf. Wilke 2007: 316). There are hardly any studies on how these directives were implemented, not even for the GDR. As had been the case before 1945, the forced conformity of the news also facilitated the existence of a national news agency with an absolute monopoly, the Allgemeine Deutsche Nachrichtenagentur (ADN), which broadcast news acceptable to the SED. Since only the SED organ, *Neues Deutschland*, was permitted to have foreign correspondents, news from abroad lay completely in the hands of the ADN. At the same time they wrote reports not meant for publication but rather to serve as confidential background information for the party leadership. Yet in spite of this key role played by the ADN, hardly any research has been done on their modus operandi.

Like the National Socialists, the SED relied less on day-to-day censorship than on channelling public opinion by their choice of journalists. The waves of purges in 1948/49 affected not only middle-class and Socialist journalists but numerous Communists as well. And once again journalists had to endure show trials intended to intimidate their colleagues. The selection of journalists on the basis of their ideological leanings was now effected less via professional associations than by schooling. While the National Socialist *Reichspresseschule* (school of journalism) had enjoyed only brief success, the Marxist-influenced journalism course at the University of Leipzig now more or less guaranteed employment, although it was still possible to enter the profession laterally. Because of this system of pre-selection, media routine was characterised not so much by daily censorship as by internalised conformity.

As was the case in other dictatorships, the GDR media left some calculated leeway for free development in a few areas, but these were particularly restricted. Satirical journals like *Eulenspiegel* were allowed to make jokes about daily life but not about the system itself. Even so, in 1988 there were as many as thirty-four weeklies and magazines published by churches and religious communities, with a total circulation of 376,000. They were, however, subject to pre-censorship and therefore some sought to align themselves with the SED (Rosenstock 2002: 325–47). A diverse underground press similar to that in Poland never developed in the GDR, either because the system was more repressive or conformity was greater. Protest via the media tended to be articulated through music or the secret reading of 'illicit literature' smuggled into large libraries or churches where it was passed on (Lokatis and Sonntag 2008: 17f.). It was not until the 1980s that illegal printers' shops produced leaflets and short-lived magazines.

Media policy in the GDR, as in the Nazi era, was still defined by directional changes, since ideological requirements were often hard to reconcile with media logic and the public's desire for entertainment. Whereas political reports comprised a large part of broadcasting time until 1953, in 1955 music accounted for more than two-thirds of programming. In the course of the following two decades radio listeners' influence increased, as GDR radio had also developed into an 'incidental' medium in which ideological harangues were deemed inappropriate (Arnold and Classen 2004: 15f.). In the interest of preserving social harmony and impelled by a sense of resignation stemming from the popularity of Western competition, a more apolitical concept of entertainment asserted itself in GDR radio during the 1980s (Larkey 2007: 17). By the same token the GDR had to respond to listeners' wishes in regard to broadcasting patterns. After the SED had replaced the old regional stations with local studios offering only limited broadcasting time, there was a great deal of criticism; the old system was revived in 1953, and 'Radio DDR' that included regional programming segments soon became the most popular channel (Dussel 1999: 134f.). As in the 1930s, listeners' demands forced the dictatorships to depart somewhat from their ideas of centralism and the belief that the state was entitled to guide the thoughts of the public (Marßolek and von Saldern 1998, Vol. 2: 131).

Much the same can be said for GDR television, which a research group has recently analysed in detail based on four thousand television programmes. Television in the GDR was originally intended to fulfil the role of 'collective agitator, propagandist and organiser for the ideas of Socialism', something Lenin had already required of the press (Steinmetz and Viehoff 2008: 16). After lengthy theoretical discussions, the number of non-political and entertaining television programmes was increased. In contrast to television series of the previous decade, the infallible Socialistic personality now took a back seat; programming became more international and adapted Western formats (ibid.: 17; 326f.).

In this process radio and television became the most important bridge between East and West. The airing of Western programming was at first opposed in the GDR only to be increasingly tolerated from the 1960s onwards. In a sense, this served as a kind of stabilising outlet and substitute for the lack of opportunities for travel (Hoff, in Hickethier 1998: 285). Attempts to spin a politically correct interpretation of Western television via *'Der Schwarze Kanal'* were a failure. Western television remained an alternative world on which the GDR remained unilaterally fixed. When innovations did occur, they were often a direct reaction on the part of GDR broadcasting to changes in Western programming, and they responded by altering their own programme formats – from crime thrillers to political roundtables.

Whereas research into viewing and listening habits was well established in the West, the SED media had little knowledge of their audience. The infrequent surveys they conducted were hardly adequate for registering Western television and radio consumption. Our present-day knowledge of GDR media behaviour is based on various sources. Surveys conducted in the West German refugee camp in Friedberg among people who were relocating from the GDR have shown that about 82 per cent of them watched Western TV programmes 'nearly every day', and a further 12 per cent watched them 'often', especially political programmes like the '*Tagesschau*' and news magazine programmes. While West German television films aroused some interest, American ones were watched less often (Dussel 1999: 176f.). Subsequent surveys conducted by Michael Meyen qualify this to a degree: according to his findings, GDR radio broadcasts accounted for about half of the listening time, as people enjoyed listening to regional news and music (Meyen 2003: 128–37).

Thus was the Cold War waged in the media. Radio especially was often utilised in this way during the 1950s and 1960s. Besides the 'Deutschlandsender der DDR' many smaller GDR broadcasters also targeted West Germans, for example the 'Deutscher Freiheitssender 904', that was intended to suggest the presence of ongoing underground activity by the recently outlawed KPD; night-time programmes for West German shift workers or 'Radio Berlin International', that was broadcast internationally in many different languages (Dussel 1999: 136). Since the number of listeners remained very low, the GDR eventually closed down these channels. It would be worth examining more closely the degree to which a West German audience tuned in to normal GDR television programming. One may assume that in addition to entertainment programmes (like Ufa films, sports or the children's programme *Sandmännche*n) people watched political programmes out of curiosity, perhaps with an ironic eye, perhaps as a 'corrective' for the Western media. Be that as it may, the influence of the Stasi on Western media has probably been overestimated by a few publications, although several journalists in the Federal Republic of Germany have discovered some evidence of Stasi activity (Knabe 2001).

As for the GDR press, one is struck by its high circulation figures: the number of daily newspapers rose from 4 million in the 1950s to 9.7 million in 1988, a number exceeded only by Japan. Many people subscribed to several newspapers. To be sure, these numbers were made possible because prices were kept low by state subsidies, as there were very few classified advertisements in Socialism. Later surveys reported that circulation was so high because people were interested in the local sections, and the papers could be used as wrapping material (Meyen 2003: 105–8). At the same time high circulation numbers may be seen as indicating a certain approval of the regime; however, emotional ties to newspapers were not unduly strong, as shown by the sharp decline in circulation after 1990. On the other hand, Western print media played almost no role in the GDR because selling and importing them was forbidden. Only the SED leadership took intense notice of the Western press and often seized upon the positions they published in order to deprecate them.

On the whole, Communist media policy in the GDR and Eastern Europe must be said to have failed. This is amply demonstrated by the rapid breakdown after 1989. The ideological standards of the Socialists corresponded neither to media logic nor the interests of the public. Socialism considered itself to be on the right side of morality because it forbade tabloid journalism, pornography and rock music. Yet the constant guidelines imposed on Communist Eastern Europe precluded any development of a popular culture comparable to that in the West, and this in turn increased imports.

The question of what role the media actually played in the collapse of Communism is difficult to answer. Western stations like 'Radio Free Europe', 'Voice of America' and 'RIAS' were important sources of information and support for the opposition. It is estimated that a third of the urban adult population and about half of the East European adult population listened to Western broadcasts after the 1950s (Johnson and Parta 2010: 345). They were especially important in the context of crises – like the Soviet invasion of Afghanistan or the catastrophe at the Chernobyl nuclear power plant in 1986. A direct influence on the protests of 1989 is stated for some countries (Ratesh, in ibid.: 225). Radio Free Europe seemed to be especially reliable, because it broadcast reports and letters from those countries, including about problems of the Western world. Simultaneously they promoted interest for and understanding of the pop-and-consumption culture of the West, and this in turn probably accelerated the turning away from Communism. One should consider whether the East European media also fostered a less politicised atmosphere that expedited rejection of the ritualised Communistic party culture and thus had a politically relevant impact in the 1980s. It is precisely this day-to-day significance of the media that offers a huge field of research for studies of Eastern and Central Europe.

The Polish underground press laid the groundwork for the radical changes that came at the end of the 1980s (cf. Aumente et al. 1999: 41–78). It used the influence of its mass circulation to good effect to question the regime's legitimacy, stabilised the work of the opposition and in 1989 laid the foundation for the dynamic spread of the *Gazeta Wyborcza* as the first Solidarność newspaper that was not forbidden (Paczkowski 1997). The media also played a great role in changes in the GDR. Western television informed the citizenry about protests and offered them an opportunity to communicate indirectly with the ruling powers and bring pressure to bear. Furthermore, the presence of Western cameras at demonstrations afforded a degree of protection against police brutality that would have completely discredited the SED regime (Czaplicki 2000). Then there was the construction that the media placed on a press conference held on 8 November 1989 by Günter Schabowski in front of television cameras. A member of the ZK, (*Zentralkomitee*, central committee), he mistakenly announced the immediate opening of the border and this led indirectly to a premature fall of the Berlin Wall.

Media and the Establishment of Democracy in West Germany

After 1945, Western Europe experienced a multifaceted transformation of its media landscape. The Western Allies reorganised the media systems in the occupied countries with a view to establishing democracy. Yet there were also changes in countries not under occupation. At the time, the experience of war and growing fear of Communism had led to growing attempts by the states to exercise control over the media, and by so doing, promote national unity. In liberated France, for example, the media experienced an increase in state ownership, control and subsidies, and in the process private radio stations were nationalised because they had collaborated with the Germans. Radio broadcasting was monopolised and largely monitored by the state in form of the newly established 'Radiodiffusion Française' (RDF; and after 1949: 'Radiodiffusion-Télévision Française', RTF). Equally marked was the influence of the French state on the newly established news agency 'Agence France-Presse' as well as on those segments of the press that received state subsidies. Structural changes were also at work in the print media. Many publishers who had collaborated with the Germans were removed. As it had above all been the Parisian press that the Germans had exploited for their own ends, the provincial press now experienced an upswing (Kuhn 2002: 27).

A glance at Italy makes clear exactly how the adaptation of Western role models after 1945 was carried out in an opinionated and pro-government manner. The Italians launched a broadcasting system modelled on the BBC and subject to public law, but after a brief phase of anti-Fascist consensus, the Christian Democratic government exerted direct centralistic influence on the stations RAI (Radio Audizioni Italia) and RAI-TV (Televisione Italia) respectively, that belonged to a state holding company. Since the Italians got most of their information from the radio, this was of great political significance. There was a certain continuity in print media, which were less popular; newspapers were polarised along party lines and former Fascists were rarely dismissed, so the old structures survived (Mancini 2005: 30–35). The fact that newspapers were mainly owned by industrial corporations strengthened the media's affinity with the Christian Democrats and cemented their dominance into the 1980s.

The media of the conquered nations Japan and Germany experienced an especially great upheaval. The victorious Western powers aimed to instrumentalise them in two ways as an aid to establishing democracy: they would teach people democratic mores by their content and format, and also by their liberal structure that had no state affiliations. In Japan, which was de facto occupied by the United States alone, the Americans applied elements of their own media model. They abolished the previous state monopoly and established a dual system in the individual prefectures that consisted of nationwide public programming financed by fees and commercial radio financed by advertising. The competition was intended to prevent any monopolisation of opinion building. In like manner the occupiers promoted American reporting formats such as interviews with the citizenry in order to make radio content more democratic (Saito, in Gunaratne 2000: 563; White 2005: 85). The transformation of the press was more short lived: although the introduction of press freedom ushered in a brief period when numerous new papers flourished, it was only a few years before the established publishers reasserted themselves and the newspaper landscape became concentrated in fewer hands.

The new media order in West Germany was similar in structure but considerably more complicated. At first the four Allied Powers worked together, but after a short time they proceeded in different ways. According to an agreement made in November 1944, all the German media were prohibited and only Allied media were published at first. In a second step, Germans were allowed to have licensed print media under Allied supervision, with the licensees having to undergo a background check (Koszyk, in Wilke 1999: 32). This complicated system of reorganisation and control shows what great significance the Allies attributed to the media in the process of 're-education'.

Historians have long rejected the concept of 'Zero Hour', since longer-range changes or continuities still played a dominant role in 1945. As far as the media are concerned, however, this concept is considered at least partly justified, since changes here were fundamental (Frei and Schmitz 1999: 184). Yet the scope of these historic media changes was quite varied. In the Western Zones many publishers and publicists with a shady past had to cease work, at least until 1948/49, or keep a low profile by working for small newspapers. Managers of leading NSDAP papers generally made a complete change, moving to related fields like advertising. This opened up great career opportunities for young, unencumbered publishers like Rudolf Augstein and Axel Springer, who had hitherto scarcely been prominent as journalists, although Springer at least came from a Hamburg publishing family (cf. Schwarz 2008: 93–128). At the same time, however, recent case studies have revealed that there was greater continuity in the personnel of the middle-class press and radio, and that professional experience counted for more than having a clean political vest. An analysis of 308 postwar journalists in Hamburg revealed a continuity of 57 per cent (Sonntag 2006: 297; Führer 2008: 118), and after 1949 not only did former publishers reappear, but key positions in many supraregional papers were in the hands of journalists who had supported National Socialism prior to 1945 (Hachmeister and Siering 2002).

On the other hand, there was a break with the past in the structure of the daily press. The retention of old newspaper names was prohibited, and licensing limitations fostered the formation of a regional press with wide circulation – and this continues to be characteristic of the German media landscape today. This resulted in a total of 178 licensed daily newspapers in 753 editions by 1948. The British granted licences to *party-affiliated* Germans, with the most recent free elections determining the ratio. The Americans, on the other hand, experimented with editorial staffs made up of journalists with different political backgrounds. Both these approaches were intended to secure democratic pluralism, but they favoured journalists with recognizable party leanings. Part of the 're-education' was an attempt to entrench Anglo-Saxon journalistic techniques. Training courses, trips to the United States and guidelines communicated standards such as the separation of news and opinion and fact-oriented objective reporting. One leading newspaper per occupation zone served as a model and a part of cultural diplomacy. Nevertheless, the success of these efforts was at first limited (cf. Gienow-Hecht 1999) and licensed print media like *Die ZEIT* criticised the Allies harshly – in particular their de-Nazification and reform programmes (Janßen, von Kuenheim and Sommer 2006: 44–67). By contrast, the newsreels remained in Allied hands until 1949, as they were apparently credited with being particularly influential.

Media content was also an important element of the Western Allies' programme of 're-education'. Radio, print media and newsreels reported on the crimes of the National Socialists, the trials of Nazi war criminals and the achievements of democracy. However, viewing the shocking documentary films about the concentration camps that were shown in 1945/46 was not compulsory, as has often been claimed, and most of the public considered them to be reliable documentation (Weckel 2006). Seen in this light, the effect of this 'education by shock' should not be underestimated. After 1946 the Allies relied more on entertaining and promotional films – for example, the so-called 'Marshall Plan Films'. But here, too the Germans countered with their own pictorial interpretation of history. Pictures of cities in rubble replaced the images of concentration camps, and this became the symbol of German victimhood (Glasenapp 2008: 106–23). Starting in the early 1950s, photographs of German refugees fleeing from the former Eastern Provinces fulfilled the same purpose (Knoch 2001: 284–323).

The Allies also worked to democratise radio programming. In place of government supervision a state-owned model was put into place, patterned on the BBC. It was to be financed by fees and administered by a board in order to prevent a renewal of state influence. The governments of the German states, however, quickly attempted to establish as much influence as possible by filling directory boards and management posts with representatives of the government and the political parties (Kutsch, in Wilke 1999: 73–79). In this way the majority parties were able to influence staffing, political commentary and critical satires (Rüden, in Rüden and Wagner 2005: 119f.).

From the 1950s onwards, media development in the German Federal Republic once again followed international trends. The market for print media declined everywhere. By 1974 newspapers in France had shrunk to half of their postwar numbers, and in the same year in Great Britain the four biggest publishers dominated two-thirds of the market (Kuhn 2002: 25; Williams 2010: 214). Thus these strong personalities in the publishing field were vicarious representatives of the media's power. Yet West German local papers that had flourished after 1949 also began to die out after 1954. Although total circulation actually grew during the 1950s, many counties now possessed only a single local paper. From an economic standpoint, this can be explained by technical innovation and rising labour costs. Seen from a historico-cultural standpoint, altered local and religious identities had opened the way to regional newspapers all could share. This both resulted from and fostered the erosion of groupings based on differing religious and ideological views.

On the other hand, the market share of tabloids grew, and 1952 witnessed the meteoric rise of the *Bild Zeitung* that patterned itself on British tabloids like the *Daily Mirror*. Within a few years it had the highest circulation of any paper in Europe. Until 1958 it almost completely eschewed political reporting and rarely took a stand on policies. Any political power it had during the early days of the Federal Republic was on the local and regional level, and its influence on national politics, even at a later date, has often been overrated (Führer 2007: 10–14). In other countries, tabloid journalism first began gathering steam in the 1960s: in Austria with the re-establishment of the *Neue Kronen-Zeitung*, and in Switzerland with *Blick*. The extent to which tabloid journalism was dependent on cultural influences can be seen in Italy where high-circulation sports journals appeared rather than big tabloids. The losers in this development were the papers of political parties and religious denominations. This was not yet foreseeable in the aftermath of 1945. In many countries, particularly the Netherlands, Austria, Italy and the German Federal Republic, there was to a certain extent a re-establishment of denominational or Social Democratic groupings that had their own print media to propagate their ideas. This state of affairs largely came to an end at the beginning of the 1960s. In Great Britain left-wing newspapers like the *Daily Herald* and *News Chronicle*, and in Germany the SPD press, disappeared almost completely – and not merely because they had failed to modernise. These left-wing papers suffered in equal measure because financing depended more and more on advertising, which tended to benefit middle-class and popular newspapers (Curran and Seaton 1985: 106). The working class now increasingly read conservative tabloids like *The Sun*, *Neue Kronen-Zeitung* or *BILD*, which probably accelerated their estrangement from the left-wing parties in the medium term. The SPD's attempt to establish a Social Democratic tabloid press was a failure (Danker et al. 2003: 161). More detailed historical studies of their impact and application are not yet available, particularly not for the German Federal Republic. Newer studies stress their opinionated, mocking arrogance and the influence of readers' social status on interpretation.

During the 1950s the media culture also passed through a transitional phase between the values of the late nineteenth century and the liberalisation that unfolded during the 1960s. Therefore governments often attempted to exercise control, especially in France and Italy, but in West Germany as well. At the same time the Adenauer government largely failed in its plans for nationwide regulatory media legislation, pro-government television and the establishment of a pro-government quality newspaper. Adenauer had more success with the *Neue Deutsche Wochenschau*, that placed the Chancellor in the spotlight with political reports that were presented in an un-political and entertaining manner – whether they were visits to foreign countries with charmingly exotic backgrounds or his birthday celebrations at home with his family (Schwarz 2002: 352–66). The political opposition, on the other hand, was confronted with the problem that their criticism was very difficult to present in a visualised manner.

This transitional character of the 1950s is also evident in West European radio. Programmes for the educated middle class continued to occupy a good deal of programming time, with musical broadcasts comprising only about half. These often consisted of classical music played by the stations' own orchestras. Although the proportion of informational programming on topics of the day increased, political reporting and commentary outside the news reports were rare, even on the BBC. In West Germany, Union politicians most prominently, but also a few Social Democrats, actually denied the right of radio broadcasters to 'propagate their own opinions'. While political commentaries on NWDR (North West German Broadcasting) became rarer, voices from the government, the parties and organisations increased (Steinmetz, in Rüden and Wagner 2005: 327–30). Political programming was not very popular in any case (Schildt 1995: 233).

More recent historical research has also studied the radio as an element of day-to-day culture. Especially in the postwar era it fostered a stable daily rhythm and feeling of normalcy, regional identity and a sense of regional belonging, and influenced gender roles, as it was a 'feminine domestic space' particularly during the day (Badenoch 2008: 125). Until the 1950s, radio was the medium that occupied leisure time most fully. On average, people listened to the radio for three hours every day, usually in company with their families in the evenings, but women often listened during the day while doing their housework. Listeners preferred light entertainment, informative programmes and local radio stations. Variety and quiz shows were especially popular, as was folk music, but news also (Schildt 1995: 214–61; Meyen 2002: 115). The triumphal progress of these popular entertainment broadcasts was facilitated by the introduction of radios with VHF (FM) frequencies. At first the number of regional programmes doubled, and then during the 1960s nationwide programming with diverse content asserted itself, broadcasting both light entertainment and more sophisticated fare.

Both the Cold War and radio technology changed international broadcasting culture during the 1950s. The introduction of VHF frequencies was especially expeditious in Germany because of the dearth of both radio sets and frequencies after the war, and this turned the radio into a regional medium. This has continued into the Internet Age, since listeners apparently prefer their radio stations to have a local orientation. At the same time the Cold War fostered the international character of radio by expanding specific foreign stations that promulgated their worldviews. Next to the big stations that emerged during the 1930s and 1940s (like Voice of America and BBC World), the Federal Republic launched the 'Deutsche Welle', a station that was to spread (West) German culture and views: first to Eastern Europe during the 1960s, and then to South East Europe, India and parts of Africa. In this way, Greek immigrants in the Federal Republic, for example, had the opportunity to communicate via the Deutsche Welle with the Greek people during the dictatorship in that country. Unfortunately, more detailed studies on the workings of the Deutsche Welle are not yet available. Important impulses continue to come from the private station Radio Luxemburg, whose trans-border modern music broadcasts appeal to young people especially.

This mélange of tradition, innovation and exchange is also evident in the cinema. In all the Western democracies fairly strict control of movies remained common into the 1950s. Thus in 1934 the American film industry, fearing state censorship, pledged itself to abide by the moral guidelines of the so-called 'Hays Code', adherence to which was monitored by the Production Code Administration. In 1949 West Germany introduced the state-authorised 'Freiwillige Selbstkontrolle der Filmwirtschaft' (FSK) based on the American model of compulsory self-censorship voluntarily undertaken, with films being scrutinised by representatives of the cinema industry and the 'public sector' (youth organisations and churches). During the 1950s the FSK forbade as many as 150 films and ordered cuts to be made in approximately 900, which amounted to a censorship rate of 5 per cent (Buchloh 2002: 210; more balanced: Kniep 2010). In addition there were cases of direct political intervention by ministries

– such as directives from the Defence Ministry in the case of war movies and from the Interior Ministry and the Chancellor's Office if films dealt with the Nazi past. The 'Inter-Ministry Committee' monitored the import of films from Eastern Europe. The state additionally exerted its influence through specific subsidies and tax breaks (Hugo, in Zuckermann 2003: 69f.). Censorship continued to be justified in the name of manners and morals. This was augmented by anti-Communist arguments or claims that rearmament and international understanding might be endangered. In many cases censorship was applied in order to prevent critical scrutiny of the past. Foreign films, too, were forbidden in the Federal Republic, with similar arguments. For instance Rossellini's masterpiece *Rome, Open City* was prohibited in West Germany until 1961, because it showed the cruelty of German Gestapo; and other films were radically shortened or incorrectly translated (like *Casablanca*).

A comparable control of the media of this period is also evident in magazines and literature, which were subject to examination by the 'Bundesprüfstelle für jugendgefährdende Schriften' (Federal Inspection Authority for Writings Liable to Corrupt the Young). Based on the Law for the Protection of Children and Youth, the Federal Ministry of the Interior and the State Ministries for Youth caused roughly six hundred books and about a thousand magazines, comics, and other media to be placed on their index between 1953 and 1963. This occurred mostly because of depictions of nudity, but also if there were negative representations of society and its elites, as in the case of Ulrich Schamoni's novel *Dein Sohn lässt grüßen* (Buchloh 2002: 132–36). In the field of cultural policy, the Adenauer era thus demonstrated a restorative character that was nevertheless in line with international tendencies.

While the number of cinemagoers in the United States and Great Britain had already decreased considerably during the 1950s, the cinema in Germany counted record numbers as late as 1956, since television did not become established as a mass medium until the following decade. There is only limited evidence for the oft-feared Americanisation of German cinema. West German films were very much more successful because they strongly mirrored the taste of the indigenous public. New German productions as well as remakes were seen by about 45 per cent of viewers, whereas American films reached only 30 per cent. Conversely, German films were quite successful in Austria, but in the rest of the world hardly at all. From an aesthetic point of view Adenauer-era cinema is considered lowbrow, and therefore it was spoken of as 'superficial cinema of pop and sentimentality' that left 'no traces' behind (Göttler, in Jacobsen, Kaes and Prinzler 2004: 171). Yet there was a certain continuity with the shattered Ufa, since former Ufa employees were part of this cinema boom (Kreimeier 1992: 365–87).

Historians have variously taken an interest in West German postwar cinema as a means of examining the culture of that time. The fact that

Heimatfilm – sentimental films usually set in idyllic rural surroundings – accounted for about a quarter of the total West German productions before 1964 was interpreted as providing a means of escapism from the ruined cities, forced displacement, and Nazi past (Wilharm 2006: 194). A great deal of attention was paid to war films, which were successful in both Western Europe and the United States. They frequently showed brave soldiers who valiantly proved their mettle by asserting themselves against their cowardly superiors. In this way these films helped to deal with both the individual and collective past, and were thus part of a historical policy that rehabilitated the Wehrmacht in the wake of German rearmament (Hugo, in Zuckermann 2003: 76; Paul 2004: 274).

Critical Turnabout: Media and Democratic Cultures past 1960

About 1960 the cinema experienced a crisis on an international scale. Genres like westerns, *Heimatfilm* and war films became less important, and at the end of the 1960s, cinemas were frequently closed down or used for showing sex films. In West Germany, approximately 800 million viewers per year had attended the cinema during the 1950s, but by the end of the 1960s there were scarcely 180 million (Grob, in Jacobsen, Kaes and Prinzler 2004: 217). This was not only the fault of television but rather of a new consumer culture, more attractively furnished homes, and opportunities for free-time activities available in cities and suburban residences (Bakker 2008: 405f.; Williams 2010: 186).

After 1960 this development gave the cinema new scope to produce art films and films with socially critical themes. In Western Europe there were similar demands for programmatic and aesthetic reform. François Truffaut's *Les Quatre Cents Coups* (1959) stood for the transition from a 'cinéma de papa' towards 'Nouvelle Vague' in France. In Great Britain, *Room at the Top* (1959) signalled a change in the direction of the British 'New Wave' cinema. In West Germany films such as *Kirmes* (1959), that took a critical view of society and the past, rang in the advent of the 'New German Film', the film d'auteur and the short art film. Such reforms were formulated by the 'DOC 59' group (1959) and the 'Oberhausener Manifesto' (1962). Even the United States joined this trend during the course of the 1960s, with 'New Hollywood' now producing films containing more social criticism. Films of this kind were prestigious and thus fostered the growth of critical attitudes at an early stage – especially among younger academics. However, these films influenced only a small number of viewers.

After 1960 the field of journalism experienced a similar transformation. Critical, social and political confidence of the press increased. In the United

States, authors like Tom Wolfe demanded a 'new journalism' that concerned itself more with subjective reporting about subcultures and social problems. In the case of the German Federal Republic, one could discern a change from 'consensus journalism' towards critical journalism, a phenomenon that Christina von Hodenberg attributes to generational change: journalists born around 1930 and strongly influenced by the establishment of democracy were now joining editorial teams of both newspapers and radio (von Hodenberg 2006). By the same token politicians changed the way they dealt with the media, attempting to involve them in a more cooperative way, as did Willy Brandt and John F. Kennedy (Münkel 2005).

Since the 1960s, the number of scandals in Western countries, brought up by investigative journalists, has increased. These media scandals challenge politicians and often force them to step down. The Spiegel Affair in 1962 had a similar impact on the political and journalistic culture in Europe to 'Watergate' in the United States. This liberalisation of journalistic work was promoted by the highest courts. In the United States the Supreme Court proved itself to be a decisive defender of press freedom in 1964 with 'New York Times vs. Sullivan', in which it found that erroneous statements about public figures were actionable only in the case of intentional falsehood and actual malice. This meant that the media no longer had to fear financial ruin from libel suits because of journalistic mistakes (Lewis 2008: 51). In West Germany the Federal Constitutional Court several times defended freedom of the press from state intervention, and the Spiegel Affair was followed by several other laws in the Federal States that protected the work of journalists.

Around 1960, photojournalism also began a transformation. Inspired by the images in *Life* magazine and by human-interest photography, pictures increasingly showed the fates of little-known individuals, with critical intent. The big weekly magazines often used contrastive arrangements of photographs to give greater emphasis to their critical accompanying texts. Instead of pictures of statesmen or the Pope, newspapers readers and television viewers were now often confronted with images of superannuated party members or empty churches (Städter, in Bösch and Hölscher 2010: 104f.). In this respect the change in aesthetics may very well have influenced the change in social attitudes. At the end of the 1960s, the Vietnam War in particular demonstrated the power of such images: photos of the massacre at My Lai or the naked girl Kim Phuc fleeing from the bombs became icons and turned the war into a moral defeat for the United States. So far little research has been done about how editorial staff selected and edited the pictures or how photo agencies marketed them (Zierenberg 2013). Hardly anything is as yet known about their appropriation or the degree to which these 'global icons' had any meaning in Eastern or Southern Europe, or even in Africa.

This critical turnabout in media culture also tends to put the innovative force of the '68 Movement into perspective. It was not the student protests that first created a critical public that grappled with deficits of democracy, problems of social injustice, or the Nazi past. It was the fact that the '68 generation had been socialised during the aforementioned period of media change and had then seized upon and exaggerated the criticism voiced by the media and taken it to extremes. Many of these '68ers aimed their protests at all established media, accusing not only the 'Springer Press' of falsifying public opinion. They put their trust in homemade flyers, posters and public presence instead. Nevertheless the '68ers frequently cooperated with the modern mass media and made use of their logic. Protests and happenings were staged for cameras, and journalists were freely admitted to events and communes, which helped to form their public image as well as their self-image. It was the media that gave these students – who were a relatively small group in society – their great significance and also shaped it: the mass media linked individual actions, turning them into a movement; they then personalised them and fostered the international exchange of protest forms (Kraushaar 2001; Vogel 2010). Also the American Civil Rights Movement benefited from its presence on television, a medium that, especially in the Southern States, broke through the conservative and racist attitudes of the local press and broadcasters (Hilmes 2004: 210f.). The same is true of the New Social Movements of the 1970s, whose local origins were given universal meaning by the media. But the terrorists of the 1970s also interacted with them: they made expert use of innovations (like videos and Polaroid pictures) and sent their blackmailing messages via the international press so as to put pressure on political leaders and influence policy. It was only because of the German media that individual terrorist groups like the Red Army Faction came to prominence. By the same token expressions like 'sympathiser' were coined in the media (Elter 2008).

The '68ers and the new social movements tried to establish their own alternative media in the 1970s. What was aimed for was a 'new type of press': papers were to be democratically produced by editorial collectives, with integrated readers' comments; circulation was to be kept small and have a local orientation; they were to be independent of advertising; and finally they were to use their critical style to stir up the readers. Even an alternative newpaper, the *tageszeitung* (called *taz*), was founded in 1979, which followed these principles and was closely linked with the new Green party (Rösch-Sondermann 1988; Büteführ 1995: 471f.; Holtz-Bacha, in Wilke 1999: 331). A few alternative local pirate radio stations emerged in Germany too, and a few of them, like Radio Dreyeckland, still exist today. Furthermore, international news services came into being as supra-regional links in several countries. Among these the first was the U.S. 'Liberation News Service' (beginning in 1967), the 'Agence de la Presse Libération' in France, the English 'People's News Service', and from 1973 the German 'Informationsdienst zur Verbreitung unterbliebener Nachrichten' (Information Service for the Dissemination of Missing News) (Stamm 1988: 72). The track record was sobering. The urban magazines in big cities like Frankfurt, Hamburg and Berlin survived to today but have been commercialised since the 1980s. The news services collapsed, with the few supra-regional papers like *Libération* in France and *taz* in Germany able to survive only in a financially ailing state and by changing their principles. By this token the *taz* abolished the rotation system among its journalists, introduced a small sports section and moved readers' letters to the back (Flieger 1992: 194). The influence of these papers on the media public remained small, but at least they contributed to a stabilisation of an alternative milieu from which the Green Party was able to profit. However the press of the 1970s and 1980s was characterised less by a swing to the Left than by political polarisation. Its positions were now more belligerent, whether they were Right or Left.

A Global Television Age?

In all industrialised countries, television is the activity that defines leisure most strongly. U.S. citizens already spent four to five hours in front of the television as far back as 1957, with Germans and Britons spending two hours watching television during the 1960s (Stumberger 2002: 118, 174). Thus for over five decades television has played a crucial role in most people's lives in these countries. Nevertheless historians have so far paid little attention to this medium. Media and communication scholars have conducted numerous studies on the history of television that address its technical development, organisation, and programming history (cf. e.g. for the FRG: Kreuzer and Thomsen 1994; and Hickethier 1998; for the GDR: Steinmetz and Viehoff 2008). On the other hand not much research has been done on the social, political and cultural significance of German television in the postwar decades. The fact that in the 1960s, when television became established as a mass medium in Western Europe, values and lifestyles underwent a fundamental change is certainly no coincidence, although processes of change in other areas like consumerism and social behaviour were likewise connected contributing factors. The influence of television on family, on gender roles, politics, sports, culture, education and religious, social and national identities has hardly ever been studied.

Early television was often described as a cannibalistic medium because it adopted several elements from older media. In this remediation, television picked up image, sound and aesthetics from the cinema, news from the newsreels, performances from the theatre and organisation, programming and reception forms from the radio. Whereas in the case of other new media, design and use had initially been quite free, wireless picture transmission immediately stepped into the footsteps of radio – up to and including being placed in the living room and having its programme schedules published in the radio programme guides. On the other hand possible alternative uses analogue to the telephone (picture telephones) or to the phonograph record (video storage) were hardly followed up.

Television, like film and radio, did not have a single inventor. It was based on a multiplicity of loosely linked individual research in various countries (cf. Abramson 1987). A foundation was laid in 1884 by the German engineer Paul Nipkow with a disc that broke up pictures into light and dark signals for purposes of transmission. He never recognised the potential of his patented invention and did not pursue it further. Beginning in the mid-1920s, Germany, Great Britain and the United States made first attempts at transmitting television signals, after radio had suggested possible means of implementation. The Berlin Radio Exhibition of 1928/29 played a prominent role in making television known to the German public, but many were disappointed by its poor picture quality. The world's first regular television operation began in 1935 in National Socialist Germany, and just before Great Britain. This enabled Nazi Germany to propagate its modernity to the world on the eve of the Berlin Olympics. Even later, international sports events continued to spur on the development of television: the 1946 Olympics in London played a defining role in accelerating the re-establishment of British television, the Football World Cup of 1954 introduced it on the European Continent, and the 1960 Rome Olympics led to the exchange of live images between Eastern and Western Europe.

The television of the 1930s differed greatly from that of today. There were usually only two hours of programming time during the evening and the transmission range hardly reached beyond Berlin, London and Paris respectively. Moreover, there were only three thousand sets before the war in London, and in Berlin a mere seventy-five in 1937 (Abramson 1987; Winker 1994: 197). In Berlin 'television rooms' allowed groups of people to view programmes on small screens, and up to ten thousand people daily were said to have watched major events like the Olympics in this way (Winker 1994: 195). Programming already exhibited characteristic elements of later developments: in addition to the news, called 'Aktueller Bildbericht' (topical picture report), there were game shows, music and comedy. Due to technical problems, only major outdoor events were broadcast live – like the coronation of Britain's King George VI in 1937 and the Nürnberg Convention of the Nazi Party in the same year. Since costs were immense and the number of viewers small, television in its early days can best be seen as a prestigious investment that promised participation and was equally opportune for both democracies and dictatorships. However, the Second World War brought an end to television in Great Britain and reduced it mainly to a form of troop entertainment in Germany.

Compared to radio, the spread of television worldwide proceeded more sluggishly. Given the high transmission costs and the prices of the sets themselves, the wealth gap obviously played a crucial role; but cultural and political factors were also important. Television grew to be a mass medium in the homelands of democracy and popular culture. First it spread in the economically powerful United States, which is why it was now internationally regarded as a sign of American modernity. In 1952, when the European Continent was still running test programmes, American television was already serving 18 million viewers. As they had done with radio, many U.S. networks invested in Latin American stations that emerged as early as 1950. In several Latin America countries, up to 80 per cent of television programmes initially came from the United States as a medium of transnational advertising (Sinclair 1999: 13f.).

At the beginning of the 1950s, Great Britain was the only European country where television had obtained a foothold. By 1953 more than half of all adult Britons could watch the coronation of Queen Elizabeth II. The beginning of the Television Age in the rest of the world depended largely on economic power and cultural self-image. In Central Europe and Japan, television grew step by step during the 1950s and became a mass medium after 1960; in the Mediterranean region this did not occur until a decade later. It spread more slowly in France because there was more resentment against the 'American medium', and in Israel it was because of objections from Orthodox Jews that the first programme, an educational one, was not aired until 1966. The spread of television was less uniform still in non-democratic countries. In Socialistic countries as well as in democratic ones, it was related to economic strength and previous media density, which explains why the number of television viewers in the GDR had already equalled that in the German Federal Republic during the 1960s. In economically weak Greece it was only in 1966 that the military dictatorship introduced propagandistic programming. Television broadcasting began a year earlier in Franco's Spain, but since a television set cost about three-quarters of the average annual income, its purchase could often be financed only by working abroad.

In industrialised countries, television ownership around 1960 did not necessarily depend upon a person's degree of wealth. Despite the high costs of sets and television fees, nearly all income groups were quite equally represented. In 1963, 53 per cent of German working-class households owned a television (a disproportionately high number), whilst among white-collar workers, civil servants and especially farmers it was less common. This can be explained by the negative attitudes of German conservatives and the well-educated bourgeoisie towards television.

Once more contrasts were very great in the case of Africa. In some countries television was introduced in the 1960s but in others it was not until the 1980s (Botswana, Somalia and Namibia) and even then it was limited to a few prestige stations in the capital cities. Even in South Africa television did not go on the air until 1976 because the regime feared that the medium would help to strengthen the anti-apartheid movement. To the present day, exceedingly low television density is characteristic of Africa, as is the widespread presence of foreign programmes that are also aired in the national languages. Radio continues to be the most important medium and connects people via regional networks.

In contrast to most other media innovations, television was a national medium from its inception and rapidly developed into a 'national socialising entity' (Fickers 2009: 401). High-frequency broadcasting limited international transmission range, and the live nature of early programming prevented the type of international exchange that had occurred in the early days of film. The fact that everyone watched programmes like the daily news reports did however structure a nationwide rhythm of life and experience, and provided food for discussion.

Furthermore, it is probable that nationwide broadcasting has contributed to the lessening significance of European dialects since the 1950s. Conversely, in countries with more than one television language (e.g. Belgium, Switzerland) separate channels tended to cement cultural differences, whereas the same-language television in different states provided a national bond – like the one between the Federal Republic and the GDR. Even the GDR was able to instil a certain degree of viewer identification with the 'homeland' through its own television programming, at least during the Honecker era of the 1970s and 1980s (Palmowski 2009: 81–89, 120–28). And although American series were internationally successful in the post-1960s, they nevertheless tended to highlight cultural 'otherness'.

From its inception, television has been considered a 'window to the world'. In actual fact, 1950s television presented primarily the world of television studios: game and quiz shows comprised a large segment of the programming, with the addition of informational formats, sports and, to a lesser extent, feature films. A more exact study of early programme content is only possible within certain limits; since very little programming material has been preserved in television archives, researchers have had to rely on programme manuscripts and television guides. It was only at the end of the 1950s that television developed its own independent profile: what had been compilations of newsreel reports now became regular evening news programmes, with newsreaders and documentation; television plays that had resembled stage performances gave way to series and made-for-television movies. Nevertheless, Germany and France still had reservations about these formats because they were considered American and trivial, but sportscasts played an important role in both Western and Socialist countries. An educational programming niche was developed for children, but as with radio, adolescents had to wait until the end of the 1960s for special 'teenager programmes'. A very conspicuous development of the 1960s was that television took on the role of counsellor and adviser – providing educational programming, health counselling and help in coping with problems. But early family entertainment series like *Familie Schölermann* were seen as vehicles for the shaping of viewers' behaviour and teaching etiquette (Hickethier 1998: 159, 216f., 227f.).

One may at least hypothesise about how television changed societal culture. It assuredly contributed to transforming the relationship between private and public spheres: a public field such as politics became more private by virtue of being aired in living rooms and also by the manner of its presentation. Conversely, television helped to publicise and politicise private matters such as family or spousal conflicts. By so doing it probably also influenced changing gender roles. Typical male-dominated public spaces such as the corner pub began to empty out during the 1950s because now men more often spent their evenings at home in the living room with their families, which led to a corresponding increase in home alcohol consumption. As radio had once done, television now structured the daily rhythm of many families, and for this reason media experts ascribe ritual functions to it. Then again, it had a certain democratic component because it held out the promise of participation: whether state function, sports final or musical event – in principle, television granted everyone seemingly direct access to happenings that were otherwise reserved for the elite. Labourers, women and people with little education were already tending to spend more time in front of the television in the 1960s (Stumberger 2002: 118–97).

Television was credited with having great influence from its very beginnings, and since the 1970s American social scientists have carried out empirical studies examining the effects of the media. According to their findings, television has a 'mainstreaming' effect: high television consumption causes ideologically diverse groups to adopt similar positions on controversial issues like abortion or minority rights (Schenk 2007: 596), precisely because television, unlike newspapers, addresses itself to a politically heterogeneous public. Since its aim is to reach everyone – at least potentially – it takes great care to focus on consensus. American studies have also examined television's emotional impact: frequent viewers tend to see the world as more violent, they have more feelings of anxiety and are therefore more likely to react aggressively to threatening situations (Bonfadelli 2004, Vol. 2: 264f.). Another aspect that was examined was the claim dating from the very beginning that television made people stupid, an accusation even levelled against the educational children's programme *Sesame Street* in the early 1970s. In the study, the so-called 'knowledge gap perspective' emerged, according to which better-educated adults and carefully fostered children profit from the media, whereas the others do not. Thus the media reinforce social differences on a cognitive level (ibid., Vol. 1: 254). However, television probably had such an impact precisely because this influence was ascribed to it; and people, not only politicians, adapted to it for that reason.

In respect of its content, television became a medium for politics at a late date and in limited measure. In every country, including most dictatorships, entertainment shows without direct political relevance were the most prevalent in television, although sports reports and crime stories were often presented within a political framework in dictatorships. During the 1950s, political commentaries, even on the BBC, were not written by the stations themselves but by politicians. Political journalism was again pioneered by American television. As early as 1947 there was a U.S. political talk show with journalists (*Meet the Press*), which was later adapted in other countries (*Internationaler Frühschoppen* in West Germany from 1953). Since newspapers were considered political media, television took over their culture of debate, which was still strictly regulated in the Federal Republic (Verheyen, in Bösch and Borutta 2006). Television in the United States also adapted some political magazine programmes from radio formats, for example *See It Now* (CBS, 1951–57), which took a stance on policies with its investigative reporting and helped to bring about the downfall of the communist-hunting Senator McCarthy. This format was picked up by the BBC with its *Panorama* (from 1953), which then in turn appeared under the same name in Germany after 1961 and established critical investigative journalism on German television. Even television in the GDR aired *Prisma* (after 1963), a moderated political magazine programme that allowed at least limited (consumer) criticism and therefore had very many viewers. It would be an important research task to do an international comparison of the style and impact of these political magazine programmes, as they doubtless contributed decisively towards politicising television and society during the 1960s and were therefore fiercely fought over by political parties. In West Germany in particular, moderators were continually being transferred, and competing programmes like *Report, Monitor* and the *ZDF-Magazin* were launched as a means of channelling criticism along party lines.

Furthermore, television transformed the 'old' media, which were now obliged to reposition themselves. Since television dominated the evenings, radio developed into an entirely 'incidental medium', primarily listened to during the day at work or in the car. It was only now, at the end of the 1960s, that the proportion of entertainment and music grew and more Anglo-American music was aired (Dussel 1999: 213). Since adolescents were buying more records, radio stations attempted to hold on to this listener group. The introduction of new radio programmes facilitated this change, since 'serious' music and cultural programmes could now be moved into time slots of their own. All this has led to a significant increase in radio listening since the mid-1970s.

Nor did television replace newspapers and magazines as many people expected. On the contrary, official commissions in West Germany found that during the 1960s income from advertising and circulation rose, even though the fact that publishing was concentrated in a few big companies had caused the demise of some traditional newspapers. In Great Britain this was mainly true for Sunday papers and the provincial press, with the latter additionally suffering from competition from giveaway papers (Williams 2010: 204). Since European newspapers were considered an endangered medium worthy of protection they received state support: in France, Austria, Italy and Scandinavia it was via direct subsidies for some segments of the press, and in other nations like Great Britain and Germany by means of tax breaks (Puppis 2007: 183f.). Television very likely contributed to an increase in the visual content of newspapers and magazines, whose pictorial matter was sometimes as much as 50 per cent (Straßner 2002: 29). It would also be well to examine more closely the extent to which television 'profoundly' changed press photography (Dewitz and Lebeck 2001: 250, 274). Press photos very probably stood on their own as unique critical and artistic commentaries because they no longer simply and primarily depicted events.

Especially hard hit by television was the cinema. Because the numbers of moviegoers had fallen drastically since the 1950s, Hollywood reacted with new recording and playback techniques, epic blockbusters (like *The Ten Commandments*), and specifically targeted young people as a group, since the older generation were more likely to be television viewers. However, television and cinema were not always competitors; in Hollywood, corporations had already had a hand in television productions during the 1950s. Yet cooperation between film and television productions continued to be problematic in Europe because the broadcasting companies produced more made-for-television films of their own (Hilmes, in Nowell-Smith 1996: 468). Nevertheless, in West Germany, too, ambitious films were often made possible only by joint financing. As was the case with radio, cinemas had to diversify during the 1980s and this was accomplished by building multiplexes incorporating several smaller cinemas that showed different films for different target groups.

Although television content was fairly apolitical on the whole, the medium was nevertheless strictly regulated and controlled by politics. In most countries the form of this control was similar to that of radio. In the United States and Latin America, television was commercially organised from its inception and essentially maintained by the big radio stations. Only later did authoritarian regimes and dictatorships in various South American countries limit its variety and tighten state control. Yet other than in Communist dictatorships, private stations continued to exist in several countries (as in Mexico), or state ownership was limited (as in Peru). In the West European democracies on the other hand, the British principle of state-owned television prevailed. Public representatives were responsible for its supervision, and its financing via licensing fees was to guarantee its independence from the state. The actual running of this system, however, turned out to be varied. While in Britain the BBC was in point of fact quite independent, the governments of France and Italy in particular exerted a great deal of influence, as did the major political parties in Germany, albeit to a lesser degree. Even in a far country like India, this system of public television was in place, but subject to especially powerful financial and administrative state control (Shrivastava 2005: 14f.). In the Netherlands, the same 'pillared' structure was applied as in radio: Liberals, Socialists, Catholics and Protestants all had their own broadcasting stations but their productions were aired on shared programming.

The political consequences of these organisational forms can be discussed only hypothetically to date. In Italy, television probably helped to buttress the decades-long dominance of the Christian Democrats, just as in France it promoted a patriotic policy under Charles de Gaulle. Some have argued that in the Netherlands television facilitated the erosion of those strongly separated political and religious milieus, which had thus far been characteristic of the Dutch society, because shared reception allowed these groups to watch the others' programmes and thus succumb to a kind of generalised relativism (Bignell and Fickers 2008: 20). Similarly, it is likely that the proportional representation of political parties turned German television into a 'consensus maker', although affinity for one party or another might have varied depending on who was holding the government majority at the time. In south-western Europe, dictatorships made use of state television to advertise their achievements. Thus the Portuguese dictator Marcello Caetano utilised the programme *Family Talks* to address the people. On the whole, however, television seems to have been apolitical and entertaining in its orientation, even during the Spanish and Portuguese dictatorships. Of course, the 'perfect world' presented on television most probably intensified people's desire to experience it in reality. This probably paved the way, at least in the long term, for an inner rejection of these regimes, as also happened in Eastern Europe.

Television can also be studied as a component of international politics and Cold War diplomacy (cf. e.g. Schwoch 2009: 3). Here the media served as a vehicle for both debate and trans-border exchanges between the blocs. From the 1950s, the Cold War led to the formation of two international broadcasting organisations in Europe – in the West the European Broadcasting Union (EBU), and in the East the 'Organisation International de Radiodiffusion et Télévision' (OIRT) (cf. Zeller 1999) – although these subsequently merged in 1993. The intention of both was to promote common programming and the exchange of programme material, and to create a European identity in the West or a Socialistic one in the East. Both achieved these objectives only in part;

people's perspectives remained focused on their own nations. Nevertheless the EBU was remarkably successful. As early as 1954 it distinguished itself with its 'Eurovision' that aired sports events like the Football World Cup, and images of the Vatican and of national cultures. Joint programmes like the *European Song Contest* tended to be exceptions, but the 'European News Exchange' provided a regular transfer of film material and thus allowed Western Europe to be united in its viewing, while the spoken commentary was left to the respective countries. In this system, sports accounted for approximately 50 per cent of the shared programmes, news material 35 per cent and cultural offerings 15 per cent (Eugster 1983: 152; Fickers 2009: 391, 408). Dictatorships like Spain and Portugal tried to find recognition via European television events. It would be well to study in more detail the exact manner in which the exchange and sharing of programmes as well as the reworking of sound tracks proceeded in order to gain new insights into the cultural coalescence of Europe. Moreover, EBU and OIRT were models for further consolidations such as the 'Asia-Pacific Union' (1964), 'Arab States Broadcasting' (1969) and the 'Organización de la Televisión Iberoamericana' (1970).

Television can also be studied as a global arena in which transnational battles for worldviews, influence and prestige were fought during the Cold War. This is true not only of the aforementioned German–German television. The first intercontinental live broadcast, the coronation of Queen Elizabeth II in 1953, was an attempt by Great Britain to use television as a means of positioning itself globally. Parts of Western Europe saw the coronation live, and copies were flown immediately to the United States and Japan so as many as 18 million American households were able to watch it (Schwoch 2009: 90f.). In 1961 the Soviet Union landed a coup with the live transmission in Europe of the first manned space flight, to which the United States responded in 1962 with its first live broadcast to Western Europe of an American astronaut on the first earth orbit (ibid.: 126). America's moon landing in 1969 was deliberately coupled with its airing on global television. In this respect the goal of demonstrating modernity to the entire world via television was closely connected to space travel.

Since 1965 the United States has been able to achieve a position of global media dominance through its news satellites. This was buttressed in the 1960s by the vision of a common global television system that would make everyone 'world citizens', sharing a common awareness of the world (Ruchatz 2003: 141; Schwoch 2009: 143). However, during the Cold War the limitations of this plan soon became clear: the Soviets refused to participate in the Intelsat organisation, instead founding their own Intersputnik group as its counterpart to integrate the Socialistic states. Even in West Germany and France, a 'world television' and live broadcasts from the United States met with reservations for fear of American dominance. There is no doubt that the Americans wanted to utilise global television to spread their values, especially to developing countries, but this was frequently criticised as 'cultural imperialism' during the post-colonial 1970s.

Not only did 'world television' famously fail, but also the attempt to successfully establish a common European broadcasting system with complete programming. This shows once again that the audience rather than media technology determines media structuring in the long term. Hence the European media public remained event-oriented. The United States certainly had more success broadcasting globally, first in countries with commercialised television, such as South America and Japan. In Western Europe, on the other hand, success was limited by anti-American feelings up to the 1960s (cf. Hilmes, in Nowell-Smith 1996: 468). The increase in the number of American television series aired in Europe during the 1970s and 1980s had consequences that were ambivalent: on the one hand, series like *Dallas* fostered anti-American prejudices; on the other, youth programmes and family series probably increased the public's fascination with the 'American Way of Life'. Furthermore, these American series stimulated the creation of adaptations in their own countries. Controversial new formats like *Sesame Street* were first aired in translation and then as remakes in several countries. West German television reacted to internationally successful U.S. series like *Holocaust* (1978) by producing similar programmes of their own like *Die Geschwister Oppermann* (1983) and *Heimat* (1984), which also dealt with the fates of families during the Nazi era, but avoided showing concentration camps (Bösch 2007). These limitations on American influence were evident even in Latin America, where most notably Brazil and Mexico sold television series of their own (telenovelas) to neighbouring countries. This demonstrates the principle of 'cultural proximity', according to which media consumers prefer things that seem to be most similar to their own culture (Sinclair 1999: 18). Even today, global television formats are most successful when national stations can link them with elements of their own culture (like *Who Wants to Be a Millionaire* or *Big Brother*), which again shows the limits of the oft-postulated Americanisation of television. Comparing the national content of such formats as well as the manner of their reception would be an excellent approach to a transnational cultural history.

The global circulation of television formats has been facilitated by the worldwide expansion of commercial channels since the 1980s. Other than in North and South America, commercial channels existed only in a few industrialised countries during the first decades of television. There was a dual system in Japan and Great Britain, where a regionally structured private channel was launched in 1955 (ITV, 'Independent Television'). ITV quickly proved financially successful and was so independent in its programming that it forced the BBC to make some reforms. For this reason businessmen and publishers in the rest of Western Europe began promoting commercial channels in the late 1950s. However, in the German Federal Republic not even Chancellor Konrad Adenauer as head of an absolute majority government succeeded in establishing a commercial channel. Many people and groups, including the churches, feared a decline of culture and morals. Also the Federal Constitutional Court judged that diversity of opinion could not be guaranteed because there were too few transmitting frequencies (Steinmetz 1996). Since viewers demanded alternatives, most Western countries introduced at least a second channel as well as regional channels, and the ensuing element of competition stimulated changes of content.

That it was precisely the 1980s that witnessed the almost simultaneous advent of commercial channels in West Germany and Western Europe has manifold causes. Cable and satellite technology made many new channels possible. In addition to that there was new legislation. In 1981 and 1986 respectively, the Federal Constitutional Court legalised commercial channels, declaring them in conformity with German Basic Law like the state-owned channels (Humphreys 1994: 237), and in Italy the Constitutional Court had already restricted the state's monopoly on nationwide broadcasting in 1976. Equally important was the change in political culture. On the one hand grassroots social movements on the political Left demanded programming variety that was viewer oriented. On the other hand the 'Conservative reversal' had gone hand in hand with calls for privatisation since 1980. In the Federal Republic this tied in with the accusation levelled by the Christian Democrats that many state-owned channels were nothing but a left-leaning 'Red Broadcasting' (Rotfunk) and that therefore it was necessary to have private television as a non-political corrective. The Social Democrats, the Greens, the churches and the trade unions were initially opposed to private channels, as they feared commercialisation, loss of quality and societal division (Humphreys 1994: 204; Bösch 2012).

The expansion of the channels proceeded in quite varied ways. In many countries numerous viewer-oriented channels emerged. Up to the 1980s about 2,500 local channels sprang up in Italy, some supported by political groups. Scandinavia and the Federal Republic saw the emergence of local channels like 'Munich TV' and 'Tele Regional Passau' (Hickethier 1998: 425). At the same time major private broadcasters appeared, and these either took over local channels, giving them niches for regional interest programmes, as was the case in Germany, or, as in Italy under Berlusconi, linked them all for nationwide broadcasting. In 1987 the largest commercial broadcaster in France actually resulted from the privatisation of the previously most important public channel, TF1. Commercial channels were frequently established in cooperation with several newspaper publishers. For example, the private channel SAT1, launched in 1984, was funded with capital from

165 newspapers and with shares of the FAZ and WAZ groups. The same was true of RTL. The big newspapers hoped to market their views across media boundaries in this way.

The establishment of commercial television is still too recent to permit an academically objective assessment of its social consequences. Facile discourses about the triviality and dearth of political content fostered by the commercial broadcasters is just as current today as is the complaint that commercial stations have aggravated the splitting of society into separate educational and cultural classes. It may be assumed that commercial broadcasting in Europe accelerated de-politicisation and social differentiation, and especially changed role models for young people. In countries such as Italy where the state-owned channels are financed by advertising to a great degree, they have copied their private competitors much more closely. Future studies will be able to examine long-term societal consequences of this development in many areas: for example, the effects of consumer culture on sports, the relationship between the sexes, and anxiety about crime levels. On the whole, the fear that the dual broadcasting system with its countless channels would lead to a fragmentation of society has not been substantiated. On the contrary, it is evident that only a few major commercial broadcasters have been successful in each country, since viewers tend to watch only a few channels on a regular basis.

With the establishment of the Internet, television has itself now become an 'old' medium and will therefore have increased relevance for historical analyses. At the same time the significance of television as a historical storage medium is growing, the more so as it increasingly chronicles history using its own sources. Seen in this light, television contributes to the constitution of events which it later presents in a historical context by using the same material as before, and it thus decisively shapes the culture of remembrance (Bösch and Schmidt 2010). The examination as well as the deconstruction of these media loops will be the responsibility of future chroniclers of contemporary history.

Epilogue

The Internet Age from the Perspective of Media History

The establishment of digital technologies, computers and Internet communication is viewed as a new turning point, and one which has already led to enormous societal changes. Since this process is still in flux, any pronouncements made about it can only be of temporary value. This is why many early books about the Internet already have a source-like character, like texts published about the cinema in 1910 or television in 1960. At the same time, the Internet shows the misperception of the future of media by many scholars of media studies up to the 1980s, who argued that the media public would become increasingly passive or that written culture would die out in the audio-visual television age.

Yet this new computer-supported form of communication can be arranged within the paradigms of five hundred years of media history, beginning with its invention. Like many modern media, the computer owes its existence not to a single brilliant inventor, but developed more or less concurrently in several countries during the course of the 1940s, proving once again that media innovations are responses to prevailing social needs. In this case the starting point was the processing of complex data, followed by the need for information and communication. In terms of the history of ideas, the groundwork for computers was also laid long ago. Indeed, media studies place the computer's origins as far back as the calculating machines of the seventeenth century, the binary numbering system developed by Gottfried Wilhelm Leibniz, and the card-punch machines of the nineteenth century that were used in administrative bureaus (Naumann 2001: 43).

Media history has often demonstrated that wars and conflicts promoted the dynamic expansion of new media and communication forms, but were not the father of media innovation per se. Military contexts did play a major role in the invention of the computer and Internet, but this must nonetheless be seen in perspective. The first functioning, freely programmable computer, the 'Z3', was developed in 1941 by the Berlin inventor Konrad Zuse without any support or recognition from the military. On the other hand, the British inventor Alan Turing used the programmable logic controller 'Colossus' to decode German ciphers. In 1946 the American 'ENIAC' was also an offspring of military research and is considered the first fully electronic all-purpose computer. One must also put into perspective the often-heard assumption that the Internet or its precursor, the American ARPA (Advanced Research Project Agency) net of 1969, was built up by the U.S. Defense Department to ensure an indestructible system of network communication in the event of a nuclear attack. In actual fact, recent studies have shown that it was developed as an academic communication network to enable the 'sharing of knowledge' among the costly computers of four universities. Nonetheless the ARPA was established and financed as a branch of the Pentagon after the 'Sputnik Shock' of 1957 (Hafner and Lyon 1998: 16).

Moreover, this involvement with military and space research explains the dominant role the United States played in this process. Also, the fact that private computers experienced their first breakthrough in the 1980s with games is open to equally disparate interpretations. On the one hand games call up associations with military simulations, but on the other hand the fact that so many games were put on the market refers to the commercial logic of media, since adolescents had recently been discovered as a consumer group. Comparatively little research has been done on the significance of administration, trade and stock markets for the progress of the digital revolution, although these had played a central role in every previous media revolution (for the United States: Cortada 2006). Postal services, newspapers, telegraphy and even radio initially created communication techniques that could transmit economic data rapidly. By the same token, commercial and ideological interests were often driving forces of dissemination. Since the Internet was not opened for commercial use until the 1990s, market logic seems to have played only a minor role initially, although the United Kingdom intended to use the Internet more for commercial transactions from the very beginning. Future socio-economical studies should analyse the consequences of computer-supported data processing and communication in more detail, starting with the 1970s and 1980s. This research should focus on the changes wrought up by large-scale data processing on work processes, self-scrutiny and control, and consequently on people's self-concepts and actions.

As this book has repeatedly demonstrated, technical inventions played a lesser role in determining the manner of media utilisation than did users' needs and their cultural, social and political leanings. This is why book printing had different effects in Asia and Europe, and societal appropriation of film and radio differed as well. Likewise, text messages, email and social networks were able to assert themselves in the digital communication media in a manner that had not been intended and did not accord with the originally planned goal of implementing data processing in administration, the economy and the sciences. What had begun in the context of politics, sciences and the economy once again developed into a vehicle for entertainment, information and social communication. Also typical was the fact that the new media first adopted the forms and contents of the old, thus forcing the latter to reposition themselves. One can already see how the digital revolution has transformed or pushed aside old media (such as video and music cassettes) and absorbed them into Internet-based communication via computer.

The Internet is considered to be both the expression of and catalyst for globalisation. Yet earlier innovations already had the character of reducing the limits of time and space, whether this was achieved by speedier communication or by condensation and storage of information. Printed books, periodicals, telegraphy, film, radio and live reports on television – like the Internet, they all began as transnational media and created new spaces for societal communication and new public spheres. At the same time media history teaches us not to overestimate the permanence of these 'border crossings'. The 'old' media tended to become more 'national' or even more 'regional' as they took root. Even the Internet, which began as a global space for academic communication, is presently being used in ways that show much more national differentiation (Stegbauer 2008: 8). Just as with the older media, formats and contents are 'translated' and adapted to the users' own cultures. Just as the old media did, this tension between transcultural communication and national adaptation will provide future opportunities for research of cultural idiosyncrasies and how they are changed by media influence.

One aspect that is considered completely new is the interactive nature of the Internet. There is no question that no medium has ever existed before that allowed so many people to participate in creating contents for public spaces or enjoy such freedom of selection. The structure and function of the public sphere, understood as a universally accessible communication space, have been fundamentally changed by virtue of being so widely accessible. Yet interactivity was a basic element already present at the creation of many old media and promoted their dynamic expansion. Even in the early pamphlets, newspapers and magazines, numerous authors quoted one another, and new speakers gained access to a newly formed public sphere through these media. The same is true for early film and radio. The extent to which publishing on the Internet will become more professional, with stronger editorial control of important pages, remains to be seen.

Although the Internet represents interactive networking, it is also perceived as a medium of private isolation, since people are meeting less often in person to have conversations but 'virtually' in the digital world instead. This, too, can be recognised in the context of media history. New media generally began by being used commonly in specific public locations before private appropriation took over. Places for this shared use were market squares (flyers), coffee houses and pubs (newspapers), reading societies (periodicals) and television viewing rooms, just as Internet cafés provided initial access to digital communication before private use of the computers became established. As the older media had done, the Internet has demonstrated that media are closely connected with personal communication. 'Social networks' like Facebook and email correspondence provide links to friends outside the medium and are thus considered a 'real life extension'. Once again, like in the age of radio or television, personal contacts in the real world have not been diminished, but have increased due to a new medium.

Although expansive in character, nevertheless the media have also stood for the exclusion of certain social groups, particularly during the early phases of their development. As numerous examples in this book have demonstrated, it was primarily men who used new media initially, although the participation of women on the public media stage of past centuries has often been underestimated. The same holds true for the beginnings of the Internet and still has some validity today. Like the old media, the Internet exhibits gender-specific contents and uses. Women primarily opt for the direct communicative functions of the Internet and produce public contents less frequently. Future diachronic studies will show the Internet, like older media, has strengthened and reshaped gender-specific roles. It has often been pointed out that the Internet offers women and minorities better opportunities of accessing public spaces because it enables incorporeal communication and dissimulation. This aspect too has a tradition reaching back at least as far as the periodical market of the eighteenth century. Be that as it may, the societal 'Digital Divide', as sociologists call it, nevertheless exists. Internet users, at least in a global perspective, are overwhelmingly better educated, younger, more affluent, and live in industrialised countries, whereas underprivileged population groups often missed the new opportunities offered by this new medium. Thus in their early phases, new media have often been seen to subvert that very promise of integration and participation which the Internet also holds out. In wealthy countries, where the majority of the populace enjoys private Internet access, one can again trace the 'Knowledge Gap Hypothesis' that likewise developed with the old media. According to this theory, educated and successful people become more clever and more successful through media use, whereas the less educated do not, since they select and process content differently.

However, future social histories of the Internet must not become too absorbed in describing such social amplification effects. It was historically much more common for new media to go hand in hand with changes in social groupings. One may call to mind the religious division that came in the wake of print, the formation of the bourgeoisie in the context of the eighteenth-century periodical market and ideological groupings that were influenced by the party-affiliated and popular press of the late nineteenth century. At first glance the Internet stands for a functional differentiation of society and the formation of special interest groups. While television and newspapers were once vehicles of nationwide communication, the Internet later seems to have fragmented society because millions of people visited different websites in a process. Yet new media technology has always left its contemporaries with an impression of confusing fragmentation – whether it was the countless single-page leaflets of the sixteenth century, films around 1900, the numerous American radio stations of the 1920s, or commercial television of the 1980s. Indeed, it was only a matter of time before a few highly visible media unfailingly stood out from this multiplicity by virtue of their scope and the number of people they could reach, and this enabled follow-up communication. Hollywood and the big press syndicates are typical examples. Yet on the Internet, too, dominant search engines, online communities and hierarchic websites are increasingly asserting themselves, enabling follow-up communication and the formation of new communities. Another argument against the idea of isolation in the private sphere is that the Internet has gone hand in hand with an ever-larger number of huge public events.

Moreover, new media often contributed to changing power structures. Discourse was media-based, and changes in the latter gave new groups of spokespersons the opportunity to shift the framework of power via new forms and rules of expression. This did not apply merely to the political sphere per se, but to many social systems and fields of knowledge whose hitherto legitimate spokesmen the media now challenged. Thus printing made it possible for laymen to discuss matters of religion in the vernacular, and newspaper and television have enabled people to form their own opinions about science, politics, the economy, and current affairs in general. Consequently, future scholars of cultural and social history will be called to examine the ways in which the Internet has called social structures into question.

Since new media have always been credited with the power to alter society, those in authority have invariably attempted to control or direct them, whether by monitoring film releases, regulating radio and television or sponsoring the press. On the other hand, the Internet is perceived as a market of opportunities, particularly free from control and censorship. Yet a glance at China demonstrates that restrictions are still a reality for many people in the world. Be that as it may, the analysis of media history has shown that controls were only partially effective and that new media made subversive communication possible. The use of Internet communication during the protests in Egypt in 2011 seems to confirm this trend. Yet although new mass media often support communicative forms of participation, this does not necessarily lead to democratisation. But at least new media forced rulers to find fresh arguments to support their political legitimacy, and provided opposition groups with fresh opportunities to speak out and thus challenge existing powers.

All new media were frequently considered as dangerous and raised similar anxieties as the computer and the Internet initially did. It was feared that they would lead to addiction, nervousness and superficiality, especially among the youth. At least computers and the Internet were not seen as posing a particular danger to women, as had been the case with novels, cinema and radio. There was also a long tradition of fear that people would lose their ability to differentiate between reality and the world of the media. Equally characteristic was the fear of negative effects on memory and attention span. Here the so-called 'Third Person Effect' comes into play: while many people believe themselves to be in command of the situation when dealing with the new media, they consider them dangerous for others, especially 'the masses'.

Another reason why newly established media were perceived as threatening lay in the fact that they accelerated communication and breached previous forms of narrative. Newspapers, films and radio already symbolised fleeting and concurrent forms of communication. In like manner the Internet was considered to be incapable of examining contents calmly and straightforwardly, allegedly losing itself in hectic snippets of information. Even so, there were always counter-movements in media history: the early market for flyers went hand in hand with the publication of great epics, the early short films led to epic blockbusters, and the principle of serialisation on television lessened the medium's transient character. It may be assumed that future media innovations will depict the Internet as unhurried, educational and socially consolidating in order to dramatise the perils of whatever new medium is emerging at that time.

The ephemeral character of the Internet must also be seen in relation to its storage capacity, which after all is an important media attribute. Accordingly, the Internet as a transient medium represents the loss of cultural memory. Yet here again a look at media history warns against too much cultural pessimism. One can assume that digital storage capabilities are perhaps even better than the capabilities of earlier media. It has often been deplored that only a fraction of the pages have come down to us from the early days of the World Wide Web, and email communication is not handed down. Compared with the first decade of film, radio and television, however, this amount is so substantial that it will provide future historians with ample research opportunities. Of course not all emails and chat conversations are handed down. Yet they represent such a surpassing number of sources compared to previous communication in person or by telephone that historical scholarship can only profit from them. Of course, this presupposes the discovery of an archiving system capable of adequately registering electronic media sources and making them accessible.

Since the mid-nineteenth century, new mass media have established and surprised the public about every thirty years. So it is not unusual that we do not know what kind of mass media will come next and consign computers, the Internet and Facebook to history. So we and coming historians will explain to our grandchildren how we survived in a world with such a simple and slow media as the Internet.

Bibliography

Abel, Richard. 2005. *Encyclopedia of Early Cinema*. London.
Abramson, Albert. 1987. *The History of Television 1880–1941*. Jefferson, NC.
Adburgham, Alison. 1972. *Women in Print: Writing and Women's Magazines from the Restoration to the Accession of Victoria*. London.
Adrians, Frauke. 1999. *Journalismus im 30-jährigen Krieg. Kommentierung und 'Parteylichkeit' in Zeitungen des 17. Jahrhunderts*. Konstanz.
Albrecht, Peter, and Holger Böning (eds). 2005. *Historische Presse und ihre Leser. Studien zu Zeitungen. Zeitschriften. Intelligenzblättern und Kalendern in Nordwestdeutschland*. Bremen.
Altenloh, Emilie. 1914. *Zur Soziologie des Kinos. Die Kinounternehmen und die sozialen Schichten ihrer Besucher. Schriften zur Soziologie und Kultur*, Vol. 3. Jena.
Anderson, Benedict. (1983) 2006. *Imagined Communities: Reflections on the Origin and Spread of Nationalism*. New York.
Arndt, Johannes. 2002. 'Pflichtmäßiger Bericht'. Ein medialer Angriff auf die Geheimnisse des Reichstags aus dem Jahre 1713. *Jahrbuch für Kommunikationsgeschichte* 4: 1–31.
———. 2006. Verkrachte Existenzen? Zeitungs- und Zeitschriftenmacher im Barockzeitalter zwischen Nischenexistenz und beruflicher Etablierung. *Archiv für Kulturgeschichte* 88: 101–15.
Arndt, Johannes, and Esther-Beate Körber (eds). 2010. *Das Mediensystem im Alten Reich der Frühen Neuzeit 1600–1700*. Göttingen.
Arnold, Klaus, and Christoph Classen (eds). 2004. *Zwischen Pop und Propaganda. Radio in der DDR*. Berlin.
Aronson, Amy Beth. 2002. *Taking Liberties: Early American Women's Magazines and their Readers*. Westport, CT.
Aumente, Jerome, et al. (eds). 1999. *Eastern European Journalism: Before, During and After Communism*. Cresskill, NJ.
Baark, Erik. 1997. *Lightning Wires: The Telegraph and China's Technological Modernisation 1860–1890*. Westport, CT.
Bachleitner, Norbert, and Andrea Seidler. 2007. *Zur Medialisierung gesellschaftlicher Kommunikation in Österreich und Ungarn: Studien zur Presse im 18. und 19. Jahrhundert*. Vienna.

Badenoch, Alexander. 2008. *Voices in Ruins: West German Radio across the 1945 Divide*. Basingstoke.
Badenoch, Alexander, Andreas Fickers and Christian Henrich-Franke (eds). 2013. *Airy Curtains in the European Ether: Broadcasting and the Cold War*. Baden-Baden.
Bakker, Gerben. 2005. The Decline and Fall of the European Film Industry: Sunk Costs, Market Size and Market Structure, 1890–1927. *Economic History Review* 58: 310–51.
———. 2008. *Entertainment Industrialised: The Emergence of the International Film Industry, 1890–1940*. Cambridge.
Balázs, Béla. (1924) 2001. *Der sichtbare Mensch oder die Kultur des Films*. Frankfurt/M.
Balogh, Anrás F., and Laszló Tarnói (eds). 2007. *Deutsche Presse aus Ungarn in der ersten Hälfte des 19. Jahrhunderts. Literatur. Theater. Sprache und Aspekte der Identität*. Budapest.
Barbier, Frédéric. 2007. Die erste Medienrevolution. Erfindung der Druckerei und Vervielfältigung der schriftlichen Sprachen in Europa von der Mitte des 15. Bis zum Beginn des 16. Jahrhunderts. In *Buch- und Wissenstransfer in Ostmittel- und Südosteuropa in der Frühen Neuzeit*, ed. Detlef Haberland. München. 23–47.
Barker, Hannah. 2000. *Newspapers, Politics, and English Society 1695–1855*. London.
Barker, Hannah, and Simon Burrows (eds). 2002. *Press, Politics and the Public Sphere in Europe and North America, 1760–1820*. Cambridge.
Baron, Sabrina A., et al. (eds). 2007. *Agent of Change: Print Culture Studies after Elizabeth L. Eisenstein*. Amherst, MA.
Bartels, Ulrike. 2004. *Die Wochenschau im Dritten Reich. Entwicklung und Funktion eines Massenmediums unter besonderer Berücksichtigung völkisch-nationaler Inhalte*. Frankfurt/M.
Basse, Dieter. 1991. *Wolffs Telegraphisches Bureau 1849 bis 1933. Agenturpublizistik zwischen Politik und Wirtschaft*. Munich.
Baumgarten, Jens. 2004. *Konfession. Bild und Macht. Visualisierung als katholisches Herrschafts- und Disziplinierungskonzept in Rom und im habsburgischen Schlesien 1560–1740*. Munich.
Behmer, Markus, et al. (eds). 2003. *Medienentwicklung und gesellschaftlicher Wandel. Beiträge zu einer theoretischen und empirischen Herausforderung*. Wiesbaden.
Behringer, Wolfgang. 1999. Veränderung der Raum-Zeit-Relation. Zur Bedeutung des Zeitungs- und Nachrichtenwesens während der Zeit des Dreißigjährigen Krieges. In *Zwischen Alltag und Katastrophe. Der Dreißigjährige Krieg aus der Nähe*, eds Benigna von Krusenstern and Hans Medick. Göttingen. 39–82.
———. 2003. *Im Zeichen des Merkur. Reichspost und Kommunikation in der Frühen Neuzeit*. Göttingen.
Beine, Manfred. 1999. Pressefreiheit und Agitation. Das Wochenblatt für den Kreis Wiedenbrück im Revolutionsjahr 1848. *Westfälische Forschungen* 49: 151–89.
Bellingradt, Daniel. 2011. *Flugpublizistik und Öffentlichkeit um 1700. Dynamiken. Akteure und Strukturen im urbanen Raum des Alten Reiches*. Stuttgart.
Benjamin, Walter. (1936) 2008. *The Work of Art in the Age of Mechanical Reproduction*. London.

Berns, Jörg Jochen. 1976. 'Parteylichkeit' und Zeitungswesen. Zur Rekonstruktion einer medienpolitischen Diskussion an der Wende vom 17. zum 18. Jahrhundert. In *Massen/Medien/Politik*, ed. W.F. Haug. Karlsruhe. 202–33.
Beyer, Franz-Heinrich. 1994. *Eigenart und Wirkung des reformatorischen Flugblatts im Zusammenhang der Publizistik der Reformationszeit*. Frankfurt/M.
Biefang, Andreas. 2009. *Die andere Seite der Macht. Reichstag und Öffentlichkeit im 'System Bismarck' 1871–1890*. Düsseldorf.
Bignell, Jonathan, and Andreas Fickers (eds). 2008. *A European Television History*. London.
Birett, Herbert. 1991. *Das Filmangebot in Deutschland. 1895–1911*. Munich.
Blome, Astrid (ed.). 2000. *Zeitung. Zeitschrift. Intelligenzblatt und Kalender. Beiträge zur historischen Presseforschung*. Bremen.
Blühm, Elger, and Rolf Engelsing (eds). 1967. *Die Zeitung: Deutsche Urteile und Dokumente von den Anfängen bis zur Gegenwart*. Bremen.
Blühm, Elger, and Hartwig Gebhardt (eds). 1987. *Presse und Geschichte II. Neue Beiträge zur historischen Kommunikationsforschung*. Munich.
Blumenauer, Elke. 2000. *Journalismus zwischen Pressefreiheit und Zensur. Die Augsburger. 'Allgemeine Zeitung' im Karlsbader System 1818–1848*. Cologne.
Böhn, Andreas, and Andreas Seidler. 2008. *Mediengeschichte*. Tübingen.
Bohrmann, Hans, and Gabriele Toepser-Ziegert (eds). 1984–2001. *NS-Presseanweisungen der Vorkriegszeit. Edition und Dokumentation*. 7 vols. Munich.
Bonfadelli, Heinz. 2004. *Medienwirkungsforschung*. 2 vols. Stuttgart.
Böning, Holger (ed.). 1992. *Französische Revolution und deutsche Öffentlichkeit. Wandlungen in Presse und Alltagskultur am Ende des achtzehnten Jahrhunderts*. Munich.
———. 1999. Das Intelligenzblatt. In *Von Almanach bis Zeitung. Ein Handbuch der Medien in Deutschland 1700–1800*, eds Ernst Fischer, Wilhelm Haefs and York-Gothart Mix. Munich. 89–105.
———. 2002. *Periodische Presse. Kommunikation und Aufklärung. Hamburg und Altona als Beispiel*. Bremen.
Bösch, Frank. 2004. Zeitungsberichte im Alltagsgespräch: Mediennutzung. Medienwirkung und Kommunikation im Kaiserreich. *Publizistik* 49: 319–36.
———. 2007. Film. NS-Vergangenheit und Geschichtswissenschaft. Von 'Holocaust' zu 'Der Untergang'. *Vierteljahrshefte für Zeitgeschichte* 55: 1–32.
———. 2009. *Öffentliche Geheimnisse. Skandale. Politik und Medien im Kaiserreich und Großbritannien 1880–1914*. Munich.
———. 2012. Zwischen Technikzwang und politischen Zielen: Wege zur Einführung des privaten Rundfunks in den 1970/80er Jahren. *Archiv für Sozialgeschichte* 52. 191–210.
Bösch, Frank, and Manuel Borutta (eds). 2006. *Die Massen bewegen. Medien und Emotionen in der Moderne*. Frankfurt/M.
Bösch, Frank, and Norbert Frei (eds). 2006. *Medialisierung und Demokratie im 20. Jahrhundert*. Göttingen.
Bösch, Frank, and Dominik Geppert (eds). 2008. *Journalists as Political Actors: Transfers and Interactions between Britain and Germany since the late 19th Century*. Augsburg.
Bösch, Frank, and Peter Hoeres (eds). 2013. *Außenpolitik im Medienzeitalter. Vom späten 19. Jahrhundert bis zur Gegenwart*. Göttingen.

Bösch, Frank, and Lucian Hölscher (eds). 2010. *Medien. Kirchen. Öffentlichkeiten. Transformationen kirchlicher Selbst- und Fremddeutungen seit 1945.* Göttingen.
Bösch, Frank, and Patrick Schmidt (eds). 2010. *Medialisierte Ereignisse. Performanz. Inszenierung und Medien seit dem 18. Jahrhundert.* Frankfurt/M.
Bourgault, Louise Manon. 1995. *Mass Media in Sub-Saharian Africa.* Bloomington.
Brandt, Hans-Jürgen. 1994. Die Anfänge des Kinos. In *Fischer Filmgeschichte Vol. 1: Von den Anfängen bis zum etablierten Medium 1895–1924.* Eds Werner Faulstich and Helmut Korte. Frankfurt/M. 86–98.
Bren, Paulina. 2010. *The Greengrocer and his TV: The Culture of Communism after the 1968 Prague Spring.* Ithaca, NY.
Briggs, Asa. 1995. *The Birth of Broadcasting, 1896–1927.* Oxford.
Briggs, Asa, and Peter Burke. 2002. *A Social History of the Media: From Gutenberg to the Internet.* Cambridge.
Broersma, Marcel. 2005. Constructing Public Opinion. Dutch Newspapers on the Eve of a Revolution, 1780–1795. In *News and Politics in Early Modern Europe*, ed. J.W. Koopmans. Leuven. 219–235.
———. (ed.). 2007. *Form and Style in Journalism: European Newspapers and the Representation of News, 1880–2005.* Leuven.
Brokaw, Cynthia J. 2005. The History of the Book in China. In *Printing and Book Culture in Late Imperial China*, eds. Cynthia Brokaw and Kai-wing Chow. Berkeley. 3–54.
Brown, Lucy. 1985. *Victorian News and Newspapers.* Oxford.
Buchloh, Stephan. 2002. *'Pervers. jugendgefährdend. staatsfeindlich'. Zensur in der Ära Adenauer als Spiegel des gesellschaftlichen Klimas.* Frankfurt/M.
Burke, Peter. 2000. *A Social History of Knowledge. Vol. 1: From Gutenberg to Diderot.* Cambridge.
Burkhardt, Johannes. 1992. *Der Dreißigjährige Krieg.* Frankfurt/M.
———. 2002. *Das Reformationsjahrhundert. Deutsche Geschichte zwischen Medienrevolution und Institutionenbildung 1517–1617.* Stuttgart.
Burns, Eric. 2006. *Infamous Scribblers: The Founding Fathers and the Rowdy Beginnings of American Journalism.* New York.
Burrowes, Carl Patrick. 2004. *Power and Press Freedom in Liberia, 1830–1970.* Trenton, NJ.
Bush, M.L. 2005. *The Casualties of Peterloo.* Lancaster.
Bussiek, Dagmar. 2002. *'Mit Gott für König und Vaterland!'. die Neue Preußische Zeitung (Kreuzzeitung) 1848–1892.* Münster.
Büteführ, Nadja. 1995. *Zwischen Anspruch und Kommerz: Lokale Alternativpresse 1970–1993.* Münster.
Buzzard, Karen. 2012. *Tracking the Audience: The Ratings Industry from Analog to Digital.* New York.
Calhoun, Craig J. (ed.). 1992. *Habermans and the Public Sphere.* Cambridge, MA.
Censer, Jack. 1994. *The French Press in the Age of Enlightenment.* London.
Chambers, Deborah, et al. 2004. *Women and Journalism.* London.
Chapman, Jane. 2005. *Comparative Media History: An Introduction – 1789 to the Present.* London.

———. 2013. *Gender, Citizenship and Newspapers: Historical and Transnational Perspectives*. Basingstoke and New York.
Charle, Christophe. 2004. *La siècle de la presse 1830–1939*. Paris.
Chow, Kai-wing. 2004. *Publishing, Culture, and Power in Early Modern China*. Stanford.
Church, Clive H. 1983. *Europe in 1830: Revolution and Political Change*. London.
Classen, Christoph. 2004. *Faschismus und Antifaschismus. die nationalsozialistische Vergangenheit im ostdeutschen Hörfunk 1945–1953*. Cologne.
———. 2007. Thoughts on the Significance of Mass-Media Communications in the Third Reich and the GDR. *Totalitarian Movements and Political Religions* 8. 547–62.
Coggeshall, William Turner. 1856. *The newspaper record. Containing a complete list of newspapers and periodicals in the United States, Canadas, and Great Britain, together with a sketch of the origin and progress of printing, with some facts about newspapers in Europe and America*, Philadelphia.
Conboy, Martin. 2002. *The Press and Popular Culture*. London.
Copeland, David. 2002. America 1750–1820. In *Press, Politics and the Public Sphere in Europe and North America. 1760–1820*, eds. Hannah Barker and Simon Burrows. Cambridge.
Cortada, James W. 2006. *How Computers Changed the Work of American Financial, Telecommunications, Media, and Entertainment Industries*. Oxford.
Cousins, Mark. 2006. *The Story of Film: A Worldwide History*. New York.
Craig, Douglas B. 2000. *Fireside Politics: Radio and Political Culture in the United States, 1920–1940*. London.
Creutz, Martin. 1996. *Die Pressepolitik der kaiserlichen Regierung während des Ersten Weltkriegs. Die Exekutive. die Journalisten und der Teufelskreis der Berichterstattung*. Frankfurt/M.
Crivellari, Fabio, and Marcus Sandl. 2003. Die Medialität der Geschichte. Forschungsstand und Perspektiven einer interdisziplinären Zusammenarbeit von Geschichts- und Medienwissenschaften. *Historische Zeitschrift* 277. 619–54.
Curran, James. 1978. The Press as an Agency of Social Control: A Historical Perspective. In *Newspaper History from the Seventeenth Century to Present Day*, eds Georg Boyce et al. London. 51–75.
Curran, James, and Jean Seaton. 1985. *Power without Responsibility: Press and Broadcasting in Britain*. London.
Curtis, Perry. 2001. *Jack the Ripper and the London Press*. New Haven, CT.
Czaplicki, Andreas. 2000. *Die Rolle der Westmedien in der Revolution in der DDR*. Mainz.
Daniel, Ute (ed.). 2006. *Augenzeugen. Kriegsberichterstattung vom 18. zum 21. Jahrhundert*. Göttingen.
Daniel, Ute, and Axel Schildt (eds). 2010. *Massenmedien im Europa des 20. Jahrhunderts*. Cologne.
Danker, Uwe, et al. 2003. *Am Anfang standen Arbeitergroschen. 140 Jahre Medienunternehmen der SPD*. Bonn.
Dann, Otto (ed.). 1981. *Lesegesellschaften und bürgerliche Emanzipation. ein europäischer Vergleich*. Munich.

Darnton, Robert. 1982. *The Literary Underground of the Old Regime.* Cambridge, MA.
Darnton, Robert, and Daniel Roche (eds). 1989. *Revolution in Print: The Press in France 1775–1800.* Berkeley.
Dewitz, Bodo von, and Robert Lebeck (eds). 2001. *Kiosk: eine Geschichte der Fotoreportage 1839–1973.* Göttingen.
Dibbets, Karel, and Bert Hogenkamp. 1995. *Film and the First World War.* Amsterdam.
Dicke, Gerd, and Klaus Grubmüller (eds). 2003. *Die Gleichzeitigkeit von Handschrift und Buchdruck.* Wiesbaden.
Diller, Ansgar. 1980. *Rundfunkpolitik im Dritten Reich.* Munich.
Doering-Manteuffel, Sabine, et al. (eds). 2001. *Pressewesen der Aufklärung. Periodische Schriften im Alten Reich.* Berlin.
Dooley, Brendan (ed). 2010. *The Dissemination of News and the Emergence of Contemporaneity in Early Modern Europe.* Farnham.
Dooley, Brendan, and Sabrina A. Baron (eds). 2001. *The Politics of Information in Early Modern Europe.* London.
Dowe, Dieter (ed.). 1998. *Europa 1848: Revolution und Reform.* Bonn.
Duchkowitsch, Wolfgang. 1978. *Absolutismus und Zeitung. Die Strategie der absolutistischen Kommunikationspolitik und ihre Wirkung auf die Wiener Zeitungen 1621–1757.* Vienna.
Duchkowitsch, Wolfgang, et al. (eds). 2009. *Journalistische Persönlichkeit. Fall und Aufstieg eines Phänomens.* Cologne.
Dussel, Konrad. 1999. *Deutsche Rundfunkgeschichte. eine Einführung.* Konstanz.
———. 2000. *Vom Radio- zum Fernsehzeitalte. Medienumbrüche in sozialgeschichtlicher Perspektive.* Hamburg.
———. 2004. *Deutsche Tagespresse im 19. und 20. Jahrhundert.* Münster.
———. 2010. Wie erfolgreich war die nationalsozialistische Presselenkung? *Vierteljahrshefte für Zeitgeschichte* 58. 543–61.
Dussel, Konrad, and Edgar Lersch (eds). 1999. *Quellen zur Programmgeschichte des deutschen Hörfunks und Fernsehens.* Göttingen.
Edwards, Mark U. 1994. *Printing, Propaganda, and Martin Luther.* Berkeley.
Egenhoff, Uta. 2008. *Berufsschriftstellertum und Journalismus in der Frühen Neuzeit. Eberhard Werner Happels Relationes Curiosae im Medienverbund des 17. Jahrhunderts.* Bremen.
Eisenhardt, Ulrich. 1970. *Die kaiserliche Aufsicht über Buchdruck. Buchhandel und Presse im Heiligen Römischen Reich Deutscher Nation 1496–1806. Ein Beitrag zur Geschichte der Bücher und Pressezensur.* Karlsruhe.
Eisenstein, Elizabeth L. (1979) 2005. *The Printing Revolution in Early Modern Europe.* Cambridge.
Eisermann, Falk. 2002. Buchdruck und politische Kommunikation. Ein neuer Fund zur frühen Publizistik Maximilians I. *Gutenberg-Jahrbuch* 77. 76–83.
———. 2003. Bevor die Blätter fliegen lernten: Buchdruck, politische Kommunikation und die „Medienrevolution" des 15. Jahrhunderts. In *Medien der Kommunikation im Mittelalter*, ed. Karl-Heinz Spieß. 289–320.
Eisermann, Thilo. 2000. *Pressephotographie und Informationskontrolle im Ersten Weltkrieg: Deutschland und Frankreich im Vergleich.* Hamburg.

Elter, Andreas. 2008. *Propaganda der Tat. Die RAF und die Medien.* Frankfurt/M.
Emery, Edwin, and Michael Emery. 1988. *The Press and America: An Interpretative History of the Mass Media.* Englewood Cliffs, NJ.
Engell, Lorenz. 1995. *Bewegen beschreiben: Theorie zur Filmgeschichte.* Weimar.
Engels, Sin-Ja. 2003. *Buchdruck in Korea und Deutschland – Jikji und die Gutenberg-Bibel: Impressionen einer 'deutsch-koreanischen Ausstellung' in der Georg-August-Universität Göttingen.* Göttingen.
Esser, Frank. 1998. *Die Kräfte hinter den Schlagzeilen. englischer und deutscher Journalismus im Vergleich.* Freiburg.
Estermann, Monika. 1999. *'O werthe Druckerkunst/ Du Mutter aller Kunst'. Gutenbergfeiern im Laufe der Jahrhunderte.* Mainz.
Eugster, Ernest. 1983. *Television Programming across National Boundaries: The EBU and OIRT Experience.* Dedham, MA.
Faulstich, Werner. 1996ff. *Die Geschichte der Medien. bisher 5 vol.* Göttingen.
———. 1998. *Medien zwischen Herkunft und Revolte. die Medienkultur der frühen Neuzeit 1400–1700.* Göttingen.
———. 2006a. *Mediengeschichte. Von den Anfängen bis 1700.* Göttingen.
———. 2006b. *Mediengeschichte. Von 1700 bis ins 3. Jahrtausend.* Göttingen.
Fellow, Anthony R. 2005. *American Media History.* Toronto.
Fickers, Andreas. 2009. Eventing Europe. Europäische Fernseh- und Mediengeschichte als Zeitgeschichte. *Archiv für Sozialgeschichte* 49. 391–416.
Filk, Christian, and Jens Ruchatz. 2007. *Frühe Film- und Mediensoziologie: Emilie Altenlohs Studie 'Zur Soziologie des Kino' von 1914.* Siegen.
Fischer, Ernst, et al. (eds). 1999. *Von Almanach bis Zeitung. Ein Handbuch der Medien in Deutschland 1700–1800.* Munich.
Fischer, Heinz-Dietrich (ed.). 1973. *Deutsche Zeitschriften des 17. bis 20. Jahrhunderts.* Munich.
Flieger, Wolfgang. 1992. *Die taz. Vom Alternativblatt zur linken Tageszeitung.* Munich.
Fortner, Robert. 2005. *Radio, Morality and Culture: Britain, Canada and the United States, 1919–1945.* Carbondale, IL.
Fox, Jo. 2007. *Film Propaganda in Britain and Nazi Germany: World War II Cinema.* Oxford.
Frasca, Ralph. 2006. *Benjamin Franklin's Printing Network: Disseminating Virtue in Early America.* Columbia, MO.
Frei, Norbert, and Johannes Schmitz. 1999. *Journalismus im Dritten Reich.* Munich.
Fremmer, Anselm. 2001. *Venezianische Buchkultur: Bücher. Buchhändler und Leser in der Frührenaissance.* Cologne.
Freund, Marion. 2004. *'Mag der Thron in Flammen glühn!'. Schriftstellerinnen und die Revolution von 1848/49.* Königstein im Taunus.
Fritzsche, Peter. 1996. *Reading Berlin 1900.* London.
Führer, Karl Christian. 1996. Auf dem Weg zur 'Massenkultur'? Kino und Rundfunk in der Weimarer Republik. *Historische Zeitschrift* 262. 739–81.
———. 2007. Erfolg und Macht von Axel Springers 'Bild'-Zeitung in den 1950er-Jahren. *Zeithistorische Forschungen/Studies in Contemporary History* 4.3.
———. 2008. *Medienmetropole Hamburg: mediale Öffentlichkeiten 1930–1960.* Munich.

Führer, Karl Christian, Knut Hickethier and Axel Schildt. 2001. *Öffentlichkeit. Medien. Geschichte.* Konzepte der modernen Öffentlichkeit und Zugänge zu ihrer Erforschung. *Archiv für Sozialgeschichte* 41. 1–32.
Führer, Karl Christian, and Corey Ross (eds). 2008. *Mass Media, Culture and Society in Twentieth-Century Germany.* Basingstoke. 97–113.
Fulda, Bernhard. 2009. *Press and Politics in the Weimar Republic.* Oxford.
Füssel, Stephan. 1999. *Gutenberg und seine Wirkung.* Frankfurt/M.
Galassi, Stefania. 2008. *Pressepolitik im Faschismus. Das Verhältnis von Herrschaft und Presseordnung in Italien zwischen 1922 und 1940.* Stuttgart.
Geppert, Dominik. 2007. *Pressekriege. Öffentlichkeit und Diplomatie in den deutsch-britischen Beziehungen (1896–1912).* Munich.
Gerbig-Fabel, Marco. 2008. Photographic Artefacts of War 1904–1905: The Russo-Japanese War as Transnational Media Event. *European Review of History* 15. 629–42.
Gernert, Angelica. 1990. *Liberalismus als Handlungskonzept: Studien zur Rolle der politischen Presse im italienischen Risorgimento vor 1848.* Stuttgart.
Gesemann, Wolfgang. 1987. Der Beginn des bulgarischen Pressewesens im Neuzehnten Jahrhundert. Bedingungen und Wirkungen. In *Zeitschriften und Zeitungen des 18. und 19. Jahrhunderts in Mittel- und Osteuropa*, eds István Fried et al. Essen. 229–41.
Gestrich, Andreas. 1994. *Absolutismus und Öffentlichkeit. Politische Kommunikation in Deutschland zu Beginn des 18. Jahrhunderts.* Göttingen.
Gienow-Hecht, Jessica C.E. 1999. *Transmission Impossible: American Journalism as Cultural Diplomacy in Postwar Germany, 1945–1955.* Baton Rogue, LA.
Giesecke, Michael. 1991. *Der Buchdruck in der frühen Neuzeit: Eine historische Fallstudie über die Durchsetzung neuer Informations- und Kommunikationstechnologien.* Frankfurt/M.
———. 2007. *Die Entdeckung der kommunikativen Welt. Studien zur kulturvergleichenden Mediengeschichte.* Frankfurt/M.
Gillessen, Günther. 1987. *Auf verlorenem Posten: die Frankfurter Zeitung im Dritten Reich.* Berlin.
Gilmont, Jean-François (ed.). 1998. *The Reformation and the Book.* Aldershot.
Glasenapp, Jörn. 2008. *Die deutsche Nachkriegsfotografie. Eine Mentalitätsgeschichte in Bildern.* Paderborn.
Gossel, Daniel. 2009. *Medien und Politik in Deutschland und den USA. Kontrolle. Konflikt und Kooperation vom 18. bis zum frühen 20. Jahrhundert.* Stuttgart.
Gough, Hugh. 1988. *The Newspaper Press in the French Revolution.* Chicago.
Grampp, Sven, et al. (eds). 2008. *Revolutionsmedien – Medienrevolutionen.* Konstanz.
Greiling, Werner. 2003. *Presse und Öffentlichkeit in Thüringen Mediale Verdichtung und kommunikative Vernetzung im 18. und 19. Jahrhundert.* Cologne.
Grendler, Paul F. 1989. *Schooling in Renaissance Italy Literacy and Learning, 1300–1600.* Baltimore.
Griep, Hans-Joachim. 2005. *Geschichte des Lesens. von den Anfängen bis Gutenberg.* Darmstadt.
Gries, Rainer. 2003. *Produkte als Medien. Kulturgeschichte der Produktkommunikation in der Bundesrepublik und der DDR.* Leipzig.

Groth, Otto. 1948. *Geschichte der deutschen Zeitungswissenschaft. Probleme und Methoden*. Munich.

Gunaratne, Shelton A. (ed.). 2000. *Handbook of the Media in Asia*. New Delhi.

Habermas, Jürgen. (1962) 1989. *The Structural Transformation of the Public Sphere. An Inquiry into a Category of Bourgeois Society*. Cambridge, MA.

Hachmeister, Lutz, and Friedemann Siering (eds). 2002. *Die Herren Journalisten: die Elite der deutschen Presse zwischen Nationalsozialismus und Bundesrepublik Deutschland*. Munich.

Haefs, Wilhelm, and York-Gothart Mix (eds). 2006. *Zensur im Jahrhundert der Aufklärung. Geschichte – Theorie – Praxis*. Göttingen.

Hafner, Katie, and Matthew Lyon. 1998. *Where Wizards Stay Up Late: The Origins Of The Internet*. New York.

Hamm, Berndt. 1996. Die Reformation als Medienereignis. In *Glaube und Öffentlichkeit*, ed. Ingo 'Baldermann. Neukirchen-Vluyn. 137–66.

Hampton, Mark. 2004. *Visions of the Press in Britain, 1850–1950*. Urbana, IL.

Hannig, Nicolai. 2010. *Die Religion der Öffentlichkeit. Medien. Religion und Kirche in der Bundesrepublik Deutschland 1945–1980*. Göttingen.

Harline, Craig E. 1987. *Pamphlets, Printing, and Political Culture in the Early Dutch Republic*. Dordrecht.

Harms, Wolfgang. 1985ff. *Deutsche illustrierte Flugblätter des 16. und 17. Jahrhunderts*. Berlin.

———. 1989. Article 'Flugblatt' and 'Flugschrift'. In *Lexikon des gesamten Buchwesens*, Vol. 2. Stuttgart.

Haucke, Lutz. 2005. *Film – Künste – TV-SHOW Film- und fernsehwissenschaftliche Studien*. Berlin.

Heidenreich, Bernd, and Sönke Neitzel (eds). 2010. *Medien in Nationalsozialismus*. Paderborn.

Heintzel, Alexander. 1998. *Propaganda im Zeitalter der Reformation. Persuasive Kommunikation im 16. Jahrhundert*. St Augustin.

Heitger, Ulrich. 2003. *Vom Zeitzeichen zum politischen Führungsmittel. Entwicklungstendenzen und Strukturen der Nachrichtenprogramme des Rundfunks der Weimarer Republik 1923–1932*. Münster.

Hemels, Joan. 1982. Pressezensur im Reformationszeitalter (1475–1648). In *Deutsche Kommunikationskontrolle des 15. Bis 20. Jahrhunderts*, ed. Heinz-Dietrich Fischer. München. 13–35.

Hensle, Michael P. 2003. *Rundfunkverbrechen. Das Hören von 'Feindsendern' im Nationalsozialismus*. Berlin.

Hett, Benjamin Carter. 2004. *Death in the Tiergarten: Murder and Criminal Justice in the Kaiser's Berlin*. Cambridge, MA.

Hibberd, Matthew. 2008. *The Media in Italy: Press, Cinema and Broadcasting from Unification to Digital*. Maidenhead.

Hickethier, Knut. 1998. *Geschichte des deutschen Fernsehens*. Stuttgart.

Higman, Francis M. 1996. *Piety and the People: Religious Printing in French 1511–1551*. Aldershot.

Hills, Daniel J. 2002. *The Struggle for Control of Global Communications*. Chicago.

Hilmes, Michele. 2004. *Only Connect: A Cultural History of Broadcasting in the United States*. Boston.
———. 2012. *Network Nations: A Transnational History of British and American Broadcasting*. New York and London.
Hirschhausen, Ulrike von. 1998. *Liberalismus und Nation. Die Deutsche Zeitung 1847–1850*. Bonn.
Hodenberg, Christina von. 2006. *Konsens und Krise. Eine Geschichte der westdeutschen Medienöffentlichkeit 1945–1973*. Göttingen.
Hoeres, Peter. 2013. *Außenpolitik und Öffentlichkeit. Massenmedien, Meinungsforschung und Arkanpolitik in den deutsch-amerikanischen Beziehungen von Erhard bis Brandt*. Munich.
Hoffmann, Steffen. 2002. *Geschichte des Medienbegriffs*. Hamburg.
Hofmeister-Hunger, Andrea. 1994. *Pressepolitik und Staatsreform. Die Institutionalisierung staatlicher Öffentlichkeitsarbeit bei Karl August von Hardenberg 1792–1822*. Göttingen.
Holzbach, Heidrun. 1981. *Das 'System Hugenberg'. Die Organisation bürgerlicher Sammlungspolitik vor dem Aufstieg der NSDAP*. Stuttgart.
Holzweißig, Gunter. 2002. *Die schärfste Waffe der Partei: eine Mediengeschichte der DDR*. Cologne.
Hörisch, Jochen. 2004. *Eine Geschichte der Medien. Von der Oblate zum Internet*. Frankfurt/M.
Horn, Sabine. 2009. *Erinnerungsbilder. Auschwitz-Prozess und Majdanek-Prozess im westdeutschen Fernsehen*. Essen.
Hoyer, Svennik, and Horst Pöttker (eds). 2005. *Diffusion of the News Paradigm 1850–2000*. Göteborg.
Huffman, James. 1997. *Creating a Public: People and Press in Meiji Japan*. Honolulu.
Hugill, Peter J. 1999. *Global Communications since 1844: Geopolitics and Technology*. Baltimore, MD.
Humphreys, Peter. 1994. *Media and Media Policy in Germany: The Press and Broadcasting since 1945*. Oxford.
Imre, Aniko, et al. (eds). 2013. *Popular Television in Eastern Europe During and Since Socialism*. New York and London.
Jacobsen, Wolfgang, Anton Kaes and Hans Helmut Prinzler (eds). 2004. *Geschichte des deutschen Films*. Stuttgart.
Jäger, Jens. 2009. *Fotografie und Geschichte*. Frankfurt/M.
Jansen, Christian and Henning Borggräfe. 2007. *Nation, Nationalität, Nationalismus*. Frankfurt/M.
Janßen, Karl-Heinz, Haug von Kuenheim and Theo Sommer. 2006. *Die Zeit. Geschichte einer Wochenzeitung 1946 bis heute*. Munich.
Jelavich, Peter. 2006. *Berlin Alexanderplatz: Radio, Film, and the Death of Weimar Culture*. Berkeley, CA.
Johnson, A. Ross, and R. Eugene Parta (eds). 2010. *Cold War Broadcasting: Impact on the Soviet Union and Eastern Europe. A Collection of Studies and Documents*. Budapest and New York.
Jungblut, Peter. 1994. Unter vier Reichskanzlern. Otto Hammann und die Pressepolitik der deutschen Reichsleitung 1890 bis 1916. In *Propaganda. Meinungskampf,*

Verführung und politische Sinnstiftung 1789–1989, eds. Ute Daniel and Wolfram Siemann. Frankfurt/M. 101–16.
Kapr, Albert. 1988. *Johannes Gutenberg – Persönlichkeit und Leistung*. Munich.
Kaul, Chandrika. 2003. *Reporting the Raj: The British Press and India, 1880–1922*. Manchester.
Kawecka-Gryczowa, Alodia and Janusz Tazbur. 1998. *The Book and the Reformation in Poland*. In *The Reformation and the Book*, ed Jean-Francois Gilmont. Aldershot. 410–431.
Käuser, Andreas. 2005. Medienumbrüche – Fragmente eines Forschungsgebiets. *Navigationen: Zeitschrift für Medien- und Kulturwissenschaften* 5. 243–60.
Kenez, Peter. 2001. *Cinema and Soviet Society: From the Revolution to the Death of Stalin*. London.
Kind-Kovács, Friederike, and Jessie Labov (eds). 2013. *Samizdat, Tamizdat, and Beyond: Transnational Media During and After Socialism*. New York.
Kinnebrock, Susanne. 1999. 'Gerechtigkeit erhöht ein Volk!?' – Die erste deutsche Frauenbewegung, ihre Sprachrohre und die Stimmrechtsfrage. *Jahrbuch für Kommunikationsgeschichte* 1. 135–72.
Kittler, Friedrich A. 1995. *Aufschreibesysteme 1800–1900*. Munich.
Klaits, Joseph. 1976. *Printed Propaganda under Louis XIV: Absolute Monarchy and Public Opinion*. Princeton.
Knabe, Hubertus. 2001. *Der diskrete Charme der DDR. Stasi und Westmedien*. Berlin.
Kniep, Jürgen. 2010. *'Keine Jugendfreigabe!': Filmzensur in Westdeutschland 1949–1990*. Göttingen.
Knoch, Habbo. 2001. *Die Tat als Bild: Fotografien des Holocaust in der deutschen Erinnerungskultur*. Hamburg.
Knoch, Habbo, and Daniel Morat. 2003. *Kommunikation als Beobachtung. Medienanalyse und Gesellschaftsbilder 1880–1960*. Munich.
Koch, Hans-Jörg. 2003. *Das Wunschkonzert im NS-Rundfunk*. Cologne.
Koch, Ursula E. 1991. *Der Teufel in Berlin. Von der Märzrevolution bis zu Bismarcks Entlassung. Illustrierte politische Witzblätter einer Metropole*. Cologne.
Köhler, Hans-Joachim. 1986. Erste Schritte zu einem Meinungsprofil der frühen Reformation. In *Martin Luther. Probleme seiner Zeit*, eds Volker Press and Dieter Stievermann. Stuttgart. 244–81.
Kohnen, Richard. 1995. *Pressepolitik des Deutschen Bundes. Methoden staatlicher Pressepolitik nach der Revolution von 1848*. Tübingen.
Komorová, Klára. 2007. Die Anfänge des Buchdrucks und der Buchkultur auf dem Gebiet der heutigen Slowakei. *In Buch- und Wissenstransfer in Ostmittel- und Südosteuropa in der Frühen Neuzeit*, ed. Detlef Haberland. München. 183–196.
König, Wolfgang. 2004. *Volkswagen. Volksempfänger. Volksgemeinschaft. 'Volksprodukte' im Dritten Reich; vom Scheitern einer nationalsozialistischen Konsumgesellschaft*. Paderborn.
Koopmans, J.W. (ed.). 2005. *News and Politics in Early Modern Europe*. Leuven.
Körber, Ester-Beate. 1998. *Öffentlichkeiten in der Frühen Neuzeit. Teilnehmer. Formen. Institutionen und Entscheidungen öffentlicher Kommunikation im Herzogtum Preußen von 1525 bis 1618*. Berlin.

Korte, Helmut. 1998. *Der Spielfilm und das Ende der Weimarer Republik. ein rezeptionshistorischer Versuch.* Göttingen.
Koszyk, Kurt. 1966. *Deutsche Presse im 19. Jahrhundert.* Berlin.
Kracauer, Siegfried. (1932) 1974. *Kino. Essays. Studien. Glossen zum Film.* Frankfurt/M.
———. (1947) 1979. *Von Caligari zu Hitler. Eine psychologische Geschichte des deutschen Films,* Frankfurt/M.
Kraushaar, Wolfgang. 2001. 1968 und die Massenmedien. *Archiv für Sozialgeschichte* 41. 317–48.
Krebs, Paula M. 1999. *Gender, Race, and the Writing of Empire. Public Discourses on the Boer War.* Cambridge.
Kreimeier, Klaus. 1992. *Die Ufa-Story. Geschichte eines Filmkonzerns.* München.
Kreuzer, Helmut, and Christian W. Thomson (eds). 1994. *Geschichte des Fernsehens in der Bundesrepublik Deutschland.* 5 Vols. Munich.
Kuhn, Raymond. 2002. *The Media in France.* London.
Kurth, Karl. 1944. *Die ältesten Schriften für und wider die Zeitung.* Brünn.
Kuskin, William. 2006. *Caxton's Trace. Studies in the History of English Printing.* Notre Dame.
Küster, Sebastian. 2004. *Vier Monarchien – vier Öffentlichkeiten. Kommunikation um die Schlacht bei Dettingen.* Münster.
Kutsch, Arnulf, and Johannes Weber (eds). 2002. *350 Jahre Tageszeitung. Forschungen und Dokumente.* Bremen.
Lang, Helmut W. 1987. Die Neue Zeitung des 15. bis 17. Jahrhunderts. Entwicklungsgeschichte und Typologie. In *Presse und Geschichte II. Neue Beiträge zur historischen Kommunikationsforschung,* eds Elger Blühm and Hartwig Gebhardt. München. 57–60.
Larkey, Edward. 2007. *Rotes Rockradio. Populäre Musik und die Kommerzialisierung des DDR-Rundfunks.* Berlin.
Latimer, Berkley Wells. 1976. *Pamphleteering in France during the Wars of Religion: Aspects of Ephemeral and Occasional Publications, 1562–1598.* Ann Arbor.
Ledderose, Lothar. 2000. *Ten Thousand Things: Module and Mass Production in Chinese Art.* Princeton, NJ.
Lee, Alan J. 1976. *The Origins of the Popular Press in England, 1855–1914.* London.
Lenger, Friedrich, and Ansgar Nünning (eds). 2008. *Medienereignisse der Moderne.* Darmstadt.
Lenoe, Mathew. 2004. *Closer to the Masses: Stalinist Culture, Social Revolution, and Soviet Newspapers.* Cambridge, MA.
Leonhard, Joachim-Felix (ed.). 1997. *Programmgeschichte des Hörfunks in der Weimarer Republik.* Munich.
Leonhard, Joachim-Felix, et al. (eds). 1999–2002. *Medienwissenschaft. Ein Handbuch zur Entwicklung der Medien und Kommunikationsformen.* 3 vols. Berlin.
Lerg, Winfried B. 1980. *Rundfunkpolitik in der Weimarer Republik.* Munich.
Lersch, Edgar, and Helmut Schanze (eds). 2004. *Die Idee des Radios: von den Anfängen in Europa und den USA bis 1933.* Konstanz.
Lewis, Anthony. 2008. *Freedom for the Thought That We Hate: A Biography of the First Amendment.* New York.

Lie, Hiu. 2003. *Die Anfänge des koreanischen Buchdrucks mit Metallettern: das königliche Druckereiamt 'Chujaso' zu Beginn des 15. Jahrhunderts*. Thunum.
Lindenberger, Thomas. 2004. Vergangenes Hören und Sehen. Zeitgeschichte und ihre Herausforderung durch die audiovisuellen Medien. *Zeithistorische Forschungen and Studies in Contemporary History* 1. 72–85.
——— (ed.). 2006. *Massenmedien im Kalten Krieg. Akteure. Bilder. Resonanzen.* Cologne.
Loiperdinger, Martin. 1993. Das frühe Kino der Kaiserzeit: Problemaufriß und Forschungsperspektiven. In *Der deutsche Film. Aspekte seiner Geschichte von den Anfängen bis zur Gegenwart*, ed. Uli Jung. Trier. 21–50.
———. 1996. Lumières Ankunft des Zugs: Gründungsmythos eines neuen Mediums. *KINtop* 5. 37–70.
———. 1997. Kaiser Wilhelm II: Der erste deutsche Filmstar. In *Idole des deutschen Films, eine Galerie von Schlüsselfiguren*, ed. Thomas Koebner. München, S. 41–54.
———. 2003. Biograph-Bilder vom Burenkrieg – Münchner Polizeizensur hört aufs Publikum. *KINtop* 14/15. 66–75.
Lokatis, Siegfried, and Ingrid Sonntag (eds). 2008. *Heimliche Leser in der DDR. Kontrolle und Verbreitung unerlaubter Literatur*. Berlin.
Longerich, Peter. 2006. *'Davon haben wir nichts gewußt!'. Die Deutschen und die Judenverfolgung 1933–1945*. Berlin.
Lorenzen, Ebba. 1978. *Presse unter Franco. Zur Entwicklung publizistischer Institutionen und Prozesse im politischen Kräftespiel*. Munich.
Lottes, Günther. 1996. Medienrevolution. Reformation und sakrale Kommunikation. In *Die Aktualität der Geschichte. Historische Orientierung in der Mediengesellschaft*, eds Stephan Kronenenbrug and Horst Schichtel. Gießen. 247–61.
Maase, Kaspar. 1997. *Grenzenloses Vergnügen. Der Aufstieg der Massenkultur 1850–1970*. Frankfurt/M.
———. 2001. Massenkunst und Volkserziehung. Die Regulierung von Film und Kino im deutschen Kaiserreich. *Archiv für Sozialgeschichte* 41. 39–77.
Mauelshagen, Franz and Benedikt Mauer (eds). 2000. *Medien und Weltbilder im Wandel der frühen Neuzeit*. Augsburg.
McDermott, Joseph Peter. 2006. *A Social History of the Chinese Book: Books and Literati Culture in Late Imperial China*. Hong Kong.
McDowell, Paula. 1998. *The Women of Grub Street: Press, Politics, and Gender in the London*. Oxford.
McLuhan, Marshall. (1962) 2011. *The Gutenberg Galaxy: The Making of Typographic Man*. London.
———. (1964) 2001. *Understanding Media: The Extensions of Man*. New York.
McReynolds, Louise. 1991. *The News under Russia's Old Regime: The Development of a Mass Circulation Press*. Princeton, NJ.
Mancini, Paolo. 2005. *Mediensystem und journalistische Kultur in Italien*. Berlin.
Marker, Gary. 1985. *Publishing, Printing, and the Origins of Intellectual Life in Russia 1700–1800*. Princeton.
Marsh, Steven. 2006. *Popular Spanish Film under Franco: Comedy and the Weakening of the State*. Basingstoke.

Marßolek, Inge, and Adelheid von Saldern (eds). 1998. *Zuhören und Gehörtwerden*. 2 vols. Tübingen.

Mauelshagen, Franz, and Benedikt Mauer (eds). 2000. *Medien und Weltbilder im Wandel der frühen Neuzeit*. Augsburg.

Meier, Gerd. 1999. *Zwischen Milieu und Markt. Tageszeitungen in Ostwestfalen 1920–1970*. Paderborn.

Melve, Leidulf. 2007. *Inventing the Public Sphere: The Public Debate during the Investiture Contest 1030–1122*. Leiden.

Mendelssohn, Peter de. (1959) 1982. *Zeitungsstadt Berlin. Menschen und Mächte in der Geschichte der deutschen Presse*. Berlin.

Mendle, Michael. 2001. News and the Pamphlet Culture in Seventeenth-Century England. In *The Politics of Information in Early Modern Europe*, eds Brendan M. Dooley and Sabrina A. Baron. London and New York. 57–79.

Meyen, Michael. 2002. *Hauptsache Unterhaltung: Mediennutzung und Medienbewertung in Deutschland in den 50er Jahren*. Münster.

———. 2003. *Denver Clan und Neues Deutschland: Mediennutzung in der DDR*. Berlin.

———. 2009. Medialisierung. *Medien und Kommunikationswissenschaft* 57. 23–38.

Minois, Georges. 1995. *Censure et culture sous l'Ancien Régime*. Paris.

Miyao, Daisuke (ed.). 2013. *The Oxford Handbook of Japanese Cinema*. Oxford.

Moon-Year, Park. 2004. A Study on the Type Casting, Setting and Printing Method of 'Buljo-Jikji-Simche-Yoyeol'. *Gutenberg-Jahrbuch* 79. Mainz. 32–46.

Morineau, Michel. 1995. Die Holländischen Zeitungen des 17. und 18. Jahrhunderts. In *Kommunikationsrevolutionen. Die neuen Medien des 16. und 19. Jahrhunderts*, ed. Michael North. Köln. 33–43.

Mörke, Olaf. 2005. *Die Reformation: Voraussetzungen und Durchsetzung*. Munich.

Mühlenfeld, Daniel. 2009. Was heißt und zu welchem Ende studiert man NS-Propaganda? Neuere Forschungen zur Geschichte von Medien. Kommunikation und Kultur während des 'Dritten Reiches'. *Archiv für Sozialgeschichte* 49. 527–59.

Müller, Corinna. 2003. *Vom Stummfilm zum Tonfilm*. Munich.

Müller, Philipp. 2005. *Auf der Suche nach dem Täter. Die öffentliche Dramatisierung von Verbrechen im Berlin des Kaiserreichs*. Frankfurt/M.

Münkel, Daniela. 2005. *Willy Brandt und die 'Vierte Gewalt'. Politik und Massenmedien in den 50er bis zu den 70er Jahren*. Frankfurt/M.

Murray, W.J. 1991. Journalism as Career Choice in 1789. In *The Press in the French Revolution*, ed. Harvey Chisick. Oxford. 161–88.

Müsse, Wolfgang. 1995. *Die Reichspresseschule: Journalisten für die Diktatur? Ein Beitrag zur Geschichte des Journalismus im Dritten Reich*. Munich.

Naumann, Friedrich. 2001. *Vom Abakus zum Internet. Die Geschichte der Informatik*. Darmstadt.

Neddermayer, Uwe. 1998. *Von der Handschrift zum gedruckten Buch. Schriftlichkeit und Leseinteresse im Mittelalter und in der frühen Neuzeit. Quantitative und qualitative Aspekte*. 2 vols. Wiesbaden.

Nickles, David Paul. 2003. *Under the Wire: How the Telegraph Changed Diplomacy*. Cambridge, MA.

Nojiri, Hiroko. 1991. *Medien in Japan*. Berlin.
North, Michael. (ed.). 1995. *Kommunikationsrevolutionen. Die neuen Medien des 16. und 19. Jahrhunderts*. Cologne.
Nowell-Smith, Geoffrey. 1996. *The Oxford History of World Cinema*. Oxford.
Oppelt, Ulrike. 2002. *Film und Propaganda im Ersten Weltkrieg. Propaganda als Medienrealität im Aktualitäten- und Dokumentarfilm*. Stuttgart.
Osterhammel, Jürgen. 2009. *Die Verwandlung der Welt: Eine Geschichte des 19. Jahrhunderts*. Munich.
Osterhaus, Andreas. 1990. *Europäischer Terraingewinn in Schwarzafrika: das Verhältnis von Presse und Verwaltung in sechs Kolonien Deutschlands. Frankreichs und Großbritanniens von 1894 bis 1914*. Frankfurt/M.
Ott, Norbert H. 1999. Leitmedium Holzschnitt. Tendenzen und Entwicklungslinien der Druckillustration im Mittelalter und früher Neuzeit. In *Die Buchkultur im 15. und 16. Jahrhundert*, ed. Barbara Tiemann. Hamburg. 163–252.
Paas, J.R. 1984. *The German Political Broadsheet 1600–1700*. 9 vols. Wiesbaden.
Paczkowski, Andrzej. 1997. Zur politischen Geschichte der Presse in der Volksrepublik Polen 1944–1989. In *Vom Instrument der Partei zur 'Vierten Gewalt'. Die ostmitteleuropäische Presse als zeithistorische Quelle*, ed. Eduard Mühle. Marburg. 25–45.
Paech, Anne, and Joachim Paech. 2000. *Menschen im Kino: Film und Literatur erzählen*. Stuttgart.
Palmowski, Jan. 2009. *Inventing a Socialist Nation: Heimat and the Politics of Everyday Life in the GDR, 1945–90*. Cambridge.
Paul, Gerhard. 2004. *Bilder des Krieges – Krieg der Bilder. die Visualisierung des modernen Krieges*. Paderborn.
——— (ed.). 2006. *Visual History. Ein Studienbuch*. Göttingen.
———. 2008/9. *Das Jahrhundert der Bilder*. 2 vols. Göttingen.
Petersen, Klaus. 1995. *Zensur in der Weimarer Republik*. Stuttgart.
Pfarr, Kristina. 1994. *Die Neue Zeitung. empirische Untersuchung eines Informationsmediums der frühen Neuzeit unter besonderer Berücksichtigung von Gewaltdarstellungen*. Mainz.
Pinkerton, Alasdair. 2008. 'A new kind of imperialism?' The BBC, Cold War Broadcasting and the Contested Geopolitics of South Asia'. *Historical Journal of Film, Radio and Television* 28(4). 537–55.
Plambeck, Petra. 1982. *Publizistik im Rußland des 18. Jahrhunderts*. Hamburg.
Plunkett, John. 2002. *Queen Victoria: First Media Monarch*. Oxford.
Poe, Marshall T. 2010. *A History of Communications: Media and Society from the Evolution of Speech to the Internet*. Cambridge.
Pompe, Hedwig. 2004. Die Neuheit der Neuheit: Der Zeitungsdiskurs im späten 17. Jahrhundert. In *Einführung in die Geschichte der Medien*, eds Albert Kümmel et al. Paderborn. 35–63.
Popkin, Jeremy D. 1990. *Revolutionary News: The Press in France, 1789–1799*. Durham, NC.
———. 2005. New Perspectives on the Early Modern European Press. In *News and Politics in Early Modern Europe*, ed. J.W. Koopmans. Leuven. 1–28.

Pöppinghege, Rainer. 2001. 'Mit mittelmaessigen Geistesgaben und Vorkenntnissen ausgerüstet': über das Verhältnis von kaiserlichen Behörden und Presse in den deutschen Kolonien 1898 bis 1914. *Jahrbuch für Kommunikationsgeschichte* 3. 157–69.

Postman, Neil. (1982) 2011. *The Disappearance of Childhood*. New York.

———. (1985) 2005. *Amusing Ourselves to Death: Public Discourse in the Age of Show Business*. New York.

Potter, Simon James. 2003. *News and the British World: The Emergence of an Imperial Press System, 1876–1922*. Oxford.

Pöttker, Horst. 2006. Journalismus als Politik. Eine explorative Analyse von NS-Presseanweisungen der Vorkriegszeit. *Publizistik* 52. 168–82.

Prutz, Robert. (1845) 1971. *Zur Geschichte des deutschen Journalismus*. Hannover.

Puppis, Manuel. 2007. *Einführung in die Medienpolitik*. Konstanz.

Radkau, Joachim. 1998. *Das Zeitalter der Nervosität. Deutschland zwischen Bismarck und Hitler*. Munich.

Rantanen, Terhi. 1990. *Foreign News in Imperial Russia: The Relationship between International and Russian News Agencies, 1856–1914*. Helsinki.

Rattner, Gelbart Nina. 1987. *Feminine and Opposition Journalism in Old Regime France: Le Journal des Dammes*. Berkeley.

Rau, Susanne, and Gerd Schwerhoff (eds). 2004. *Zwischen Gotteshaus und Taverne. Öffentliche Räume in Spätmittelalter und Früher Neuzeit*. Cologne.

Raymond, Joad (ed.). 1999. *News, Newspapers, and Society in Early Modern Britain*. London.

———. 2001. *The Invention of the Newspaper: English newsbooks, 1641–1649*. Oxford.

———. 2003. *Pamphlets and Pamphleteering in Early Modern Britain*. Cambridge.

Read, Donald. 1999. *The Power of News: The History of Reuters*. Oxford.

Reeves, Nicolas. 1997. Cinema, Spectatorship and Propaganda: Battle of the Somme and its Contemporary Audience. *Historical Journal of Film, Radio and Television* 17. 5–28.

Reichardt, Rolf. 2008a. 'Das größte Ereignis der Zeit'. Zur medialen Resonanz der Pariser Februarrevolution. In *Medienereignisse der Moderne*, eds Friedrich Lenger and Ansgar Nünning. Darmstadt. 14–40.

———. 2008b. Plurimediale Kommunikation und symbolische Repräsentation in den Französischen Revolutionen 1789–1848. In *Revolutionsmedien – Medienrevolutionen*, eds Sven Grampp et al. Konstanz. 231–75.

Reinermann, Lothar. 2001. *Der Kaiser in England: Wilhelm II. und sein Bild in der britischen Öffentlichkeit*. Paderborn.

Renner, Andreas. 2000. *Russischer Nationalismus und Öffentlichkeit im Zarenreich 1855–1875*. Cologne.

Repgen, Konrad. 1997. Der Westfälische Friede und die zeitgenössische Öffentlichkeit. *Historisches Jahrbuch* 117. 38–83.

Requate, Jörg. 1995. *Journalismus als Beruf. Entstehung und Entwicklung des Journalistenberufs im 19. Jahrhundert. Deutschland im internationalen Vergleich*. Göttingen.

———. 1999. Medien und Öffentlichkeit als Gegenstände historischer Analyse. *Geschichte und Gesellschaft* 25. 5–33.

——— (ed.). 2009. *Das 19. Jahrhundert als Mediengesellschaft*. Munich.
Retallack, James. 1993. From Pariah to Professional? The Journalist in German Society and Politics, from the Late Enlightenment to the Rise of Hitler. *German Studies Review* 16. 175–223.
Richardson, Brian. 1994. *Print Culture in Renaissance Italy: The Editor and the Vernacular Text, 1470–1600*. Cambridge.
Ries, Paul. 1977. The Anatomy of a Seventeenth-Century Newspaper. *Daphnis* 6. 171–232.
———. 2001. The Politic of information seventeenth-century Scandinavia. In *The Politics of Information in Early Modern. Europe*, eds Brendan M. Dooley and Sabrina A. Baron. London and New York. 237–269.
Rösch-Sondermann, Hermann. 1998. *Bibliographie der lokalen Alternativpresse: Vom Volksblatt zum Stadtmagazin*. Munich.
Rosenberger, Bernhard. 1998. *Zeitungen als Kriegstreiber? Die Rolle der Presse im Vorfeld des Ersten Weltkrieges*. Cologne.
Rosenstock, Roland. 2002. *Evangelische Presse im 20. Jahrhundert*. Stuttgart.
Ross, Corey. 2006. Mass Culture and Divided Audiences: Cinema and Social Change in Inter-War Germany. *Past & Present: A Journal of Historical Studies* 193. 157–96.
———. 2008. *Media and the Making of Modern Germany: Mass Communications, Society, and Politics from the Empire to the Third Reich*. Oxford.
Rosseaux, Ulrich. 2004. Die Entstehung der Meßrelationen. Zur Entwicklung eines frühneuzeitlichen Nachrichtenmediums aus der Zeitgeschichtsschreibung des 16. Jahrhunderts. *Historisches Jahrbuch* 124. 97–123.
Roth-Ey, Kristin. 2011. *Moscow Prime Time: How the Soviet Union Built the Media Empire that Lost the Cultural Cold War*. New York.
Rubinger, Richard. 2007. *Popular Literacy in Early Modern Japan*. Honolulu.
Ruchatz, Jens. 2003. Spiel ohne Grenzen oder grenzenlose Spielerei? Eurovision – Intervision – Mondovision. In *Medienkultur der 60er Jahre. Global – lokal*, eds Irmela Schneider, Thorsten Schneider and Tina Bartz. Wiesbaden. 121–47.
Rüden, Peter von, and Hans-Ulrich Wagner (eds). 2005. *Die Geschichte des Nordwestdeutschen Rundfunks*. Hamburg.
Rutz, Rainer. 2007. *Signal: Eine deutsche Auslandsillustrierte als Propagandainstrument im Zweiten Weltkrieg*. Essen.
Sachsse, Rolf. 2003. *Die Erziehung zum Wegsehen: Fotografie im NS-Staat*. Dresden.
Saenger, Michael Baird. 2005. The Birth of Advertising. In *Printing and Parenting in Early Modern England*, ed. Douglas A. Brooks. Aldershot. 197–219.
Sawyer, Jeffrey K. 1990. *Printed Poison: Pamphlet Propaganda, Faction Politics, and the Public Sphere in Early Seventeenth-Century France*. Berkeley.
Scannell, Paddy, and David Cardiff. 1991. *A Social History of British Broadcasting*. Vol. 1. Oxford.
Schanze, Frieder. 1999. Der Buchdruck eine Medienrevolution? In *Mittelalter und frühe Neuzeit: Übergänge. Umbrüche und Neuansätze*, ed. Walter Haug. Tübingen.
Schanze, Helmut (ed.). 2001. *Handbuch der Mediengeschichte*. Stuttgart.
Schenk, Michael. 2007. *Medienwirkungsforschung*. Tübingen.
Schildt, Axel. 1995. *Moderne Zeiten: Freizeit. Massenmedien und 'Zeitgeist' in der Bundesrepublik der 50er Jahre*. Hamburg.

Schilling, Michael. 1990. *Bildpublizistik in der frühen Neuzeit. Aufgaben und Leistungen des illustrierten Flugblattes in Deutschland bis um 1700.* Tübingen.
Schmidt, Anne. 2006. *Belehrung – Propaganda – Vertrauensarbeit: zum Wandel amtlicher Kommunikationspolitik in Deutschland 1914–1918.* Essen.
Schneider, Bernhard. 1998. *Katholiken auf die Barrikaden? Europäische Revolutionen und deutsche katholische Presse 1815–1848.* Paderborn.
Schneider, Franz. 1966. *Pressefreiheit und politische Öffentlichkeit. Studien zur politischen Geschichte Deutschlands bis 1848.* Neuwied am Rhein.
Scholz, Leander. 2004. Die Industria des Buchdrucks. In *Einführung in die Geschichte der Medien*, et al. eds Albert Kümmel. Paderborn. 11–34.
Scholz Williams, Gerhild, and William Layfer (eds). 2008. *Consuming News: Newspapers and Print Culture in Early Modern Europe 1500–1800.* Amsterdam.
Schönhagen, Philomen. 1998. *Unparteilichkeit im Journalismus. Tradition einer Qualitätsnorm.* Tübingen.
Schort, Manfred. 2006. *Politik und Propaganda: Der Siebenjährige Krieg in den zeitgenössischen Flugschriften.* Frankfurt/M.
Schöttker, Detlev (ed.). 1999. *Von der Stimme zum Internet. Texte aus der Geschichte der Medienanalyse.* Göttingen.
Schramm, Martin. 2007. *Das Deutschlandbild in der britischen Presse 1912–1919.* Berlin.
Schröder, Thomas. 1995. *Die ersten Zeitungen. Textgestaltung und Nachrichtenauswahl.* Tübingen.
Schultheiß-Heinz, Sonja. 2004. *Politik in der europäischen Publizistik: Eine historische Inhaltsanalyse von Zeitungen des 17. Jahrhunderts.* Stuttgart.
Schults, Raymond L. 1972. *Crusader in Babylon: W.T. Stead and the Pall Mall Gazette.* Lincoln, NE.
Schulz, Manuela. 2005. *Zeitungslektüre und Landarbeiterschaft. Eine kommunikationsgeschichtliche Studie zur Verbreitung des Zeitungslesens im 19. und 20. Jahrhundert.* Bremen.
Schwarz, Hans-Peter. 2008. *Axel Springer: Die Biografie.* Berlin.
Schwarz, Uta. 2002. *Wochenschau. westdeutsche Identität und Geschlecht in den fünfziger Jahren.* Frankfurt/M.
Schwoch, James. 2009. *Global TV: New Media and the Cold War, 1946–69.* Urbana, IL.
Scribner, Robert W. 1981. *For the Sake of Simple Folk: Popular Propaganda for the German Reformation.* Cambridge.
Segeberg, Harro (ed.). 2004. *Das Dritte Reich und der Film.* Munich.
Seong-Rae, Park. 2004. An Invention with Little Innovations. *Gutenberg-Jahrbuch* 79. Mainz. 26–31.
Shrivastava, K.M. 2005. *Broadcast Journalism in the 21st Century.* New Delhi.
Siemann, Wolfram. 1985. *Die deutsche Revolution von 1848/49.* Frankfurt/M.
———. 1987. Ideenschmuggel. Probleme der Meinungskontrolle und das Los deutscher Zensoren im 19. Jahrhundert. *Historische Zeitschrift* 245. 71–106.
Simonson, Peter, Janice Peck, Robert T. Craig and John Jackson (eds). 2012. *The Handbook of Communication History.* London.
Sinclair, John. 1999. *Latin American Television: A Global View.* Oxford.

Sklar, Robert. 2002. *A World History of Film*. New York.
Sloan, William David, and Julie Hedgepeth Williams. 1994. *The Early American Press, 1690–1783*. Westport, CT.
Smith, Anthony. 1979. *The Newspaper: An International History*. London.
Sohn, Pow-Key. 1972. Early Korean Printing. In *Der gegenwärtige Stand der Gutenberg-Forschung*, ed. Hans Widman. Stuttgart. 217–31.
———. 1998. Invention of the Movable Metal-Type Printing in Koryo: Its Role and Impact on Human Cultural Progress. *Gutenberg Jahrbuch* 73. 25–30.
Sommerville, C. John. 1996. *The News Revolution in England: Cultural Dynamics of Daily Information*. Oxford.
Sonntag, Christian 2006. *Medienkarrieren. biografische Studien über Hamburger Nachkriegsjournalisten 1946–1949*. Munich.
Sösemann, Bernd. 2000. *Theodor Wolff. Ein Leben mit der Zeitung*. Munich.
——— (ed.). 2002. *Kommunikation und Medien in Preußen vom 16. bis zum 19. Jahrhundert*. Stuttgart.
———. 2007. Journalismus im Griff der Diktatur. Die 'Frankfurter Zeitung' in der nationalsozialistischen Pressepolitik. In *Diener des Staates. 'Widerstand zwischen den Zeilen' im Dritten Reich*, ed. Christoph Studt. Münster. 11–39.
Spahn, Martin. 1908. Die Presse als Quelle der neuesten Geschichte und ihre gegenwärtigen Benutzungsmöglichkeiten. *Internationale Wochenschrift für Wissenschaft. Kunst und Technik*. 1163–70 and 1211–20.
Spieker, Markus. 1999. *Hollywood unterm Hakenkreuz. Der amerikanische Spielfilm im Dritten Reich*. Trier.
Stahr, Gerhard. 2001. *Volksgemeinschaft vor der Leinwand. Der nationalsozialistische Film und sein Publikum*. Berlin.
Stamm, Karl-Heinz. 1988. *Alternative Öffentlichkeit. Die Erfahrungsproduktion neuer sozialer Bewegungen*. Frankfurt/M.
Standage, Tom. 1998. *Das viktorianische Internet. Die erstaunliche Geschichte des Telegraphen und der Online-Pioniere des 19. Jahrhunderts*. St Gallen.
Stegbauer Christian. 2008. Raumzeitliche Strukturen im Internet. *Aus Politik und Zeitgeschichte* 39. 3–9.
Stein, Peter. 2006. *Schriftkultur, eine Geschichte des Schreibens und Lesens*. Darmstadt.
Steinmetz, Rüdiger. 1996. *Freies Fernsehen. Das erste privatkommerzielle Fernsehprogramm in Deutschland*. Konstanz.
Steinmetz, Rüdiger, and Reinhold Viehoff (eds). 2008. *Deutsches Fernsehen Ost. Eine Programmgeschichte des DDR-Fernsehens*. Berlin.
Stieler, Kaspar. 1969. *Zeitungs Lust und Nutz. Neudruck der Original-Ausgabe von 1695*. Bremen.
Stöber, Gunda. 2000. *Pressepolitik als Notwendigkeit. zum Verhältnis von Staat und Öffentlichkeit im wilhelminischen Deutschland 1890–1914*. Stuttgart.
Stöber, Rudolf. 2000. *Deutsche Pressegeschichte. Einführung. Systematik. Glossar*. Konstanz.
———. 2003. *Mediengeschichte. Die Evolution 'neuer' Medien von Gutenberg bis Gates: Mediengeschichte. Die Evolution 'neuer' Medien von Gutenberg bis Gates*. 2 vols. Wiesbaden.

Straßner, Erich. 2002. *Text-Bild-Kommunikation*. Tübingen.
Studt, Christoph (ed.). 2007. *'Diener des Staates' oder 'Widerstand zwischen den Zeilen'?: die Rolle der Presse im 'Dritten Reich'*. Berlin.
Stumberger, Rudolf. 2002. *Fernsehen und sozialstruktureller Wandel*. Munich.
Thogmartin, Clyde. 1998. *The National Daily Press in France*. Birmingham, AL.
Thomaß, Barbara. 2007. *Mediensysteme im internationalen Vergleich*. Konstanz.
Thompson, John B. 1995. *The Media and Modernity: A Social Theory of the Media*. Stanford, CA.
Thompson, J. Lee. 1999. *Politicians, the Press and Propaganda: Lord Northcliffe and the Great War, 1914–1919*. London.
Uphaus-Wehmeier, Annette. 1984. *Zum Nutzen und Vergnügen – Jugendzeitschriften des 18. Jahrhunderts. Ein Beitrag zur Kommunikationsgeschichte*. Munich.
Vande Winkel, Roel, and David Welch (eds). 2007. *Cinema and the Swastika: The International Expansion of Third Reich Cinema*. New York.
Virilio, Paul. 1989. *War and Cinema: The Logistics of Perception*. London.
Vittinghoff, Natascha. 2002a. *Die Anfänge des Journalismus in China 1860–1911*. Wiesbaden.
———. 2002b. Unity vs. Uniformity: Liang Qichao and the Invention of a 'New Journalism' for China. *Late Imperial China* 23. 360–95.
Vogel, Meike. 2010. *Unruhe im Fernsehen. Öffentlich-rechtliches Fernsehen und Proteste in den 1960er Jahren*. Göttingen.
Vogel, Sabine. 1999. *Kulturtransfer in der frühen Neuzeit: Die Vorworte der Lyoner Drucke des 16. Jahrhunderts*. Tübingen.
Wagner, Robert G. 1995. The Role of the Foreign Community in the Chinese Public Sphere. *China Quarterly* 142. 423–43.
Waibel, Nicole. 2008. *Nationale und patriotische Publizistik in der Freien Reichsstadt Augsburg. Studien zur periodischen Presse im Zeitalter der Aufklärung 1748–1770*. Bremen.
Walkowitz, Judith R. 1994. *City of Dreadful Delight: Narratives of Sexual Danger in Late-Victorian London*. London.
Walravens, Hartmut. 2007. *Buch- und Druckwesen im kaiserlichen China sowie in Zentralasien. Korea und Japan: eine annotierte Bibliographie*. Stuttgart.
Waschik, Klaus. 2010. Virtual Reality. Sowjetische Bild- und Zensurpolitik als Erinnerungskontrolle in den 1930er-Jahren. *Zeithistorische Forschungen* 7.
Weber, Johannes. 1997. *Avisen. Relationen. Gazetten: der Beginn des europäischen Zeitungswesens*. Oldenburg.
———. 1999. Der große Krieg und die frühe Zeitung. Gestalt und Entwicklung der deutschen Nachrichtenpresse in der ersten Hälfte des 17. Jahrhunderts. *Jahrbuch für Kommunikationsgeschichte*. 23–61.
Weckel, Ulrike. 1998. *Zwischen Häuslichkeit und Öffentlichkeit. Die ersten deutschen Frauenzeitschriften im späten 18. Jahrhundert und ihr Publikum*. Tübingen.
———. 2006. Nachsitzen im Kino: Anglo-amerikanische KZ-Filme und deutsche Reaktionen 1945/46 – über Versuche kollektiver Beschämung. *Berliner Debatte Initial* 17. 84–99.
Weise, Bernd. 1989. Pressefotografie. *Fotogeschichte* 31. 15–40; *Fotogeschichte* 33. 27–62.

Welch, David. 2000. *Germany, Propaganda and Total War, 1914–1918: The Sins of Omission'*. New Brunswick, NJ.
———. 2001. *Propaganda and the German cinema, 1933–1945*. London.
Welke, Martin. 1977. Zeitung und Öffentlichkeit im 18. Jahrhundert: Betrachtungen zur Reichweite und Funktion der periodischen deutschen Tagespublizistik. In *Presse und Geschichte: Beiträge zur historischen Kommunikationsforschung*, ed. Elger Blühm. München. 71–99.
Welke, Martin, and Jürgen Wilke (eds). 1999. *Der Weg zur freien Presse in Deutschland*. Frankfurt/M.
———. 2008. *400 Jahre Zeitungen. Ein Medium macht Geschichte. Die Entwicklung der Tagespresse im internationalen Kontext*. Bremen.
Welke, Sabine. 1971. *Die Frau und die Anfänge des deutschen Zeitungswesens. eine Studie zur Geschichte der Publizistik des 17. Jahrhunderts*. Vienna.
Wendt, Reinhard. 2007. *Vom Kolonialismus zur Globalisierung. Europa und die Welt seit 1500*. Paderborn.
Wenzlhuemer, Roland (ed.). 2010. Global Communication: Telecommunication and Global Flows of Information in the Late 19th and Early 20th Century. *Historical Social Research* 35.
Wetzel, Hans-Wolfgang. 1975. *Presseinnenpolitik im Bismarckreich. 1874–1890; das Problem der Repression oppositioneller Zeitungen*. Bern.
Weyrauch, Erdmann. 1995. Das Buch als Träger der frühneuzeitlichen Kommunikationsrevolution. In *Kommunikationsrevolutionen, Die neuen Medien des 16. und 19. Jahrhunderts,* ed. Michael North. Köln. 1–15.
White, James. 2005. *Global Media: The Television Revolution in Asia*. New York.
Wiener, Joel H. 1969. *The War of the Unstamped: The Movement to Repeal the British Newspaper Tax, 1830–1836*. Ithaca, NY.
——— (ed.). 1988. *Papers for the Millions: The New Journalism in Britain, 1850s to 1914*. New York.
Wilharm, Irmgard. 2006. *Bewegte Spuren: Studien zur Zeitgeschichte im Film*. Hanover.
Wilke, Jürgen. 1984. *Nachrichtenauswahl und Medienrealität in vier Jahrhunderten. eine Modellstudie zur Verbindung von historischer und empirischer Publizistikwissenschaft*. Mainz.
———. 1986. Auslandberichterstattung und internationaler Nachrichtenfluß im Wandel. *Publizistik* 31. 53–90.
——— (ed.). 1992–1996. *Massenmedien in Lateinamerika*. 3 vols. Frankfurt/M.
——— (ed.). 1999. *Mediengeschichte der Bundesrepublik Deutschland*. Bonn.
——— (ed.). 2000. *Grundzüge der Medien- und Kommunikationsgeschichte, von den Anfängen bis ins 20. Jahrhundert*. Köln.
———. 2007. *Presseanweisungen im zwanzigsten Jahrhundert. Erster Weltkrieg – Drittes Reich – DDR*. Cologne.
Williams, Kevin. 2010. *Get Me a Murder a Day! A History of Mass Communication in Britain*. London.
Willmann, Heinz. 1974. *Geschichte der Arbeiter-Illustrierten Zeitung. 1921–1938*. Berlin.
Windt, Franziska, Jürgen Luh and Carsten Dilba. 2005. *Die Kaiser und die Macht der Medien*. Berlin.

Winkler, Karl T. 1998. *Wörterkrieg. Politische Debattenkultur in England 1689–1750.* Stuttgart.
Winker, Klaus. 1994. *Fernsehen unterm Hakenkreuz: Organisation. Programm. Personal.* 1994. Cologne.
Winseck, Dwayne R., and Robert M. Pike. 2007. *Communication and Empire: Media, Markets and Globalization, 1860 –1930.* Durham, NC.
———. 2008. Communication and Empire. Media, Markets, and Globalization, 1860 – 1910. In *Global Media and Communication* 4. 7–36.
Witte, Karsten. 1998. The Indivisible Legacy of Nazi Germany. *New German Critique* 74. 23–31.
Wittmann, Frank, and Rose Marie Beck (eds). 2004. *African Media Cultures – Transdisciplinary Perspectives.* Cologne.
Wobring, Michael. 2005. *Die Globalisierung der Telekommunikation im 19. Jahrhundert. Pläne. Projekte und Kapazitätsausbauten zwischen Wirtschaft und Politik.* Bern.
Wohlfeil, Rainer. 1984. Reformatorische Öffentlichkeit, Literatur und Laienbildung im Spätmittelalter und in der Reformationszeit. In *Literatur und Laienbildung im Spätmittelalter und in der Reformation*, eds Ludger Grenzmann and Karl Strackmann. Stuttgart. 41–54.
Würgler, Andreas. 2009. *Medien in der Frühen Neuzeit.* Munich.
Wyver, John. 1989. *The Moving Image: An International History of Film, Television, and Video.* New York.
Youngblood. Denise J. 1992. *Movies for the Masses: Popular Cinema and Soviet Society in the 1920s.* Cambridge.
Yukawa, Shiro. 2010. *Das Verschwinden des materiellen Prozesses. Eine vergleichende Mediengeschichte der japanischen Schreib- und Druckkultur.* Erfurt.
Zahlmann, Stefan (ed.). 2010. *Wie im Westen. nur anders. Medien in der DDR.* Berlin.
Zaret, Daivd. 2000. *Origins of Democratic Culture: Printing, Petitions, and the Public Sphere in Early Modern England.* Princeton.
Zeller, Rüdiger. 1999. *Die EBU – Internationale Rundfunkoperationen im Wandel.* Baden-Baden.
Zierenberg, Malte. 2013. Die Ordnung der Agenturen. Zur Verfertigung massenmedialer Sichtbarkeit im Pressewesen. 1900–1940. In *Fotografien im 20. Jahrhundert. Verbreitung und Vermittlung*, eds. Annelie Ramsbrock, Annette Vowinckel and Malte Zierenberg. Göttingen. 44–65.
Zika, Charles. 2007. *The Appearance of Witchcraft: Print and Visual Culture in Sixteenth-Century Europe.* London.
Zimmermann, Clemens (ed.). 2006. *Politischer Journalismus. Öffentlichkeiten. Medien im 19. und 20. Jahrhundert.* Ostfildern.
———. 2007. *Medien im Nationalsozialismus. Deutschland 1933–1945. Italien 1922–1943. Spanien 1936–1951.* Vienna.
Zuckermann, Moshe (ed.). 2003. *Medien. Politik. Geschichte.* Göttingen.

Index

1968, 154–155

Acres, Birt, 104, 106
Adams, Samuel, 63
Adenauer, Konrad, 149, 151, 165
advertisement, 10, 22, 32, 40, 45, 49–51, 79–80, 83, 91, 98 f, 107, 110, 112, 114–115, 121, 143, 146, 149, 154, 157, 161, 166. *See also Intelligenzblätter*
Africa, 92, 96–97, 99–101, 150, 153, 157–158
Albrecht, Duke, 52
Alexander II., Tsar, 61, 78
alphabetisation, 22, 24, 30. *See also* illiteracy
Altenloh, Emilie, 107
Anderson, Benedict, 31, 68
Anneke, Mathilde Franziska, 76
aristocracy, 47, 54, 59, 61, 65, 91. *See also* monarchy
Arndt, Ernst Moritz, 69
Augstein, Rudolf, 146
Australia, 92, 95– 97, 105
Austria, 11, 43, 45, 49, 57, 60, 67–68, 70, 74, 78, 82, 89, 133, 148, 151, 161

Bain, Alexander, 92
Balazs, Bela, 120
Beaverbrock, Lord, 112
Behringer, Wolfgang, 39, 56
Belgium, 71, 111, 158
Benjamin, Walter, 120
Berlusconi, Silvio, 165
Bismarck, Otto von, 87, 89, 96, 106
Blucher, Gebhard Leberecht von, 69
Bly, Nellie (Elizabeth Cochrane), 85
Bonaparte, Napoleon, 66, 67, 68, 72
book, 9, 13–25, 32, 35–38, 40, 42, 45, 59–61, 70, 85, 97–99, 103–104, 112, 151, 168–169
Brandt, Willy, 153
Brant, Sebastian, 26
Briggs, Asa, 7
Brissot, Jaques, 65
broadsides. *See under* leaflets
Brusse, Marie Joseph, 81
Buchner, Georg, 72
Bülow, Bernhard von, 87, 89
Burke, Peter, 7
Burkhardt, Johannes, 57
Butler, Josephine, 84

Caetano, Marcello, 162
Carolus, Johann, 39, 40

Caxton, William, 22
Ceaușescu, Nicolae, 139
censorship
   109, 111–112, 118–119, 123, 133–134, 150–151
   see under film
   newspapers/press/periodicals, 43–44, 46, 48–49, 64, 66–70, 72, 75, 78, 98, 111–113, 123–126, 137, 140–141
   printing (early), 28–29, 32, 37
   radio, 116, 123, 183, 140–141, 145
   self-censorship, 67, 70, 109, 88, 134, 141
   telegraphy, 93
   television, 161
Chamberlain, Joseph, 86
Chapman, Jane, 7, 84
Charles X., King, 71
China, 2, 12–18, 20, 31, 87, 94, 97–99, 171
Christian Democrats. *See under* Conservatives
church
   19th century, 71, 75
   20th century, 115–116, 141, 150, 162, 165
   printing (early), 16, 28–30, 32–38, 43
   See also Reformation
Churchill, Winston Spencer, 131
cinema. *See under* film
city (culture), 9, 82–84, 116, 119, 152
class
   lower, 59, 67–68, 98, 107, 135
   middle/ bourgeois, 24, 42, 52, 54–55, 58, 59–61, 71, 74, 84, 86, 97, 103, 107–108, 110, 115, 119, 121–129, 141, 146, 149, 157, 170
coffee houses/pubs, 24, 47, 51, 58–61, 65, 74, 90, 107, 129, 156, 169
colonialism, 91– 94, 99, 101–102, 130, 164
computer, 167–173
concentration of media ownership, 88, 94, 118, 120, 125, 161
Concini, Concino, 28
conservatives, 66–67, 74–75, 77, 80, 84, 88, 90, 108, 118, 121–122, 145, 157, 162, 165
Cooke, William Fothergill, 92
correspondent (foreign), 9, 40, 44–46, 59, 79, 85–86, 95, 98, 101–102, 141
crime, 50, 79, 83, 108, 132, 136
Czechoslovakia 42, 69, 140

da Vinci, Leonardo, 32
de Gaulle, Charles, 131, 162
de la Reviere Manley, Mary, 53
democracy, 8, 61, 113, 116, 122, 131, 145–147, 150, 153–154, 156–157, 161
Denmark, 41–42, 49, 79, 109, 117, 130
Desmoulins, Camille, 65
Deutsch, Karl W., 68
dictatorships, 4–5, 8–9, 12, 123–144, 157, 160–163

Eastern Europe
   16th–19th century, 22, 36, 60, 69, 96
   20th century, 96, 113, 137–145, 150–151, 156, 162
   See also Czechoslovakia/Poland and Russia/Soviet Union

economic crisis, 94, 116, 118, 119–121, 125
Edison, Thomas, 104
Edward VII., King, 86
Eisenstein, Elisabeth L., 19, 32, 138
Eisermann, Falk, 28
Elisabeth II., Queen, 157, 163
England. *See under* Great Britain
Erzberger, Matthias, 88

family, 47, 79, 85–86, 127, 155, 159, 164
Faulstich, Werner, 7, 20, 36
Fichte, Johann Gottlieb, 69
film, 4–5, 7, 9–11, 120, 139–140, 155–156, 163, 168, 171–172
    audience, 9, 106–109, 111, 118–119, 132–135, 151–152, 161–162
    censorship, 109, 111–112, 118–119, 122–123, 133–134, 138, 150–151
    cinema, 4, 9, 103–109, 111, 117–120, 128, 132, 135, 161
    Cold War, 137–140, 143, 147, 150–152
    film (early), 77, 101, 103–113
    propaganda, 111–113, 132–136
Force, Charles L., 100
fourth estate/fourth power, 3, 59, 80, 87, 100–101
France
    17th/18th century, 40–43, 47–51, 53, 57, 60, 64–68
    19th century, 3, 69, 71, 73–80, 82
    20th century, 82, 84, 87–90, 92–93, 96, 99, 105–107, 119, 121, 130–131, 145, 148–149, 152, 154, 156, 158, 161–163, 165
    film (early), 104–107, 109, 111–112, 117, 119
    printing, 20–23, 25, 28–29, 31, 36, 37
Franklin, Benjamin, 50, 63
Franklin, James, 50
Fritsch, Ahasver, 55, 56

Galilei, Galileo, 32
Gallois, Leonard, 3
Gates, Bill, 93
GDR, 9, 11, 137, 139–144, 155, 157–158, 160
George IV, King, 73
George VI, King, 156
Geppert, Dominik, 87
Gerlach, Ludwig von, 75
Giesecke, Michael, 14, 21, 33 38
Girardin, Emile, 76
globalisation, 91–102, 105–106, 153–154, 157, 162, 169
Goebbels, Joseph, 120, 123, 126, 128, 129, 135, 136
Gorres, Joseph, 69, 75
Gottsched, Johann Christoph, 53
Great Britain
    17th/18th century, 40–45, 47–51, 53–54, 57, 59–60, 62, 65–67
    19th century, 11, 70–73, 75, 77–78, 81, 84–86
    20th century, 9, 11, 82–90, 92–96, 99, 105–107, 109, 111–112, 115–117, 119–120, 128–132, 147–148, 151–152, 154–157, 160–164, 168
    film (early), 105, 106–107, 109–113
    printing, 19, 22–23, 28–29, 31–32, 35
Greece, 69, 157

Gutenberg, Johannes, 13, 18, 19,
  20, 21, 23, 24, 26, 28, 30, 35,
  37, 39, 40, 70

Habermas, Jürgen, 8, 52, 58, 59, 61
Habsburg Empire. *See under* Austria
Hamilton, Alexander, 63
Hammann, Otto, 89
Hammerstein, Wilhelm von, 88
Hardenberg, Karl August Freiherr
  von, 68
Harline, Craig E., 28
Hatin, Eugene, 3
Havelock, Eric Alfred, 33
Hearst, William R., 9, 88, 101
Heine, Heinrich, 72
Hepworth, Cecil, 117
Hett, Benjamin, 83
Hitler, Adolf, 120, 128, 133, 136
Hobhouse, Emily, 86, 101
Hodenberg, Christina von, 153
Hollywood 117–118, 133–135, 152,
  161, 171
Horgan, Stephen H., 83
Hörisch, Jochen, 7
Huck, August, 88
Huffman, James, 97
Hugenberg, Alfred, 118, 120, 121,
  122, 133
Hungary, 42, 69, 113, 139
Hunt, Frederick, knight, 3

illiteracy, 25, 47, 65, 101, 138
imprints, 29, 32, 67
India, 93–94, 97, 113–115, 150,
  162
influence of media, 17–19, 30–38,
  57–61, 118–119, 121, 131,
  135–136, 158–160
Intelligenzblätter, 50–51, 59, 67
Internet, 3, 12, 93, 150, 162,
  166–173

Italy
  17th–19th century, 40, 60, 67, 71
  20th century, 89, 105, 108–109,
    113–114, 123–126, 129–
    130, 132, 134, 145, 148–
    149, 161–162, 165–166
  film (early), 105, 108–109
  printing, 20–25, 28–29, 31

Jack the Ripper, 83
Japan, 2, 12–14, 16–17, 77, 93,
  97–99, 101, 105–107, 113–
  117, 125, 127, 143, 146, 157,
  163–164
journalism
  beginning of, 44, 45–46, 50, 53,
    56, 64–65
  investigative, 65, 79–81, 83,
    153, 160
  modern, 9–11, 63–66, 67,
    70–73, 76, 78, 80–83,
    85–91, 98–101, 111, 121,
    123–124, 126–127, 135,
    137, 140–141, 143–144,
    146–148, 152–155, 160
  profession, 4, 46, 81–82, 126,
    141
  See also correspondent (foreign)

Kaul, Chandrika, 97
Kennedy, John F., 153
Kittler, Friedrich A., 103
Kleist, Heinrich von, 69
Köhler, Hans-Joachim, 35
Korea, 13–19, 30
Korte, Helmut, 118
Kotzebue, August, 69
Kracauer, Siegfried, 119, 120

Lang, Fritz, 118
Lange, Helene, 84

Latin America, 12, 50, 69, 96–97, 114, 157, 161, 164
Lazarsfeld, Paul F., 4
leaflets, 2, 5, 10, 20, 25–28, 39–40, 44–46, 56–57, 61, 74, 142, 154, 169–171
   characteristics, 25–28
   content, 25–29
   in the French Revolution, 64–69, 73–74
   in the Reformation, 28, 35–56
Leibniz, Gottfried Wilhelm, 167
Lersch, Edgar, 116
liberalism, 3, 44, 49, 70–71, 73–75, 77–78, 81, 88, 90, 100, 109–111, 121–122, 124, 127, 131, 146, 149, 162
libraries, 11, 15, 33, 54, 60–61, 97, 142
Lincoln, Abraham, 95
Ludewig, Johann Peter, 59
Lumière, Auguste u. Louis Jean, 104, 105, 107
Luther, Martin, 32, 35–36

Mann, Thomas, 130
Marat, Jean Paul, 65
Maria Theresia, Empress, 42
Marx, Karl, 75
Maximilian I, 28
Mazzini, Guiseppe, 71
McCarthy, Joseph, 160
McLuhan, Marshall, 4, 13, 30–33
media policy. *See under* freedom of press, propaganda, censorship, 4, 8, 28, 34, 36, 57, 68, 105, 111–113, 117, 123–136, 138, 141–142, 148–149, 156–157
Méliès, George, 109
Metternich, Klemens von, 68
Meyen, Michael, 143

monarchy, 8 40, 64–66, 70, 86, 107, 127. *See also* aristocracy
moral weekly. *See under* periodicals
Morse, Samuel, 92
Mosse, Rudolf, 9, 88, 124
Mussolini, Benito, 124, 126, 129

National Socialism, 122–130, 132–136, 138–143, 146, 156
nationalism, 23–25, 27, 30–32, 48, 54, 58, 60, 62, 68–76, 78–80, 88, 91–96, 98, 106–107, 109, 116, 118, 121, 158, 163–164, 169
Neddermeyer, Uwe, 19, 21
Netherlands
   17th/18th century, 41–44, 46–47, 59, 64, 66
   19th/20th century, 71, 77–78, 80–81, 114, 131–132, 148, 162
   printing, 27–28, 37
news agencies, 45, 74, 89, 92, 95–97, 102, 112, 121, 123–125, 137, 139, 141, 145
   Associated Press (AP), 95
   Havas/Agence France Press (AFP), 95–96, 112
   Reuters, 93, 95–97
   TASS, 139
   Wolffs Telegraphisches Bureau (WTB), 89, 95–96, 123
newspapers, 3–5, 39–61, 169
   17th century, 39–48, 55–56
   18th century, 48–51
   circulation, 47–48, 64–65, 66, 67, 72–75, 77–79, 98, 104, 110, 121–122, 136, 137, 148, 161
   content, 44, 47, 50–51, 94–95, 110, 121, 127, 153, 161

international transfer, 41–43,
62–69, 97–101, 113, 127,
131, 138, 145, 165
   mass media, 77–84, 92, 95, 98,
101, 105, 171
   political press, 44–45, 63, 72–
76, 78–80, 87, 90, 121–126,
131, 137, 139, 140–141,
146, 148–149, 160, 170–171
   popular/tabloids, 78–79, 121,
130, 148–149
   readership/perception, 47, 51–
52, 59, 68–69, 122, 148,
159, 170
newsreels, 132, 134–135, 149
Nikolaus I, Tsar, 60
Nipkow, Paul, 156
North America. *See under* United
States
Northcliffe, Lord, 9, 80, 85, 88, 112
Norway, 84, 90, 130

Ottoman Empire, 23, 27, 42, 69, 93

pamphlets. *See under* leaflets
Panowsky, Erwin, 120
Papen, Franz von, 117
parliaments, 8, 43, 45, 57, 75–76,
87, 95
partisanship of the press, 45–46, 50,
56, 58, 63, 66, 74, 78, 80–81,
116
Paul, Gerhard, 10
Paul, Robert W., 104
Pearson, Cyril, 88
Pender, John, 131
periodicals, 39–61, 77, 170
   circulation, 104, 121, 161
   education, 50–52
   entertainment, 98, 120
   ideology, 76–77, 82, 127, 141,
161, 213

   influence, 56, 58, 60–61, 74–
75, 103–104, 151, 170–171
   international transfer, 64, 69, 98
   moral weeklies, 52–54, 60
   satire, 75–76, 123, 130–131,
141
   women's magazines, 52–54, 76,
79
Peter the Great, Tsar, 22, 42
Peucer, Tobias, 55
Philippe, Louis, 71
phonograph, 6–7, 12, 77, 115–116,
156, 160
photography, 10, 12, 77–79, 82–84,
86, 89, 101, 112, 120–122,
126–127, 135–136, 140, 147,
153, 161
Pike, Robert M., 93–94
Pitt, William, 67
Pius II, Pope, 24
Poland, 28, 35, 42, 69, 139–141,
144
Portugal, 16, 23, 37, 114, 162–163
postal service, 20, 39–41, 49, 58,
93–94, 168
Postman, Neil, 32, 34, 95
Potter, Louis de, 71
Powell, Elisabeth, 53
press,
   control of, 112, 125–126, 141
   freedom of, 43–44, 48–50, 53,
63–67, 70–72, 74–76, 78,
81, 95, 99–100, 109, 111,
123, 126–127, 135, 146, 153
   international transfer, 22–24,
30, 35
   invention of, 1, 13–14, 19–21,
23–24, 28, 30, 34–35, 37, 40
   perception, 19–20, 23–24
   printers, 2, 15–17, 22–26, 37,
40–42, 44, 46, 50, 67

printing (early), 1–2, 4–7, 9–11, 13–38, 168
printing locations, 2, 15, 22–23, 29, 33, 37, 40–41, 44, 70, 142
significance, 17–18, 30–38
technique, 13, 15–16, 21, 23, 30–31, 39
propaganda
 Early Modern Period, 26, 28, 34, 57
 Modern Period, 68–69, 111–113, 116–117, 123–136, 138, 140–141
 See also censorship, GDR, National Socialism, revolution
Prudhomme, Louis-Marie, 64
public sphere
 Early Modern Period, 18, 24, 26, 47, 51–52, 58–61, 65–66
 Habermas' model, 8, 52, 58–59, 61
 Modern Period, 72, 75, 83–85, 90–91, 98, 101, 108–110, 137, 144–147, 154–156, 159, 164, 169, 170–173
 See also reading societies and coffee houses
publisher, 47, 64, 66, 77, 80, 82, 85, 88–89, 91, 97–98, 101, 112, 121, 124, 140, 145–148
Pulitzer, Joseph, 82, 85, 88, 101

radio, 4, 9–11, 31, 113–117, 123–125, 170–172
 invention of, 104, 113–114, 156
 organization, 114–115, 143, 147–148
 politics, 116–117, 128–131, 142, 148

 programme, 115, 128–132, 156, 158–160
 use/significance of, 4, 116–117, 128–131, 137–140, 142–147, 149–150, 153–162, 168–172
Read, Donald, 96
reading societies, 30, 33, 47–48, 58–61, 67, 69, 108, 171
Reformation, 5, 34–37, 58
Renaudot, Theophraste, 47
Repgen, Konrad, 46
revolution
 1789, 7, 29, 44, 52–53, 64–65
 1830, 62, 70–73
 1848, 44, 73–74
 1917, 114, 137
 American Revolution, 62–64, 73
Richelieu, Armand, cardinal, 28, 43
Richter, Eugen, 88
Riefenstahl, Leni, 132, 135
Riis, Jacob A., 83
Robespierre, Maximilian de, 66
Rockefeller, John D., 86, 129
Roosevelt, Franklin D., 128
Russell, William Howard, 101
Russia/Soviet Union
 19th century, 69, 77–78, 81, 85
 20th century, 92, 96, 98, 111, 137–140, 163
 printing/press (early), 22, 41–42, 47, 56, 60
Russwurm, John B., 100

Sachsse, Rolf, 126
scandal, 64, 67, 84–85, 86–87, 89, 122, 125
Schamoni, Ulrich, 151
Schanze, Frieder, 33
Scherl, August, 9, 80, 88, 121

Schleiermacher, Friedrich, 69
Schubart, Friedrich Daniel, 50
Shaw, Flora, 86
Siebenpfeiffer, Philipp, 71
Skladanowsky, Emil and Max, 104
social democracy, 75, 78, 84, 88, 89–90, 110, 122, 125–126, 135–136, 141, 148–149
South Africa. *See under* Africa
South America. *See under* Latin America
Spahn, Martin, 5
Spain
    early printing, 20, 23, 27, 27–28, 45–46
    modern period, 114–115, 123–124, 129, 132–135, 157, 162–163
Springer, Axel, 9, 146
Stalin, Joseph, 138
standardisation, 15–16, 18, 27–32, 34, 56, 104, 109, 147, 159
stars, 86, 108, 117, 135
Stead, William Thomas, 81, 83–84, 98
Stieler, Kaspar, 55
subscription, 47, 51, 60, 82
Sweden, 41–43, 46, 49, 109, 130
Switzerland, 20, 23, 37, 40, 57, 69, 99, 116, 130, 134, 148, 158, 160, 180, 215

Tarbell, Ida, 86
tax, 49, 62, 63, 67, 72, 77, 79, 151, 161
Taxis, Franz von, 20
telegraphy, 10, 73, 77–78, 92–95, 97, 101–103, 113–114, 121, 168–169
television, 155–166
    commercial channels, 146, 157, 164–166, 171
    content, 142, 158–161
    exchange of programmes, 138–139, 142–143, 157–158, 162–165
    influence, 152, 153, 157–160, 166, 172–173
    invention of, 156–158
    research on, 4–12, 167
    state-owned channels, 146, 161–162, 165–166
    utilisation, 142–143, 155–156, 159, 169
Thiers, Adolphe, 71
Thompson, John, 106
Truffaut, François, 152
Turing, Alan, 168
Turkey, 114. *See also* Ottoman Empire

Ullstein, Leopold, 9, 88, 124 172
underground media, 5, 29, 64, 139, 141, 144
United States, 2, 8, 11
    film (early), 104, 107, 109, 111, 113
    print media 17th/18th century, 27, 47, 50, 53, 62–63, 65, 67
    19th century, 70, 73, 81–82
    20th century, 82–84, 88, 90, 93–94, 100–101, 113–114, 116, 121, 127–128, 130, 139, 147, 150, 151–154, 156–158, 160–163
universities, 20, 22, 29, 33, 43, 81, 84, 110, 114, 168
use of media, 4, 10–12, 60–61, 137–138, 141–143, 164–166, 169

Vargas, Getúlio, 128
Victoria, Queen, 86, 106, 147

violence (presentation of), 22, 54, 66, 71, 73, 79, 82–83, 85, 98, 108, 111, 130, 131–132, 135, 144–145, 147, 159

war, 2, 8, 10–11, 22, 26–27, 34–35, 37, 42–46, 48, 57, 62–63, 65–66, 68–69, 76–77, 86, 90, 101, 103, 105–107, 167
  American War of Independence, 48, 62–66
  Cold War, 10, 137–165
  colonial wars, 101–102
  First World War, 77, 90, 103–112, 131
  Peasants' War (1525–1526), 34–36
  Second World War, 123–137, 156
  Thirty Years' War, 44–46, 57
Weber, Johannes, 57
Weckel, Ulrike, 54
Weise, Christian, 55–56, 59
Wekhrlin, Wilhelm Ludwig, 50
Wheatstone, Charles, 92
Wilhelm I, Emperor, 86
Wilhelm II, Emperor, 86–87, 106, 109

Wilkes, John, 49
Wilson, Sarah, 86
Winseck, Dwayne, 93
Wirth, Johann Georg August, 72
Wolfe, Tom, 153
Wolff, Theodor, 110
women, 59, 61, 73, 84–86, 111, 118, 127, 135, 150, 170, 172
  female journalists, 47, 53–55, 76, 85–86
  public sphere, 59, 84, 107–108, 170
  use of media, 47, 52, 107–108, 149–150, 159
  women's movement, 84–86
  women's periodicals, 52–54, 76, 84
world financial crisis. *See under* economic crisis

youth/children, 34, 51–52, 84, 98, 107–108, 111, 119, 123, 143, 150–151, 158, 159, 164, 172–173

xylography, 16–18

Zuse, Konrad, 168

CPSIA information can be obtained at www.ICGtesting.com
Printed in the USA
BVOW06*1536120715
408374BV00006B/51/P

9 781782 386254